To Sallie & Sam,

Foreign Service Jewels

With warm regards,

Jewell Fenzi

22 December
1994

MARRIED TO THE FOREIGN SERVICE

An Oral History of the American Diplomatic Spouse

TWAYNE'S
ORAL HISTORY SERIES

Donald A. Ritchie, Series Editor

JEWELL FENZI
with CARL L. NELSON

MARRIED TO THE FOREIGN SERVICE

An Oral History of
the American Diplomatic Spouse

TWAYNE PUBLISHERS   NEW YORK
Maxwell Macmillan Canada Toronto
Maxwell Macmillan International New York Oxford Singapore Sydney

Twayne's Oral History Series No. 13

Married to the Foreign Service: An Oral History of the American Diplomatic Spouse
Jewell Fenzi with Carl L. Nelson

Copyright © 1994 Foreign Service Spouse Oral History, Inc., 1824 16th Street,
N.W., Washington, D.C. 20009 (202-387-4024)

Twayne Publishers   Maxwell Macmillan Canada, Inc.
Macmillan Publishing Company   1200 Eglinton Avenue East
866 Third Avenue   Suite 200
New York, New York 10022   Don Mills, Ontario M3C 3N1

Library of Congress Cataloging-in-Publication Data

Fenzi, Jewell.
    Married to the foreign service : an oral history of the American
diplomatic spouse / Jewell Fenzi with Carl L. Nelson.
        p.   cm.—(Twayne's oral history series ; no. 13)
    Includes bibliographical references (p.   ) and index.
    ISBN 0-8057-9123-X   ISBN 0-8057-9122-1 (pbk)
    1. Diplomatic and consular service, American—History.
    2. Diplomats' wives—United States—Interviews.   I. Nelson, Carl L.,
    1948-   . II. Title. III. Series.
JX1706.Z7F46   1994
327.73'0092'2—dc20   94-8303
                                                           CIP

10 9 8 7 6 5 4 3 2 1 (hc)

Printed in the United States of America

To Guido,
for taking me along

To Sallie and Sam —
for a multitude
of reasons.
        With much love,
        Click and Judy
December, 1994

Contents

Illustrations

1. Stewart and Catharine Johnson with young Catharine (Tita), Cairo, 1926
2. Anna Durkee Smith Kemp, undated
3. Lilla Grew Moffat in Hancock, New Hampshire, 27 July 1927
4. Anita Grew English with John Polando and Russell Boardman, Constantinople, 1931
5. Ambassador to Liberia Elbert G. Mathews and his wife, Naomi, Roberts Field, Monrovia, August 1959
6. Dr. Beatrice Berle visiting the children's ward of Hospital dos Servidores do Estado in Rio de Janeiro, March 1961
7. Julia and Paul Child, Oslo, 1959
8. Assistant Secretary of State for African Affairs Joseph Palmer II and Margaret Palmer, 1966
9. Edward R. Murrow, Marvin Breckinridge, and William L. Shirer donning ice skates, Amsterdam, January 1940
10. Bernetta, Estrellita, Anita, Carol, and Christina Jones with their teacher, "Mrs. Jones," Bhopal, 1957
11. Coretta Scott King, Dorothy (Steb) Bowles, and Yetta Weisz at Roosevelt House, New Delhi, 1969
12. Mary Louise Barker bound for Brisbane, 1943
13. John Stewart Service and Lisa Green at U.S. Senate Tydings subcommittee loyalty hearings, 23 June 1950
14. Chief of Protocol Lenore Annenberg, Judy Motley and daughters, and Langhorne A. Motley at his swearing-in ceremony as ambassador to Brazil, 1981
15. Elizabeth (Elsie) Grew Lyon, Hancock, New Hampshire, 20 August 1987
16. The first AAFSW board of directors, Washington, D.C., 1960
17. Mrs. Christian A. Herter conversing with her successor, Mrs. Dean Rusk, 21 February 1961
18. Marion Post Wolcott, c. 1939

Foreword

Long cast in the role of supporting actor, the spouse of an American Foreign Service officer was nevertheless integrally responsible for an embassy's functioning. The wives—and in later years the husbands—of Foreign Service officers had a definite script of protocol to follow, an audience to entertain, and critics who regularly reviewed their performance. Although neither employed nor paid for their assigned tasks, they shared the hardships, dangers, and adventures of diplomatic life and made their own contributions to American foreign relations. Over time, their quasi-official role changed considerably, in large measure as a result of the consciousness-raising of the women's movement. Still, their story remained largely unknown to those outside of diplomatic circles until oral history interviews allowed Foreign Service spouses to recount their past and present status within the Department of State and at last offered them center stage.

Oral history may well be the twentieth century's substitute for the written memoir. In exchange for the immediacy of diaries or correspondence, the retrospective interview offers a dialogue between the participant and the informed interviewer. Having prepared sufficient preliminary research, interviewers can direct the discussion into areas long since "forgotten," or no longer considered of consequence. "I haven't thought about that in years" is a common response, uttered just before an interviewee commences with a surprisingly detailed description of some past incident. The quality of the interview, its candidness and depth, generally will depend as much on the interviewer as the interviewee, and the confidence and rapport between the two adds a special dimension to the spoken memoir.

Interviewers represent a variety of disciplines and work either as part of a collective effort or individually. Regardless of their different interests or the variety of their subjects, all interviewers share a common imperative: to collect memories while they are still available. Most oral historians feel an additional responsibility to make their interviews accessible for use beyond their own research needs. Still, important collections of vital, vibrant interviews lie scattered in archives throughout every state, undiscovered or simply not used.

Twayne's Oral History Series seeks to identify those resources and to publish selections of the best materials. The series lets people speak for themselves, from their own unique perspectives on people, places, and events. But to be more than a babble of voices, each volume organizes its interviews around particular situations and events and ties them together with interpretative essays that place individuals into the larger historical context. The styles and format of individual volumes vary with the material from which they are drawn, demonstrating again the diversity of oral history and its methodology.

Whenever oral historians gather in conference, they enjoy retelling experiences about inspiring individuals they met, unexpected information they elicited, and unforgettable reminiscences that would otherwise have never been recorded. The result invariably reminds listeners of others who deserve to be interviewed, provides them with models of interviewing techniques, and inspires them to make their own contribution to the field. I trust that the oral historians in this series, as interviewers, editors, and interpreters, will have a similar effect on their readers.

DONALD A. RITCHIE
Series Editor, Senate Historical Office

Preface

By the 1990s, as never before, women had assumed leadership roles in the U.S. Congress and at the highest levels of the presidential administration. But these successes did not occur in a vacuum; instead they were part of an unfinished history of modern American women that goes back a century and more. *Married to the Foreign Service* explores one strand of this history, the experiences of the spouses of America's Foreign Service officers in the twentieth century.

Based on oral histories rich in exciting memories and perceptive insights into how foreign affairs have been conducted, it provides a valuable resource for anyone interested in the growing independence and political maturity of American women. Here are Julia Child, who began her cooking career as a Foreign Service spouse in Paris; Marvin Patterson, who broadcast for Edward R. Murrow and CBS Radio in wartime Europe before her marriage to a diplomatic officer; the labor activist and presidential consumer adviser Esther Peterson, also the spouse of a longtime Foreign Service official; and scores of other women, well known and unknown, all Foreign Service spouses, who made contributions to the conduct of U.S. foreign policy at home and abroad. Their unique experiences and recollections reveal much about the challenges of representing this country overseas, the social dimensions of Washington and the government in peace and war, and the internal pressures that the Department of State places on the lives of its married personnel.

It is the examination of these pressures that gives the book an even larger significance. Spouses of Foreign Service officers have given generously of their talents during this century, but without compensation and often without even recognition of their contributions. Jewell Fenzi traces how, until the 1960s, a system existed that deemed spouses to be "unofficially official" members of embassy and mission staffs. She explains the official government policy, which, with a growing feminist consciousness as impetus in the early 1970s, removed spouses from any obligations to assist with the duties of a diplomatic assignment.

But while that policy, which persists into the 1990s, officially released spouses from implicit obligation to the government, it did not deal with the status of the spouse willing to contribute to the work of a Foreign Service post. These women continue to seek formal recognition of their status from the Department of State, including paychecks.

In the surge of interest about the role of women in U.S. history during the past two decades, the place of women in the foreign policy and diplomacy of the nation has received little attention until recently. Of all the activities of the government, foreign affairs have seemed a secure male bastion rarely influenced by a feminine presence. Woman ambassadors and policy makers—Clare Booth Luce, Eleanor Dulles, and Jeane Kirkpatrick come to mind—were pioneers, exceptions to the rule expressed in the cliché "striped-pants diplomats."

During the 1980s, however, scholars began slowly and tentatively to investigate how women have had an effect on foreign relations. As so often occurs with the history of American women, once the record was opened striking evidence emerged that feminine participation has been greater than was earlier understood.

Along with research into the role of women in foreign policy, scholarly investigation of the wives of the presidents—which had been largely sporadic and anecdotal before the 1980s, with the publication of only a few biographies of famous First Ladies such as Abigail Adams, Mary Todd Lincoln, and Eleanor Roosevelt—went forward. Even in the 1990s, careful and thorough inquiries into the influence, and contributions, of presidential spouses has not occurred, even though several books have surveyed the history of First Ladies as a whole, with special emphasis on the twentieth-century development of the institution. Volumes on Lady Bird Johnson, Ellen Wilson, and Edith Roosevelt have been published.

In 1993 historians, and the nation, watched as Hillary Rodham Clinton attempted to restructure the nation's health care system. Tentative exploration has begun into the accomplishments of wives of state governors and college presidents. The result has been a keen new interest in the place of the spouse in a political marriage. It is thus very fitting that the role of spouses in yet another area of public service should now be the subject of historical investigation.

This book is a timely and informative examination of the role of women in a neglected aspect of foreign policy and a welcome contribution to the literature on the marriages of government officials. It brings a group of independent and self-reliant women out of the historical shadows, providing a new perspective on the human dimensions of U.S. foreign affairs, while at the same time advancing a compelling argument that government policy toward spouses in the Foreign Service needs to be overhauled at an early date.

LEWIS L. GOULD
Eugene C. Barker Centennial Professor in American History,
University of Texas at Austin

Acknowledgments

Portions of this book were published in the *Foreign Service Journal* as articles by Jewell Fenzi and Carl L. Nelson: "The Duke in Baghdad" (August 1991); "The Great Divorce: Why the 'Hands-off' Policy Did More Harm Than Good for Spouses" (June 1992); "Bon Appétit: Julia Child—From Foreign Service Wife to French Chef" (November 1992).

I owe special thanks to the more than 500 women and men, primarily with Foreign Service affiliations, who contributed to the Foreign Service Spouse Oral History Program, and to the Marpat Foundation for generous support.

Thanks also are due to: Dr. Joan D. Challinor, for her continuing support and permission to quote from her dissertation on Louisa Adams; Dr. Lewis L. Gould, Department of History, University of Texas at Austin, for guidance in women's history; Marc Pachter, deputy assistant secretary for external affairs, Smithsonian Institution, and the Biography Group of Washington, D.C., for thought-provoking and stimulating conversation, and for building confidence; Donald A. Ritchie, associate historian, U.S. Senate, and past president of the Oral History Association, whose initial support led to the launching of the Foreign Service Spouse Oral History Program; Dr. William Z. Slany and Paul Claussen, Office of the Historian, U.S. Department of State, for help with official documentation; and Mark Zadrozny and Cindy Buck of Twayne Publishers.

Additional funding was provided by the Association of American Foreign Service Women; Association for Diplomatic Studies and Training; Diplomatic and Consular Officers Retired; Una Chapman Cox Discretionary Fund, Director General of the Foreign Service; Betty Dillon; Holsey Handyside; and two major anonymous donors. The program, and the book, would not have been possible without their assistance.

I owe a large measure of gratitude to staff members of several specialty libraries, who were cheerfully courteous in responding to my inquiries, including Willa Baum of the regional oral history office, Bancroft Library, University of California at Berkeley; Dr. Patricia King, Arthur and Elizabeth Schlesinger Library on the History of Women in America, Radcliffe College, Cambridge,

Massachusetts; Dennis Bilger, Harry S. Truman Library, Independence, Missouri; Agnes Peterson, Hoover Institution on War, Revolution, and Peace, Stanford University, California; and the Townshend, Vermont, public library for its collection of feminist literature.

Oral history, of course, needs interviewers with tape recorders and patient transcribers. From the Foreign Service Spouse Oral History Program, I would like to thank: Joan Bartlett (New England representative), Priscilla Becker, Linda Bell, Annabel Ebersole, Ruth Kahn, Penne Laingen, the late Hope Meyers, Patricia Norland, Patricia Squire, Margaret Sullivan, Suzanne Swanson, Mary Louise Weiss, and Monique Wong. Additional, and much appreciated, interviews were conducted by Patricia Barbis and Pamela Burdick; Marian Phillips from the Greenwich, Connecticut, Public Library Oral History Project, who interviewed Anita English; and Maurice Weisz from the Labor Diplomacy Oral History Project at the Association for Diplomatic Studies and Training. Catharine Bell, Marion S. Bergesen, Robert Lewis, and Beatrice Meyerson interviewed their mothers. The time-consuming task of transcription profited greatly from the tireless efforts of Caroline Farquhar; other transcribers included Peg Davies, Marion Henderson, Penne Laingen, Marta Schlely, Joleen Schweitzer, and Patience Spiers. Kristie Miller and Joan Williamson gave steadfast support in a variety of roles. My thanks to all of them.

Over the six years of the program, the following individuals, and doubtless many more, provided invaluable assistance: H. Eugene Bovis, Shelley Getchell, Donna Hartman, Anne Kauzlarich, Dorothy Kidder, John Kormann, Mary Brown Lawrence, Lilla Lévitt, Ruth Little, Stephen Low, Cecil and Elsie Lyon, Naomi Mathews, Nancy Matthews, Marvin Patterson, Richard B. Parker, Flora Pitts, Martha Ross, Jack and Caroline Service, Christine Shurtleff, Sally Stout, and Inge Wolf.

Finally, my affectionate thanks to my spouse for years of staunch support, and to my children, Cammillo Fenzi and Ruth Fenzi Reeder—and to Ruth's husband Tom Reeder—for reversing the traditional parental role and giving *me* good advice.

Any errors, however, are my own.

Introduction

I do not wish you to accept an embassy to England . . . .

Abigail Adams

Abigail Adams was unhappy during the early summer of 1783. She already had been separated from her husband, John, for five years, while he pursued the diplomatic interests of the newly confederated United States in Paris and The Hague. With London as a possible new appointment, Abigail's greatest fear was that her husband would be pressed into further service of her new country's foreign interests, and as a result, she could be reunited with him only by hazarding the long ocean voyage to Europe.[1]

"I do not wish you to accept an embassy to England, should you be appointed," Abigail wrote to John on 20 June from the Adamses' home in what is now Quincy, Massachusetts. "This little cottage has more heart-felt satisfaction for you than the most brilliant court can provide." This sentiment also demonstrated the remarkable common thread of separation from their husbands that united the Foreign Service wives of the past and the present. In 1968, when her husband drew a Vietnam assignment, Abigail's seven-times great-granddaughter Catherine (Casey) Peltier wound up in the Philippines, 1,000 miles away.

In the same letter, Abigail explained the reasoning behind her complaint, reasoning that did not prevail and led directly to her historical position as America's first Foreign Service spouse. "[A] well-ordered home is my chief delight, and the affectionate domestic wife with the relative duties which accompany that character my highest ambition," she wrote.[2] If John would not, or could not, come home, then Abigail resolved to join him in Paris, in "the disinterested wish of sacrificing my personal feelings to the public utility." The role of the diplomatic spouse, in her view, amounted to "the earnest wish I had to soften those toils which were not to be dispensed with, and if the public welfare required your labors and exertions abroad, I flattered myself, that if I could be with you, it might be in my power to contribute to your happiness and pleasure."[3] While two centuries old, Abigail Adams's views on the role of the spouse in the Foreign Service retain great relevance in the 1990s.

In the years since, America's diplomats—and diplomatic historians—have consistently overlooked the personal side of U.S. foreign relations. Yet in the last three decades in particular, and with the women's movement as catalyst, many foreign affairs agency wives have begun to open their diaries and memories to reveal the important contributions of spouses to the success of American diplomacy abroad.

As its principal source, this book drew on more than 170 oral history interviews conducted by the Foreign Service Spouse Oral History Program during the late 1980s and early 1990s. The program was established in 1986 as a collaborative effort to record the memories of women whose service experiences dated back to the years immediately prior to World War I. The Foreign Service spouse's place in history—her public and private accomplishments abroad and her contributions as a support system for U.S. foreign relations—has been virtually unknown outside the Foreign Service, and only partially appreciated within it. As a group, though, the collective remembrances of these spouses chronicled political, economic, and social changes of the twentieth century from a new and heretofore undocumented perspective.

The initial purpose was to assemble archives of tape-recorded interviews and written materials—letters, journals, articles, books, and photographs—documenting the lives of the spouses of employees of the U.S. foreign affairs agencies. Interviewing began with four narrators, women in their seventies who had spent a collective 100 years as Foreign Service wives while serving in 25 countries. All lived in Washington, D.C., where they were accessible for interviews. Interviewers were principally Foreign Service women, spouses of both active and retired officers, whose years with the service had spanned periods long enough for them to have participated in the drastic changes in the role of wives within it.

Transcripts of the interviews make up the Association of American Foreign Service Women Oral History Collection in Washington, D.C. Copies have been placed in the National Foreign Affairs Training Center in Arlington, Virginia, in Georgetown University's Lauinger Library in Washington, D.C., and in the Arthur and Elizabeth Schlesinger Library on the History of Women in America at Radcliffe College in Cambridge, Massachusetts.

On a personal note, two principal reasons underlie the genesis of this book and of the Foreign Service Spouse Oral History Program. The first and most immediate reason for making this material available was to add a voice to the chorus advocating official recognition of the diplomatic spouse. The second resulted from my 30-year observation that no comprehensive history existed of Foreign Service wives.

When my husband retired from the Foreign Service in the mid-1980s and we returned to Washington, I ventured to the Library of Congress and retrieved only a meager computer printout weighted heavily with cookbooks, books by foreign diplomatic wives, and a few vanity press publications. One of the most relevant titles turned out to be a one-act play called *A Diplomatic Tea*, written by Isabella Key Reeves, performed by the Casper, Wyoming, chapter of the Daughters of the American Revolution, and published by Oil City Press in 1938.[4] It was apparent that, 200 years after Abigail and Louisa Adams's correspondence and journals were written, they remained the best record of the lives of American diplomatic spouses.

Louisa (Mrs. John Quincy) Adams's life in czarist Saint Petersburg, for instance, encompassed all of the rigors of diplomatic life then and now. She endured prolonged separation from her family and husband at an isolated post. She endured illness, the death of a child, the deaths of family members thousands of miles away, miscarriages, depression, financial hardship, a lengthy search for adequate housing, and untrustworthy domestic help, all amid the necessity of providing due deference to host country dignitaries. In addition, in the early nineteenth century she suffered two profound psychological perils: months without communication from home, and rigorous travel. In February 1815, alone with her son and two servants, she embarked on a 40-day trek to Paris across the frozen steppes in a horse-drawn Russian sleigh. John Quincy Adams had left her behind to pay the bills, pack up the household, and follow him to Paris as best she might.

Through it all, both she and her husband, bitingly ambitious, viewed these diplomatic hardships as paving a route to the U.S. presidency. As Joan Ridder Challinor points out in her study "Louisa Catherine Johnson Adams: The Price of Ambition" (1982), the pair had "absolutely no money" when John Quincy Adams was offered a seat on the Supreme Court, yet he turned it down, suggesting instead that they stay on in Saint Petersburg without salary.[5]

My personal experience over 30 years was that diplomatic life could still be exceptionally harsh emotionally and physically on those who practice it. The first career spouse I encountered abroad offered a poignant example. I saw her only once socially. At a large embassy reception, she stood alone, chain-smoking, eyes wide with fright. As she shredded butt after butt with yellowed fingers, tobacco flakes and bits of paper littered the floor around her. An "incident in Cuba" was responsible, we were told.

Yet almost without fail, Foreign Service women of that earlier generation, when queried about their diplomatic years, declared them to be exciting, fulfilling, and adventurous. In one oral history interview, an ambassador's spouse (service entry date 1947) used the word *wonderful* 18 times to describe her service experiences, which included: a honeymoon cut short by a call from "Mother State"; sailing pregnant through a gale to her first post, which had been devastated by World War II; unsatisfactory boarding school experiences for her children; life at a high–security-risk embassy threatened by terrorists; separation from her husband, who served in a war zone; and performing double hostess duties while her husband was deputy chief of mission for unmarried ambassadors. Another ambassador's spouse (service entry date 1967) demonstrated a growing generation gap when she used the term *difficult* 25 times to describe her continuing Foreign Service "adventure."

Another example revealed the contrasts in the preoccupations of different generations of spouses. It came from a letter penned at the American embassy in Stockholm in 1951:

Had a dinner party last night, small, just seven of us, but we had a lot of fun. Fru Olafson came to serve, and I must say I feel glad now of the effort and money we spent over the last few years getting our silver (Holmes and Edwards, but most people think it is Jensen's sterling because it is a copy of one of his patterns) and the Rosenthal china (a year in the making) and the convent set of dinner mats, plus the silver gotten in Peru by selling all my old clothes. The table looks so lovely, with the candles burning and the silver swan bowl, which I filled with yellow and white chrysanthemums. We had martinis and tiny cheese puffs, and small caviar sandwiches. Then I had ox-filet of beef marinated in French dressing and cut in thin strips. Tossed in hot butter, then taken out, mushrooms and green olive strips put in, and all put together with garlic, onion juice, etc., and sweetbreads. With that rice ring, and around it, rings of fresh (frozen) peas, each ring with a gay small braised tomato in the center. It is all served on one platter and so goes quickly. For dessert I made vanilla ice cream, just like our great-grandmothers used to freeze, rich and smooth and yummy. With strawberries and lady fingers, coffee, brandy and chartreuse finished us all up. Oh yes, cream soup with sherry and red wine with the meat. AND scotch and soda afterwards. With being hostess and having to drink all that, no wonder I am writing you with a hangover.[6]

In the 1990s spouse correspondence is more likely to echo the attitudes expressed in the *SUN* (*Spouses' Underground Newsletter*), published by Francesca Kelly at whatever post she found herself, and including such irreverent titles as "How I Nearly Killed My Husband in Language Class," "Let's Go and Call a Shrink," and the trials and tribulations of "Rebecca Long Fairchild, Foreign Service Spouse," who in one episode mistook the ambassador for a veterinarian.

Even more startling are the vast differences in events recorded by spouses and those their husbands recalled for a Foreign Service officer oral history program. After reading the transcript of Laurent Morin's interview, his wife, Ann Morin, an authority on women ambassadors, commented, "We are talking about two people happily married who have lived a long life together. Reading my husband's transcript and then mine, you would think you were reading about two different lives at a different set of posts. There was *no relationship* between the events we recorded in our two interviews. It was startling. My most devastating experience was the loss of a child, which my husband had not even mentioned. I insisted that he include it when he edited his transcript."

A dissimilarity in public perception of the Foreign Service as a series of effortless encounters with the rich, famous, and powerful, and diplomatic life's true demands on spouses—coping with CODELs (congressional delegations) and other American VIP visits abroad—was characterized in Marilyn Holmes's 1993 interview. As spouse of the chargé d'affaires in Rome in 1978, Marilyn Holmes recalled her personal efforts to ensure the success of Rosalynn Carter's visit as official U.S. representative to the funeral of Pope Paul VI. Marilyn readied Villa Taverna, the ambassador's residence, for Mrs. Carter's stay and adroitly managed a social schedule fraught with political pitfalls.

We were very shorthanded. In Europe, in August, everybody was on leave, including our ambassador. Allen, my husband, relied on me heavily to put together Mrs. Carter's schedule. I had to make the arrangements at Villa Taverna, where she would be staying. There was no domestic staff, so I grabbed any of the maintenance people I could find at the embassy and stuffed them into a uniform. "You're going to be a maid." "You're going to be a butler." Mrs. Carter was not going to leave the villa because of the paparazzi and the notoriety of the press in Rome, and, of course, this was not a joyful visit since it was for the funeral. There were also security problems because of the [Aldo] Moro kidnapping in March of that year, and as it happened security would not release her from the residence.

So we had the problem of who she was going to see, and when, and how, and how that would play in local politics. The Vatican let it be known that the dean, Cardinal Sinn, wished to call on Mrs. Carter. He was Filipino and very much wanted to discuss with her his concerns about the Philippines. Well, there was a great political battle going on between Sinn and his fellow cardinals. And the Vatican foreign minister thought he should see Mrs. Carter to discuss legitimate affairs of state, namely, human rights, so the two factions in the Vatican were warring.

I would get back to my man in the Vatican and say, "Why don't you send a delegation? You can all have tea with Mrs. Carter." "Well, who's going to walk in first?" "Well, I don't know. You know the protocol, who meets her first and how they address her," and on and on. It was actually very amusing, but I had to coordinate the actual tea, which did happen. Meanwhile, I was trying to figure out whether there would be any pastries or tea. Because the servants who weren't servants didn't have a clue in the kitchen.

And then I would be back on the telephone with the Vatican saying, "Yes, I think we can accommodate you. Cardinal Sinn will walk in first, and then the foreign minister will come in second." That kind of thing.

I managed Mrs. Carter's entire social calendar from the ambassador's residence, with my fake domestics running around in their uniforms. It was a lot of work, I must say, but she was extraordinarily gracious, helpful, cooperative, didn't know enough to do to be nice to people, and followed it up with the nicest thank-you letters and signed photographs, which had been taken with everyone. Certainly a very positive visit.

At eight o'clock the night before she left for Washington, she called and asked me to jog with her. I pulled on my old running clothes and drove over to the residence. Fortunately, the gardens of Villa Taverna are huge, and there was plenty of room to jog. Well, there was Rosalynn Carter, perfectly made up, in knockout running gear, looking as if she were ready for the cameras to roll!

She talked while we jogged, which I found difficult to do, and I was totally impressed with her knowledge of affairs in Washington. She knew exactly what was going on, especially on the Hill, and could cite the bills by their numbers. She knew everything.

I have dealt with first ladies from Jacqueline Kennedy to Nancy Reagan and found Rosalynn Carter and Lady Byrd Johnson to be the most gracious. Mrs. Carter is, I think, more politically astute than her husband and would have made a good president.

Spousal experiences in American diplomatic history during the past eight decades contained several institutional milestones. The first, the Rogers Act of 1924, created the modern Foreign Service and in the process merged the diplomatic corps and the consular corps, which was responsible for commercial matters and the welfare of U.S. citizens abroad. World War II witnessed an enormous expansion in diplomatic endeavor and not incidentally created new opportunities for women and spouses to contribute as professionals. A management reform study by Henry M. Wriston, former president of Brown University, resulted in the "Wristonization" program, which brought high-level civil servants into the Foreign Service and sent them abroad with wives who had never anticipated living overseas. The fear and repression of the McCarthy era made scapegoats out of well-prepared, educated, and dedicated Foreign Service officers and took their spouses down to defeat as well. Up until 1970 spouses, if recognized at all, were identifiable in the Department of State register by an apocryphal "m." at the conclusion of an officer's biographical sketch. Ironically, the beginning of spouse listings in the register was followed five years later by the classification of the entire document as a national secret, to protect the identities of U.S. intelligence agents serving undercover as economic or political officers. In 1972 a change in the status of women in general, and of diplomatic spouses in particular, was exemplified by the "Policy on Wives" instituted by the foreign affairs agencies.

Those spouses who gained experience abroad also served at home in Washington, and their insights gathered in both venues offered unique perspectives into how the bureaucracy worked. Beginning in 1960, tours in Washington had provided spouses with opportunities to take meaningful action—such as transforming the Foreign Service Wives' Group from an elite luncheon gathering into a broader formal organization, the Association of American Foreign Service Women. In the 1970s a group of dedicated spouses lobbied Congress and the State Department for pension benefits for divorced spouses and the establishment of the Family Liaison Office in Washington to address family concerns. Community liaison offices soon mushroomed in missions abroad. In the 1980s and 1990s, while on Washington assignment, spouses devised the "Foreign Service associate" proposal to enhance spouse employment opportunities and lobbied, without success, for spouse paychecks. It was this kind of involvement that prompted one spouse of a midcareer officer to observe that she "had been abroad too long."

Oral history offered a particularly effective format for these recollections and made it possible to gather and disseminate a large body of material in a relatively short period. The interviews revealed that women had indeed played a large role in international relations throughout nine decades of American foreign affairs and had had a profound impact both at home and abroad. Equally important, the interviews offered spouses an awareness that their experiences had value in the larger scheme of international relations. What they do, and did, counted.

The interviews have preserved the private insights of spouses such as Théophania (Fanny) Chipman. Upon her marriage in the 1930s, she acquired a prominent father-in-law who insisted she quit her job with the Inter-American Commission of Women, because "women who were married should stay at home," even though her new husband's salary as a third secretary proved inadequate. She soon found herself in Joseph Stalin's Moscow, where in the winter newspapers bundled around feet served commonly as shoes for many Russians. Elizabeth (Betty) Moffat White vividly recalled the "beautiful, blue-green, green-blue china" eyes of Adolf Hitler in Berlin in the midthirties. Evacuation, an inherent risk in diplomatic life, became the metaphor for the democratization of the Foreign Service, from Edith O'Shaughnessy's flight from Mexico City in 1914 on the private train of the president of Mexico, to the thousands of evacuees who fled turmoil in the Middle East in the late 1970s, prompting the spouse of a high-ranking official to use her considerable influence to set up an evacuation crisis center in the Department of State.

But Foreign Service life also presented limitless opportunities and at times was just good fun. Television's "French Chef," Julia Child, used her tenure as a diplomatic spouse during the late 1940s and 1950s in Paris, Marseille, Bonn, and Oslo to launch her career of changing the way Americans think about food. June Hamilton, in the 1960s, gained a footnote in jazz history when she introduced the legendary Duke Ellington to the musical rhythms of the Middle East, even though his performance in Baghdad coincided with a successful coup against the Iraqi government.

This narrative tells these and many more spouses' stories in roughly chronological fashion. Because of space limitations, not all 170 interviews could be used, and some receive more emphasis than others. In every case, the selection process was undertaken with an eye toward capturing the broader outlines and common elements of the experience of being a Foreign Service spouse and the wide variety of contributions they made to American diplomacy.

While by the 1990s a significant number of men—700, according to the Family Liaison Office—served in the role of foreign affairs agency spouse, this narrative is concerned primarily with the experiences of women. The wives' participation as "a key group not even on the payroll" in "the ceremonial side of diplomacy," to quote former Deputy Undersecretary of State for Administration William B. Macomber, Jr., was of necessity intimately intertwined with the evolving role of women in society.[7] The changing nature of women's views toward their own appropriate involvement in U.S. diplomacy and society at large, combined with the responses to those changing perceptions by men in the Foreign Service establishment and the bureaucracy itself, together produce a narrative of subtle tension, punctuated with the sudden and imperative demands of international and national political events and crises.

"[A]ny man's life . . . can be but a cold and colorless thing if it affords no intimate glimpse of the personalities involved," former Undersecretary of State Joseph C. Grew wrote in his nearly 1,600-page memoir, *Turbulent Era*, in 1952.[8] But his daughter Lilla Grew Moffat (Lévitt) remembered 35 years later, "My mother would have liked much more of us, much more of a personal nature in my father's book." This narrative attempts to fill in those human, personal gaps and to give real substance to the engaging and difficult tasks that have been the spouse contribution to American diplomacy.

The text, a broad-brush sweep through the twentieth century, relies to a large degree on the memories of the narrators, women who usually are introduced in the decade they entered the service. Many of their stories, of course, could not be independently verified from historical sources. But all of the interviews were taped and transcribed, and all of those interviewed signed deeds of gift placing the transcripts in the public domain for the use of future researchers. For this study, the spoken language of the transcripts has been edited—but minimally—to enhance the readability of the text. In every case, the thoughts and emphases of the interview subjects remain unchanged.

A NOTE ON NAMES

Keeping track of the names of the wives whose stories are told here posed a formidable obstacle. Some grew up in the service, then married Foreign Service officers. Others entered foreign affairs agencies while single and later married officers. Divorced women reverted to—and some young spouses kept—their maiden names. And Foreign Service widows remarried.

Lilla Grew Moffat (Lévitt), for example, daughter of the distinguished veteran diplomat Joseph C. Grew, posed such a dilemma. As a child and young adult in the service, she was Lilla Grew. On her marriage to Jay Pierrepont Moffat in 1927, she became Lilla Moffat. Following his death in 1943, she left Foreign Service life and remarried, becoming Lilla Lévitt.

She is introduced in the text by her full name, which also appears in the Appendix, the list of women and men interviewed for the Foreign Service Spouse Oral History Program. Subsequently, she is referred to as Lilla Moffat, her name as a Foreign Service spouse. The names of other women have been handled in similar fashion.

TWILIGHT OF THE "OLD" AND DAWN OF THE MODERN FOREIGN SERVICE

The Foreign Service was my life.

Lilla Grew Moffat (Lévitt)

Around the time of World War I, the U.S. diplomatic service, while poised on the brink of the accelerating change that characterizes it even today, remained an insular world drawn from the upper reaches of society. The officers and spouses of this small world, selected primarily from the Ivy League universities and the likes of Miss Porter's School, prized assignment to the prestigious posts in Europe. Family "quality," personal wealth, political acquaintances, and financial achievement determined who became an American diplomat, and for that matter, his spouse.

From Abigail Adams's time until World War I, little had changed in the Foreign Service. The diplomatic and consular corps, still separate physical entities, were composed largely of men of independent means. The representational responsibilities of statecraft meant that the job cost the officeholder in real money terms. Of course, throughout the nineteenth century, communications improved dramatically, and travel from post to post underwent a remarkable transformation. Abigail Adams's storm-tossed, month-long journey across the Atlantic, in a good boat with a sound "copper bottom," [1] was replaced in the age of steam with first-class travel in floating cities called ocean liners (and later in the jet age by a cramped, economy-class airplane seat). But the role of the diplomatic spouse retained a comfortable character and a slow pace devoted to formal entertainment and servant supervision, a lifestyle that only began to crack with the technological and political upheavals—beginning with World War I—that mark the twentieth century.

It was a closed and rarefied society. The diplomatic list of 1922 named 300 officers, including 100 military attachés, who were traditionally single. [2] Only

1

five women officers entered the service in the 1920s. Foreign Service officers were assigned to posts that averaged three officers and few dependents. The hallmarks of diplomatic life—tasteful furnishings, engraved sterling, fine crystal, fragile bone china, and monogrammed linens—were provided by the family. Only in 1919 did the State Department begin to pay the costs of sending families and household goods abroad. There were no overseas American schools, no access to U.S. medical facilities, no commissaries, and no paid home leave. For the wives, transfers from one post to another involved long voyages on ocean liners with nursemaids, governesses, steamer trunks, and mounds of luggage as traveling companions. The spouses were a tight-knit group, and their children, many of whom grew up to pursue Foreign Service careers themselves, thought, as children do, that the situation was normal.

Wives in this upper-class milieu, as in society at large, had few options beyond the traditional family support role. As in the larger culture, they took on their husbands' status, but their role of "unofficially official" spouse demanded an active participation in whatever culture they found themselves. To a large degree, these spouses assumed, almost without question, that their appropriate function was to provide, particularly socially, an official representation of U.S. diplomacy, even without any formal status of their own.

In 1914 one wife in Mexico City chronicled events in a rare published account of everyday American diplomatic life before World War I. Edith O'Shaughnessy, wife of the chargé d'affaires to Mexico, Nelson O'Shaughnessy, in daily correspondence to her mother described conditions during these years of civil strife in Mexico.

Diplomatically, this was a very volatile time. The revolutionaries Emiliano Zapata and Venustiano Carranza were moving in on Mexico City, while Francisco (Pancho) Villa was marauding in the North. U.S. relations with the government of President Victoriano Huerta were collapsing. These events led eventually to the U.S. invasion of northern Mexico in an unsuccessful attempt at apprehending Villa.

In one account, Edith O'Shaughnessy tells of a weekend excursion in March 1914 from Mexico City to Vera Cruz on the Caribbean coast, where her husband had scheduled meetings with U.S. Navy officials aboard the USS Mayflower. The party made a side trip, however, to a massive prison at nearby San Juan. To reach the commandant's quarters, they were obliged to skirt thick masonry walls where narrow slits, only inches wide, led into unlighted, unaired dungeons. "Human sounds came faintly from these apertures," Edith O'Shaughnessy wrote.

"[Then] we went up on the great parapets, the norte blowing fiercely—I in my black Jeanne Hallé hobble-skirt and a black tulle hat, as later we were to go to tea on the Mayflower. We walked over great, flat roofs of masonry

2

in which were occasional square, barred holes. Peering down in the darkness, thirty feet or so, of any one of these, there would be, at first, no sound, only a horrible, indescribable stench mingling with the salt air. But as we threw boxes of cigarettes into the foul blackness there came vague, human groans and rumbling noises, and we could see, in the blackness, human hands up-stretched or the gleam of an eye. If above, in that strong norther, we could scarcely stand the stench that arose, what must it have been in the depths below? About 800 men live in those holes. . . .

"I know there must be prisons and there must be abuses in all communities; but this pest-hole at the entrance to the great harbor where our ships lie within a stone's-throw seems incredible.

"Afterward, the contrast of tea, music, and smart, ready-to-dance young officers on the beautiful Mayflower rather inclined me to stillness. I was finding it difficult to let God take care of His world!"[3]

A month later, on the night of 22 April 1914, President Huerta called at the U.S. embassy residence—where earlier his men had confiscated weapons and ammunition—to invite the chargé d'affaires and his wife to his son's wedding the following day. Although the O'Shaughnessys had maintained cordial relations with Huerta and his wife, it was the only time the president had visited the residence during the chargé's tenure in Mexico City. Because of deteriorating diplomatic relations, the O'Shaughnessys were to be evacuated the day after the wedding, aboard Huerta's personal train, again to Vera Cruz, where American ships were anchored. On 24 April Edith O'Shaughnessy wrote to her mother "from the train, after our sudden departure last night":

"But I must go back to Wednesday night—our last night in Mexico City—when I was too tired for feeling or thought. In the morning Nelson decided that, under the circumstances, he would not, could not, go to the Huerta wedding. Then I decided to go alone. [A member of the embassy staff] went with me in the automobile. I put on my best black things, long white gloves, and pearls, and got through the crowd in front of the embassy, and went to the president's house in the Calle Alfonso Herrera, enfolded and exhilarated by dazzling air. I got there to find myself the only foreigner, of course, [with] only three or four other women, the wives of cabinet ministers and generals. The men were mostly in full uniform. Madame Huerta came in, looking very handsome and dignified in a becoming dress of delicate pomegranate color veiled partly with black lace—a good dress. The dark, bright-eyed bride, in a dress with a good deal of imitation lace, arrived nearly three-quarters of an hour late. Immediately after her arrival the president entered, in his slouch-hat and the celebrated gray sweater.

"He quickly greeted the guests, called his wife, 'Emilia,' and then turned to me. 'Mrs. O'Shaughnessy,' he said, and indicated a place near the table where the marriage contract was to be signed. So I rose, and stood with the family during the ceremony which he had put through at a lively pace. . . . After the ceremony we all went out to get into the automobiles and . . . started off through the dazzling streets to the distant 'Buen Tono' church which had been put at the disposition of the president for the wedding. On our arrival the president, who had gone ahead, appeared to help us out of the motor; then, saying to me in Spanish, 'I have something to do,' he disappeared. I never saw him again.

"Our train was supposed to go at nine o'clock, but we did not leave until eleven-thirty. Our diplomatic colleagues and a very few others who knew of our going were there to see us off, in the dimly lighted, gray station. At ten I begged our friends to go; we have masses of letters and telegrams [to deliver for them]. A forty-three thousand dollar fund, my jewels and money of our own and other people's, I carried in the black hand-bag with the gilt clasps which you gave me in Paris. McKenna from the embassy guards the codes as if they were infants. No sovereign of Europe could have planned and executed this departure of ours more royally than Huerta did.

"But at Guadalupe, the first stop just outside the city, a painful incident occurred. About twenty-five persons, American friends, were waiting there to board the train and continue the journey with us. But Nelson had given his word of honor, when he received the safe-conduct, that no person or persons other than the personnel of embassy and consulate should avail themselves of this privilege. So rarely was faith kept with Huerta that it seemed hard that it should be done in this crucial hour and at the expense of our own people. We intended, however, to save even honor; but as our train rolled out of the station I felt, to the full, 'the fell clutch of circumstance.'

". . . We have passed Tejería, the last Mexican station; the sand-hills and spires of Vera Cruz will soon be distinguishable. I have just looked out of the window, my eyes dim with tears. Far up the broken track the blessed white flag of truce can be seen approaching—our people, our men, coming for their own."

"Vera Cruz, April 25
We had left Huerta's train at the break in the tracks and, with Captain Huse and the other officers as a military escort, I walked down the track about two kilometers. The rails were torn up, but the road-bed was undestroyed and as we walked along in the blazing sun, with scrubby, dusty palms and cactus in the grayish fields on either side, my back turned to the Mexican train, I was divided between joy and sorrow—joy to see and be with my own again and

the haunting thought of poor, distracted Mexico, and of our own people, whom we had been obliged to leave to heaven knows what fate. It is easy to be the last out of the danger zone, but very, very hard to be the first. I hope that another time, if fate puts us again in such strange places, we will be the last to go.

"We finally got to our own train, which was run by a poor, dilapidated, leaking, propped-up engine, all that was left. The Mexicans had been quick about the machines, and every locomotive had been seized by them and sent away, after which they had destroyed those kilometers of track. Everybody climbed into the relief train, and there came the question of getting our luggage from one train to another. So, to make a very long story short, several cutthroat-looking peons, casting deadly glances at los gringos, transferred a lot of the hand-luggage, aided by the men of the party. All I possess of value, except that left at the embassy, was contained in a single, large trunk, reposing in the cactus-fields in the enemy's lines, watched over by the same shambling, dark-browed, cutthroat Mexicans who helped to transfer the small baggage.

"Captain Huse said afterwards, 'You didn't realize what danger we were in.' I asked him, 'Are we at war with Mexico?' And he answered, 'I don't know.' Adding, 'They say not; but when one armed force opposes another armed force, and many are killed, we are rather of the opinion that it is war.' "[4]

PERILS OF FAMILY LIFE

In addition to evacuation, the perils of childbirth often accompanied these women of the early Foreign Service to and from, and at, their posts. They and their husbands were sometimes called upon to perform skills more useful in frontier, rather than diplomatic, life. The memories from 1918 and 1919 of Catharine Johnson (Cluett) are a case in point. Before her husband, Stewart Johnson, was killed in a motor accident in Cairo in 1926, she had accompanied him on assignment to Guatemala City, San José (Costa Rica), Caracas, and Berlin. It was their exit from Costa Rica, their journey to and from Venezuela, and the birth of their daughter that dramatized the primitive conditions faced by Americans abroad. In a 1982 interview with her daughter, Catharine Johnson recalled:

Costa Rica had a revolution in early December 1918, and during it the citizens attacked the legation, trying to climb the iron fence. Stewart contacted the State Department.

Two days later a battleship arrived, and some of the crew came to the rescue. We took a steamer at Port Limon and then boarded the cruiser *USS Salem*, who fired a salute as we boarded the ship, and were given the captain's quarters.

I was taken ill on the voyage. The ship's doctor, Lieutenant Commander Harrison, was very interested in my violently nauseated condition. Shortly, I coughed up an eight-inch worm (the doctor said it's very unusual to exit from the mouth, usually it's from the other end), and the next day I vomited its mate, several inches longer. Dr. Harrison said he would preserve them for the Smithsonian Institution.

After we docked at a private plantation at the mouth of the Mississippi and trained to Chicago, I was in St. Luke's Hospital recovering for several weeks, as it was also discovered that I was pregnant. Meanwhile, Stewart went to Washington and learned that Caracas, Venezuela, would be our next post. . . .

[In Caracas], our social life was quiet because of my pregnancy. . . . But when the legation had a July 4th celebration for all U.S. citizens in Venezuela—even though we thought the baby might arrive that day—I was hostess, dressed in flowing chiffon. The baby, our daughter Catharine, waited until July 6th and has been known as Catita or Tita, after being called Catalinita by her Venezuelan nurse. The doctor insisted that I not go to the clinic for the birth, because of our social position, so the clinic came to the legation. Stewart was present at her birth, which proved valuable later on.

In a series of letters to her parents, Catharine Johnson chronicled birthing and postnatal practices in Caracas. She wrote to her mother a week after Tita's birth on 6 July 1919, mistakenly dating the letter 1918: "Here it is just a week today since 'Tita' arrived, and you must excuse [the] pencil and writing as I haven't even been allowed to sit up yet. As for me now I feel finely, the only thing that troubles me are the stitches which are coming out today." [5]

Catharine's birthing experience included thirteen hours of labor, followed by an additional three under chloroform before the doctor intervened with forceps, assisted throughout by her husband, who learned basic midwifery skills in the process. Her new, and unexpectedly healthy, daughter was named even before Catharine recovered from the anesthesia. But on doctor's orders, she spent the next six weeks in bed.

She resumed her story in the 1982 interview:

After less than a year in Caracas, we were transferred to Washington in November 1919. We returned on a freighter, again in the captain's quarters, and were the only passengers. But at the next port, Cartagena [Colombia], Harry A. Frank, the author of *Vagabonding in the West Indies* and other travel books, and his wife boarded the ship.

At 4:30 the next morning, Frank woke the Johnsons to say that his wife was having a baby. Since Stewart Johnson had witnessed Tita's birth, he accompanied Catharine to the Franks' cabin to assist. The galley was not yet open, so there was no hot water; sherry was the only painkiller. Catharine Johnson continued:

After the baby was born, we sent the father to our cabin for my sewing basket, and I used my nail scissors and white silk thread. Stewart, who knew the procedure, said to tie the thread near the baby and another near the placenta and wait for the pulse to stop. We made the father [cut the umbilical cord]. That night, the baby was brought to the dining room and placed in the center of the dining table as a centerpiece, with his arms and legs kicking and waving.

Stewart and Catharine Johnson, young Catharine (Tita), and Mira, the greyhound, in the gardens of the American Legation, Cairo, Egypt, 1926. Courtesy of Tita Bell.

TALES OF FOUR MARRIAGES

The Johnsons' assignment of less than a year to Caracas was highly unusual in the Foreign Service at this time. For young officers in particular, whether in the consular or diplomatic corps, overseas postings could stretch into many years away from the United States. Just as today, many young officers married into the local culture, even though attracting an American spouse was tacitly preferred by the Department of State: further assignments would uproot the foreign-born spouse from her native background, placing her in the uncomfortable position of representing the United States in a culture as alien to her as the American one.

Whether American or foreign-born, spouses of this generation tended to be of the same socioeconomic background as their officer husbands and often brought desired, and career-enhancing, wealth to a Foreign Service marriage. Three narratives from the World War I period illustrate the differing attitudes spouses brought to the diplomatic duties expected of them.

The first is drawn from the correspondence between Bernette Chase Kemp, called Nettie, Anna Smith Kemp, and the consular officer Edwin Carl Kemp. The women were close friends in Melrose, Massachusetts, during the early years of the century. When Bernette married Carl Kemp in 1909, the friendship expanded to include him and was naturally carried on through voluminous correspondence when he joined the consular corps in 1914; the couple went first to the French possession of St. Pierre et Miquelon off the Canadian Atlantic coast, and later to Tunis, Tunisia. Nettie died of influenza in November 1918, shortly before the armistice. A year later Carl Kemp convinced Anna, then a near-spinster approaching 30, to cast aside a settled New England lifestyle and marry him in Paris, before setting up housekeeping at his post in Bucharest, Romania.

Nettie Kemp's early letters to Anna from Tunis described everyday life in the World War I–era consular corps in North Africa. On 5 December 1916 she revealed an ambivalent attitude toward the representational responsibilities (which have persisted into the 1990s) and, although a trained nurse, an unwillingness to help in treating war wounded because doing so almost certainly would have overwhelmed her frail health.

"I shall make my calls with Carl beginning this p.m. [even though] my calling clothes are too light and bright for this weather. The wife of the resident general is in mourning and not receiving but we're commencing with the next in rank and going down the lot. No one outside the necessary officials and the Consular Corps. Otherwise we'd have 150 to make. And I'm going to make my health a reason for not making the others. Although as a matter of fact I'm better than for a long time and fat for me, everybody here thinks I look delicate so I'm going to work it for what it's worth. All the women here are working themselves ill in hospital work. . . . Of course, over here I keep my past history [as a trained nurse] dark, but it amuses me to keep up with these amateur nurses and their troubles."[6]

Three years later, following Nettie Kemp's untimely death from influenza, Anna set sail alone—a rarity for her generation—from New York on board the Patria, bound for Marseilles, where Carl Kemp met her, then overland to Paris, where they were married on 26 November 1919 (Anna, whose comprehension of French was nonexistent at the time, did manage to answer "oui" at the appropriate points), and finally by train to Carl's assigned post in Bucharest. The trip began, Anna Smith Kemp wrote to her sister Mae, with scenes reminiscent of Abigail Adams's first ocean voyage more than a century earlier.

"On Board the Patria, November 1919 . . . After we left the harbor Thursday we ran into a storm and for three days were on end all the time.

"I spent Friday and Saturday flat on my back and didn't care what happened. Everything fell over that wasn't hitched and even the stewardess was ill. . . . No one could get any service at all when they were ill. The food is impossible and everyone much disgruntled with everything. It is a very good introduction to what I shall find from France on, I suppose.

"During the storm a man from the steerage jumped overboard but it was so rough they made no attempt to get him. Two people went insane and one man who was confined got away and caused much excitement one night. So, you see, life is hardly dull.

"17 November . . . We passed the Azores and Gibraltar and have been following the African coast. After that we had more rough weather, the boat standing on end day and night. Saturday it calmed down and another man jumped overboard. It seems to be the habit on board this ship. They stopped, made a circle several times, threw over life buoys, but no one appeared. The next night the crazy boy nearly finished his parents so they had to put him in a straightjacket.

"The food and service still continue poor. Afternoon tea has just been

Anna Durkee Smith Kemp, Boston, undated. Courtesy of Janet Kemp Doell.

served and after washing my cup and spoon myself I managed to drink some today. It improves the flavor to have the china fairly clean.

"This old tub either has no cargo or is a very wobbly ship. We had such a list at Gibraltar I was all worn out holding it down on the other side. There are three 'vamps' on board. Donald [a distant cousin] will explain to you what they are. The Captain is very attentive to one.

"People at my table are all worn out trying to find out why I am roaming around alone. They ask all the direct questions they can and then try the indirect method. Finally, they wanted to know if I were a Romanian princess traveling incognito.[7]

Anna Kemp went on to spend 28 years in the Foreign Service, the last 12 as wife of the consul general in assignments to Canada, Germany, and, finally, Jamaica after World War II.

The second narrative involves the marriage of a foreign-born spouse to an American officer. Aida Schoenfeld was the daughter of a Scottish expatriate father based in Montevideo, Uruguay, and a Scottish mother who herself had been born in Valparaiso, Chile.

The courtship and shocking introduction to the duties of Foreign Service life experienced by Aida Schoenfeld displayed the same sharp contrast between days spent in the genteel occupations of an upper-class wife and the harsh rigors of international travel and representational responsibilities. She was born in Uruguay, had an excellent command of the Spanish language and culture, and was educated in British schools in Montevideo and England, becoming in a sense a truly international spouse. She thrived in the service.

Shortly after her marriage in September 1915 to Hans Frederick Arthur (Turo) Schoenfeld, 19-year-old Aida received a rude introduction to the political workings of the State Department when a new U.S. minister to Uruguay arrived in the person of Robert Emmett Jeffrey, whose political connections had clinched the job. "He was a political assignment and knew absolutely nothing about diplomacy, and his wife knew less," Aida remembered in a 1982 interview. "She had been married to this man for four months. She was about half his age and they came from Little Rock, Arkansas."

[The appointment] was by William Jennings Bryan [Secretary of State, March 1913 to June 1915, who liked to appoint "deserving Democrats"]. Mr. Jeffrey told us one night that he was offered two posts, and he didn't know which to accept. One was Buenos Aires, and the other was Montevideo. And so he telephoned his wife before he left, and he said, "Which one would you like to go to?" And she said she thought Montevideo sounded more romantic. They knew absolutely nothing about where it was or anything.

She was the daughter of the proprietor of the hotel in Little Rock. Anyway, they came, but that marriage didn't last very long. She was very unhappy, and so she departed the scene. And he said he was going to blow his brains out— he was going to commit suicide because she'd left him. But finally, he was persuaded to go back to the United States, so Turo was in charge for quite some time. . . . Turo said that Mr. Jeffrey would sit at his desk where he had four spittoons at each corner, and it didn't matter where he sat, he never missed! Terrible!

Mrs. Jeffrey wanted to see the asylum, the penitentiary and the maternity hospital. We drove to these three places in one day, and I remember it was just the most horrible thing. I had nightmares about this for weeks later. I had to go along because she spoke no Spanish. I had to go, so I went.

A final narrative concerns another foreign-born spouse, Yvonne Jordan, a Frenchwoman born in Brittany in 1897, whose job as an interpreter led to marriage and a lifetime as a Foreign Service spouse.

With the devastation of World War I finally over in the spring of 1919, France was faced with the prospect of hundreds of thousands of American soldiers being stranded in Europe until the shipping capacity on North Atlantic routes could bring them home. One of these stranded officers was Curtis Calhoun Jordan, a University of Southern California graduate serving in the American army. While awaiting repatriation from France, Curtis Jordan not only found a wife, whom he returned to marry two years later, but also in Paris took the exams to become a Foreign Service officer and passed them. In a 1987 interview, Yvonne Jordan told the story of meeting Curtis. He was a police commissioner in Brittany, an officer in the American army, and she was an interpreter in a jewelry store owned by a childhood friend. He came into the store with his captain, a Catholic who wanted to buy a rosary for his wife. Yvonne showed the captain various rosaries and said, " 'If you buy this more expensive one, I will give you a nice case for it.' Well, my English was not perfect, and Curtis did not understand me perfectly. He thought I said 'kiss.' He asked, 'What do I have to buy to get one?' 'Get what?' I asked. 'Why, a kiss,' he replied."

Yvonne Jordan, like her native-born American spouse counterparts, had that love of travel and ability to fit into foreign cultures that are hallmarks of the successful Foreign Service wife. Her honeymoon was at her first post in American-ruled Haiti. Nearly 70 years later, she recalled her impressions.

As I say, I'm the perfect sponge. I'm very adaptable. While we were in Haiti and my husband was chargé d'affaires, we had a visit from an American warship and, of course, were entertained by the admiral. After dinner, the men went for their usual drink, and the women sat all around one little room.

I can still see them. I was the only non-American-born. They talked. I spoke English fluently when I was married. I never had any difficulty with the language, but they were talking about things I knew nothing about. I went home that night and I said to my husband, "Now, no more French magazines. I want to be an American completely and be more informed than I am now about American life."

And I've never stopped. I'm truly American, but that was the night that it struck me most forcibly.

More than the other couples introduced in this chapter, the Jordans foreshadowed the future Foreign Service. Although Curtis Jordan entered the diplomatic corps, he served over half of his career in consular work at posts such as Barcelona, Spain, Madras, India, and San Luis Potosí, Mexico, and had a tour in remote Laurenço Marques (now Maputo), Mozambique. Yvonne Jordan, still fiercely loyal, at 91, to her dashingly handsome late husband, insisted that "since life was the same in all of the major capitals," they consciously chose consulate positions at more remote posts to be "more in touch with the people of the country."

If Yvonne and Curtis Jordan represented the emerging Foreign Service, one woman who became a spouse in the decade following World War I was a member of the elite that had dominated U.S. foreign affairs for well over a century and continued to do so until the years immediately after World War II. Lilla Grew, by her marriage, epitomized the entangled "extended family" of the Foreign Service's genealogical tree of her time. For example, Lilla Grew's husband, Pierrepont Moffat, was Elizabeth (Betty) Moffat White's brother; and Elizabeth Lewis married John Moors Cabot, a cousin of the Grews' mother (see chapter 2).

There were many relationships, some close, others more tenuous, and every member of the close-knit Foreign Service had almost instinctively absorbed the values of the social class, which, at this time, crossed international boundaries with few difficulties. The glue that held them together was perhaps best expressed by Lilla Moffat: "The Foreign Service was my life."

Lilla Grew Moffat in the garden of the Grew home, Hancock, New Hampshire, 27 July 1927. Courtesy of Bachrach.

ANCESTRAL TIES

Lilla Grew Moffat was descended from Benjamin Franklin and was the grand-daughter of the American impressionist painter Lilla Cabot Perry, a close friend of Claude Monet. She grew up in the Foreign Service with a high-ranking father, attended finishing school in Switzerland, and remembered as "home" marble palaces in Copenhagen and Constantinople (now Istanbul) as well as Lilla Cabot Perry's comfortable farmhouse in Hancock, New Hampshire. Lilla's early years were spent with governesses and in finishing schools; her education was private and predominantly European, although she graduated from Holton Arms and attended the Corcoran School of Art in Washington, D.C.

Among her early memories, Lilla recalled that she and her three sisters "happened" to be in Hancock, on home leave, when World War I broke out. Her mother, Alice Perry Grew, "rented a house in Boston and left us there with our governess, and my grandparents just across the street. Then my mother went back to Berlin to be with my father."

During the war, she traveled eight times across the Atlantic, which was infested with German submarines and torpedoes. She wanted to move us children to Switzerland, but my grandmother Perry, her mother, wouldn't hear of it.

"You'll take those children away over my dead body," she said.

So my poor mother had to be separated from her children. She had to keep going back and forth between husband and children for four years, at great risk. It was very hard on her. . . . My mother had no easy life [in the Foreign Service], but she managed it well.

Of the three surviving sisters, Lilla, more than her siblings, viewed her mother as an inspiration for her own role as a Foreign Service wife.

While she was at the Corcoran, Lilla became engaged to Pierrepont Moffat, 11 years her senior, a friend of her parents, and one of Washington's most eligible bachelors in the mid 1920s. "All my friends knew him, and he had a great place in the world I moved in then in Washington," she remembered. "To become engaged ahead of any of my classmates, and then to him, took care of that feeling of inadequacy, inferiority, you know, that I had as a Foreign Service child." They were married 27 July 1927 in the garden of the Grews' Hancock home.

Pierrepont Moffat's office was at the White House, his job the modern equivalent of chief of protocol to President Calvin Coolidge. Lilla Moffat, 19, moved gracefully from the classroom to friendship with Grace Coolidge, the president's wife. Her new husband, on the other hand, disliked the job intensely.

Calvin Coolidge became president in 1923, when the expanding demands of protocol made necessary the first formal appointment of a Foreign Service officer to the White House as aide in charge of protocol. Proper social credentials and a reputation for brilliance made Pierrepont Moffat a prime candidate, but the appointment was for him almost a career-ending move. "He had to plan dinner parties, receptions, and that sort of thing, and decide who should be invited," Lilla Moffat remembered in 1987. "He had such a time. When the lists were closed, and the maximum number had been reached and couldn't be exceeded, various officials would call wanting to have family and friends invited. Pierrepont always had to say no. The pressures being brought on him were so great—threats and everything else—that he was ready to leave the service. It was only when Pierrepont learned that he had the understanding and support of the president that he agreed to stay." Pierrepont Moffat's distaste for the social side of diplomatic life was an irony not lost on Foreign Service wives, then or now.

AN AWESOME TERM

"What, exactly, is protocol, this awesome term?" asks Hope Ridings Miller, doyenne of the Washington society reporters in the 1930s and 1940s, in her book Embassy Row. *"Strictly speaking, it is a name given to a variety of written documents and is derived from the Greek protos, meaning 'first,' and kolla, meaning 'glue.' Originally, 'the protocol' referred to the first leaf glued to a manuscript as a guide to its contents.... Technically, protocol is the body of ceremonial rules to be observed in written or personal association between heads of state or their emissaries, with full clarification as to forms and customary courtesies for all international intercourse." Viewed practically, protocol is a way of organizing relationships so that no one of rank is offended. "We need protocol," quipped an anonymous diplomat, "because we can't all get through the door at the same time."* [8]

To the wives of the Foreign Service in the 1920s, when the service began to open up to those of lesser wealth and social position, it seemed that people of all sorts were clamoring to get "through the door" by any means possible, while maintaining the civility demanded of polite society. Yet the first official handbook, "Social Usage in the Foreign Service," was not printed by the Department of State until June 1957. Its text bears a striking resemblance to the current "Diplomatic Social Usage: A Guide for United States Representatives and Their Families Abroad" (1984).

An Efficiency Report by One Who Knows

Regardless of the reforms that were coming, the life of one consular spouse in the early 1920s revealed that the old world was still firmly entrenched. Her biting commentary appeared anonymously in the January 1923 number of the American Consular Bulletin, *predecessor of the* Foreign Service Journal. *Titled "A Consul's Wife: An Efficiency Report by One Who Knows," the one-page essay was a scathing indictment of a diplomatic system ruled by patronage:*

"She acquired a prime qualification for her position by being born in the United States of parents, grandparents and other ascendants also born therein. She married into the service young. . . .

"She crossed the Atlantic alone, met her husband and proceeded to some islands where her tea tables formed a neutral ground for warring factions and nationalities. After months, with a baby in her arms, she was again upon the ocean now under the stark terror of the submarine. In a hot, ugly and dirty tropical town her home was for four years the only spot where a wandering American could get a hearty welcome and decent food. When the fort blew up and bullets rained upon the roof and it was feared that the stores of dynamite would go off and wreck the town she was interested but unafraid. This time with two babies, she was again upon the sea and not far away when a submarine downed the Carolina. . . .

"[S]he made more friends for her husband than he ever made for himself. In another port she made some scanty social life grow where none had grown before; because she had been kind to a bank bookkeeper's wife her husband was warned to withdraw his little all and did it two hours before the bank failed.

"She speaks one foreign language with amazing fluency and has a store of useful words in several others.

"On an income of about $4,000 she has kept her end up with acquaintances spending from three to ten times that and *has saved some money* [emphasis in original].

"But are these the best things that can be said about her? Not and decidedly not. She has looked after the consul's food, cared for his health, fought him to make him buy new clothes and keep his old ones pressed, but the finest manifestation of her genius is that she has never taken any interest in the business of the consulate. She has never liked unduly nor disliked at all any vice consul nor clerk nor the wife of any. She has never expressed an opinion on any of the political or international questions that have been raging around her nor seemed to know that they existed. She has never asked what income Jones declared nor what age Miss Ann put on her registration. She lived in a consulate for four years, passed the office door some forty times a day but never crossed its threshold except when she was invited and has never been heard to say, 'Other consuls get promoted through political influence.'

"Yet the law says, 'The government cannot accept services gratuitously rendered.' "[9]

THE ROGERS ACT OF 1924

In the same January issue, the Bulletin editorialized: "Hearings have actually begun on the Rogers bill. On Monday, 11 December, the Secretary of State appeared before the Committee on Foreign Affairs of the House of Representatives to present his views . . . for the reorganization and improvement of the Foreign Service. . . . Under Secretary of State Joseph C. Grew hailed the Rogers bill as 'an instrument for God, Country, for Peace and for Trade.'"[10]

The Rogers Act, introduced by Massachusetts Rep. John Jacob Rogers, was enacted 24 May 1924 and became effective a short five weeks later. Its provisions merged the diplomatic and consular corps, created a ranked and evaluated hierarchy within the new Foreign Service, and controlled entry through rigorous examinations. It also clamped a firm lid, through publication of a schedule of fees for services in the 1925 Register of the Foreign Service, on the "spoils" lining the pockets of overseas consular officers. Further, to guarantee future good behavior, the act required that "every secretary, consul general, consul, vice consul of career, or Foreign Service officer, before he receives his commission or enters upon the duties of his office, shall give to the United States a bond . . . in a penal sum not less than the annual compensation allowed to such officer."[11]

The political impetus that culminated in the Rogers Act had created a broad structural framework for a new style of diplomatic life. There were, of course, the immediate strains of merging the elite, old-school diplomats with their less well endowed consular colleagues. But placing the Foreign Service on a more stable foundation had opened the door for a new class of diplomat, whose qualifications were assured through examined merit and whose participation was not predicated upon independent wealth. For the wives of both kinds of officer, change was in the offing. But the old social world held on with tenacity.

After gaining suffrage in 1920, a few women pressed for admission as officers but met with stout resistance from the Foreign Service establishment. Although women were deemed unsuitable for officer status, in part "because of social, political, or climatic reasons," these factors "seemed to have little bearing on where women clerical personnel were hired or sent," Homer Calkin wrote in 1977.[12] Lucille Atcherson, who had ranked third on the 1922 diplomatic service examination and had been appointed an officer that year, languished in Washington for three years before her controversial appointment as third secretary in Berne, Switzerland, in 1925.[13]

For a woman, being the wife of a Foreign Service officer meant not being eligible for entry into the service itself. Marriage, which later would result in immediate termination from the service, was not the source of contention it would become *because there were so few women in the Foreign Service. The number of married couples both having jobs in the State Department in the early days is best characterized by a 1913 memo: "There is not a single case of such double doin's in this dept."* [14] *It was only possible for both members of a married couple to hold government jobs if they were in different departments. When the Great Depression came, the Economy Act of 1932 became the basis for dismissals, mainly of wives who could rely on the government salary of a spouse. In 1934 Secretary of State Cordell Hull reported to the president that, of the 40 employees dismissed from the State Department, 37 were women.* [15]

2

A DIPLOMATIC DEPRESSION

Nobody would believe what was said to me in those days, and nobody has ever said it since. When I walked into my first day's meeting with the ambassador, he said, "Well, I hope you'll be useful to me. I will certainly throw you out if you're not."

Elizabeth Cabot

The 1930s and the Great Depression brought a new kind of spouse into the Foreign Service, women of independent accomplishment who gave up—or were forced by the economic climate to give up—professional and political careers to join their new Foreign Service officer husbands abroad. The character of the officers themselves was changing as well, in a diplomatic corps that no longer required substantial family wealth for entry. At the same time, the meager stipend of several thousand dollars awarded new officers acquired a new attractiveness.

One new spouse of 1936, Fanny Chipman, exemplified this trend. Also known in the service by her given Greek name, Théophanie or Théophania, (Fanny) Bunand-Sevastos was born in France in 1905. As a child and young woman, she lived among the artistic notables of Parisian society and modeled for her uncle, the sculptor Antoine Bourdelle, when he created his famous tribute, La France, to the first American soldiers arriving in Europe during World War I. At about the same time, Chipman posed for another of Bourdelle's works. "Perhaps I shouldn't talk about that because it's in the nude," she recalled.

But, I suppose it doesn't make any difference because I don't look anything like it now. That I can assure you! Bourdelle was very funny about it. "You mustn't tell anyone about this." He always felt it was going to be detrimental to my getting a husband. So I never told anybody—until recently my cousin and I started talking about this. I think at 82 I can mention it. It's part of a frieze inside the Marseille Opera. I've never seen it in place, but it is in the [Bourdelle] Museum in the life size. It's called *La Naissance de Venus*—the Birth of Venus. The Venus is a friend of ours—my mother's actually. Again, I couldn't be the Venus. I was too slender, believe it or not. I am just the nymphs that support the arms of the Venus. I consider it a very beautiful relief. All the detail of it is very poetical.

By the time of her marriage in 1935, Fanny had lived in the United States, and Washington, for almost a decade, the first six months of which she was the Washington-based executive secretary of the Inter-American Commission of Women, an early feminist organization, headed by Doris Stevens, under whose auspices she attended several international conferences in Europe and South America.

"Society in Capital at Notable Bridal," trumpeted the New York Times on 21 June, "Miss Fanny Bunand-Sevastos is Married to N. B. Chipman of U.S. Foreign Service." The changes marriage brought about in her life could hardly have been more dramatic.

The Chipman family were Washington "cave dwellers"—families who'd lived here a long time. Mrs. Chipman was a Norris from Virginia; Mr. Chipman had been here always.

Mr. Chipman wanted me to stop working. He was very conservative about that sort of thing—you know, women who were married should stay at home. There was nothing for me to do: we had a two-room apartment. I argued with him. "First, we need the money." Norris was a third secretary. "Secondly, I can't quit that way. I know all about the Commission. I have to pass all I know to somebody else." We agreed that I would work only part-time. I was able to train someone to take my place. Then we went to Russia.

THE OLD AND THE NEW

In many ways, the Great Depression had put the Foreign Service on hold. While hiring continued, sparingly, newcomers to the service found themselves in an uneasy situation. Young officers frequently were told they had a post if they could get themselves there. Foreign Service salaries, though modest, drew in some of the brightest of their generation, men who lacked vast personal fortunes but nonetheless inherited the "striped-pants" image of their predecessors. Young women who married into the service at this time had attended schools such as Columbia, Oberlin, Reed, Smith, the universities of Missouri and Southern California, Vassar, and schools abroad.

Their relationship to the service was personified by the experiences of Elizabeth Lewis Cabot. She provided the best example of the assumption by officers, almost all of whom were men, that a wife would unquestioningly perform in the "two for the price of one" role expected of spouses throughout most of this century. Most defined their social position by their husbands' accomplishments, to which they contributed significantly. Elizabeth Cabot, who had graduated from Vassar in 1927, was working at the Museum of Modern Art in New York in 1930.

My mother asked me to come to Mexico for Christmas to visit her. She was married to the manager of the light and power company in Mexico City—it was her second marriage—so even though I had not been there for a while, I had all sorts of friends and connections in Mexico.

When I arrived, it was just at the moment of a turnover in the embassy. Ambassador Dwight Morrow was leaving. And an interesting new ambassador came, whose name was J. Reuben Clark, Jr., a Mormon. He'd been undersecretary of state, a very able man who came down to settle some very tedious and confusing financial patterns with Mexico. Being a Mormon, he and his wife lived very simply. At the embassy [residence], there was no coffee, there was no tea, no alcohol ever served. Guests arriving for the ambassador's parties were directed across the lawn, usually to Joe Sattherwaite's little house, for their drinks—he was one of the secretaries. Then they would go back to the residence. The ambassador always reimbursed Joe.

Since I had a great many connections in Mexico, the embassy asked me to stay for a year and be the social secretary and introduce Mrs. Clark to some of the confusions of diplomacy. I got my training there, because Arthur Bliss Lane was the counselor, a very definite, astute, old-fashioned career man, who simply taught me what goes on in an embassy. Then I tried to help Mrs. Clark.

By that time Jack [John Moors Cabot] was at the embassy, and I decided that I wouldn't go back to New York. We were married about eight months later, and Jack was immediately transferred to Rio de Janeiro, Brazil. The State Department, instead of keeping us in Mexico, promptly shifted us, you see. Today they let a wife, who has a connection with a country, either return to that country or stay in it. But in those days the rule was adamant.

We were fortunate to be living in Brazil during the Depression, but the State Department was unkind to us. Without warning, we would have a month's salary withheld. They would simply announce that we would be refused the next check, and we had to live an extra month without pay, until Jack got his salary for the following month. My mother paid the hospital expenses when I had a baby, and fortunately she paid for a nursemaid. I was expected to be "on tap," to be available to help with visitors and do the usual embassy business just as soon as I had the baby.

When we arrived in Rio [in 1932], the ambassador, Edwin V. Morgan [ambassador for 21 years, 1912–33], lost no time in letting us know that we were to spend our entire time linking and connecting with Brazilians. Nobody would believe what was said to me in those days, and nobody has ever said it since. When I walked into my first day's meeting with the ambassador, he said, "Well, I hope you'll be useful to me. I will certainly throw you out if you're not. I want you to get out of this embassy. I want you to join clubs. I want you to find a place to live. I want you to meet people. And I want you to take a few trips around. I want you to come back in four weeks and tell me what you have done, and then I'll decide whether you're useful to me."

You know, we never worked harder or better. My husband was a great tennis player, so right away we joined all the top tennis clubs, which meant that you connected with people all over Brazil. We took trips up and down the coast, from north to south in little coastal steamers. Everywhere we went, we saw to it that we were meeting Brazilians. We remembered their names, and we stored it all up for the ambassador. And people were naturally nice to us because the embassy was very small and Jack was the only secretary.

In Rio, I had to go to the market, I had to move around—there was no such thing, luckily, as a PX [post exchange], which I think are a disaster. However, at the time I thought shopping that way was a nuisance. But there was less pressure. Husbands had more leisure time to help wives, and the hours in the embassy were shorter. We got up very early and worked in the cool of the morning. At about noon everybody went to the beaches, where we met people and got the diplomatic news. We got all the gossip of the city and the gossip of politics. At about two o'clock we had a meal, and then everybody had a siesta. The embassy reopened at five, and we worked until nine at night because it would be cool again. Then the parties started at nine. We were attuned to the life the Brazilians led.

Elizabeth and John Moors Cabot learned their job well. He became minister to Finland, ambassador to Sweden, Colombia, Brazil, and Poland, and eventually deputy assistant secretary of state for inter-American affairs.

SWIMMING THE BOSPORUS

Anita Grew English, daughter of Ambassador to Turkey Joseph C. Grew (who served as undersecretary of state twice in his career), in the late 1920s shared her father's love of adventure and his understanding of the personal connections that undergird American diplomatic institutions. For spouses, and for officers' children, the "old school" could create a romantic lifestyle as close to that of European royalty as was likely for Americans. But the privileged position held by the offspring of the ambassador could be rudely shattered when the daughters, as they often did, became the spouses of entry-level Foreign Service officers.

Anita English's experiences in "growing up fast" demonstrated a wide contrast between her leisurely life of privilege in Turkey beginning in 1927 and her life as a new Foreign Service spouse in Budapest five years later. "Constantinople (now Istanbul) was quite magical and glamorous, and I loved it all," she said. With Joseph Grew, she waited through a long night on a Turkish airfield for Russell Boardman and John Polando to complete their historic nonstop 50-hour flight from New York to Istanbul in July 1931, a flight that, at 5,011.3 miles, broke the long-distance record.[1] Later, with her father's encouragement, Anita was the first person to swim the Bosporus.

From their summer house, father and daughter often swam the mile-wide strait that separates Europe from Asia. But it was Anita who became, in August 1931, the first person to swim the 19-mile length of the Bosporus, the waterway that connects the Black Sea with the Sea of Marmara, in the process gaining herself worldwide headlines. "I loved long-distance swimming, because you see I swim breaststroke and always look around and enjoy what I'm seeing," she recalled.

One day I said that I'd love to swim from the Black Sea to the Marmara, and he [Joseph Grew] latched onto that. I tried one year and didn't quite make it. The headlines in a certain American newspaper had said, "Girl Fails in Swim," and I didn't like that. But I still had the idea to swim from one sea to the other.

It was a pleasant swim because from the Black Sea the current comes down through the Bosporus. I would not call it much of a feat if you know the currents. There wasn't any fear of not being able to make it because if you wanted to stop, you were very near the shore. But it was exciting because it was the first time anybody had done it.

Anita Grew English with John Polando (left) and Russell Boardman, Constantinople, 1931. *Courtesy of Jane Boardman Teglas.*

Anita English's self-effacing description of her swim took on a somewhat different character when described by her father in his memoirs, Turbulent Era. *Joseph Grew grasped the historic importance of her feat. After following his daughter in the support boat, he rushed immediately, "without putting on [his] coat and tie," to inform the waiting press.[2]*

"One very nice thing," Anita English remembered, "Boardman and Polando were very touched that we waited on that airfield for so many hours. So after my record-setting swim, I got a cable from the two of them, together, which I thought was very sweet. They said, ' . . . we wish we could have waited for you as you waited for us.' "

A short year later, her life changed drastically. She got married in Istanbul, to Robert English, and went from the carefree existence of an ambassador's daughter to a new reality of running the small household of a lower-level Foreign Service officer in Budapest. "There were so many changes," English recalled, "for one thing, the split-up of the family. At one time, we were on four different continents, my parents on one, and the three daughters each on another."

When I married we went to Budapest. I think they gave it to us as a wedding gift. But [Robert] was so sick. He spent the first year being very, very sick, and it was a tough time. For me, Budapest was getting used to a totally different life. I'd never had to think in terms of the mechanics of living. I'd been looked after. Then, suddenly, I had to run a house and look after things and a very sick husband. I grew up fast . . . and things crowded in.

Budapest was the beginning of changing times in another way, too. I remember [in 1934] my husband coming back from the office one day and saying, "We've got to have lunch with the new German secretary and his wife. They want to have a quiet lunch just with us. Be very discreet, just do more listening, be very discreet." And he knew then what I didn't realize, didn't know enough to realize, that they wanted to make contacts because they were Nazis infiltrating.

THE FISH FORK SYNDROME

As the Foreign Service cast its recruitment net more widely in American society, a need arose to groom the new breed of young officers to be diplomats. The Rogers Act of 1924 had authorized creation of the Foreign Service Officers Training School. (In the 1990s its direct descendant is the National Foreign Affairs Training Center.) By 1932 Cornelia B. Bassel had become assistant to the director of the small institution. She brought distinguished social and political credentials to her new position as arbiter of diplomatic rules, particularly on the social side. Called Nele (pronounced "kneel"), she was the sister-in-law of John W. Davis, the Democratic presidential candidate in 1924. A southern lady of the old school born in Clarksburg, West Virginia, Bassel traced her ancestry to pre–Revolutionary War America and had been in Washington since her service in the War Department during World War I. Her command of French and German was extensive.

While her official position was limited to training Foreign Service officers, as an extension of her interest in and fondness for these fledgling diplomats she voluntarily became the social mentor for their young wives. "Miss Bassel was a glorious lady," remembered Dorothy Kidder, a great-niece of Theodore Roosevelt.

She taught us manners and behavior and protocol and general good demeanor, and I loved Miss Bassel, she had such style; she was wonderful. And I'm always grateful to Miss Cornelia Bassel for what she did teach me. We had four months in Washington before we went to our first post, Sydney, Australia. Those were the days of the grandes dames, Mrs. Beale, Mrs. Bliss, and Mrs. Bacon, and through the friendships of my parents and Randy's we were invited to their houses, albeit we were seated well below the salt, but we did have an awfully entertaining beginning in the Foreign Service.

The Diplomatic and Consular Officers Retired (DACOR) organization's unpublished "History of DACOR Bacon House" noted:

Throughout the 1930s and 40s "The Three B's," [the wealthy socialites] Mrs. Robert Woods Bliss, Mrs. Truston Beale and Mrs. Robert Low Bacon, dominated Washington society. It was said that anyone wishing to become part of Washington's social whirl would first drop their cards on "The Three B's" before calling at the White House. While known for their hospitality and generosity in supporting the arts, each saw to it that her historic home would be preserved for future generations. Mrs. Bliss bequeathed her home, Dumbarton Oaks, site of conferences held in 1944 to discuss proposals for creation of the United Nations to Harvard University as a center for the study of Byzantine and pre-Columbian art. Mrs. Beale gave Decatur House on Lafayette Square [across from the White House], home to naval hero Commodore Stephen Decatur, three secretaries of state, a vice president and several members of Congress, to the National Trust for Historic Preservation. Mrs. Bacon willed her home to the Bacon House Foundation, which she created in 1975 as an educational institution dedicated to "fostering international understanding."[3]

While Cornelia Bassel was firmly in control of the training, and to some degree the reputations, of young Foreign Service officers, and by extension their spouses, a 1938 article in the Daughters of the American Revolution (DAR) National Historical Magazine *described only her influence on the officers, making no mention of their wives. "There is no other position like hers in all the world," the article explained. "She is the assistant to the director of the nation's Foreign Service Officers' Training School and at this post she comes in constant contact with the smart young men Uncle Sam is training for key positions in the Foreign Service."[4]*

In spite of the DAR omission, Miss Bassel's vigilant correspondence followed the young women halfway around the globe. Naomi Mathews recalled in a 1986 interview:

I can remember one evening in Sydney when Consul General Tom Wilson was having Prime Minister [Sir Robert Gordon] Menzies to dinner. He said, "Now, honey"—he always called me "honey"—"You must remember not to go rushing into the dining room first." As if I would! "You must wait and come last with the prime minister." Little bits of diplomatic protocol, all along he would teach me. He would write to Miss Bassel and tell her whether I did well or not. Then she would write me and say Mr. Wilson said that you did very nicely or maybe you should remember to do this or that. It was really kind of wonderful that someone was taking an interest. I wasn't the only one I'm sure, but she took more interest in me because I was in Sydney with her

Ambassador to Liberia Elbert G. Mathews and his wife, Naomi, arrive in the middle of the night at Roberts Field, Monrovia, Liberia, August 1959. *Courtesy of Naomi Mathews.*

very good friend and her Georgetown neighbor [when he was on Washington assignment], Tom Wilson.

Not everyone was a fervent supporter of Miss Bassel. She gave no formal courses, and she dispensed her knowledge selectively. "Cornelia Bassel was a terrific social snob," scoffed a Foreign Service widow, a Smith graduate, resident of Washington's fashionable Georgetown neighborhood, and local patron of the arts. "She was her own private spy, keeping abreast of everything that was going on. My husband had to produce five letters of recommendation for me."

She also was selective in her attentions. A foreign-born spouse recalled in a 1989 conversation:

I had been so well received in the United States, but Miss Bassel was prejudiced against foreign wives. My husband met me here in Washington, and I said to her, "Well, at least he chose me in his own country." She also objected to my being in the feminist movement. In Miss Bassel's defense, I must say that she had such a maternal feeling for the young officers, she felt my husband should have married a nice American girl, an Avis Bohlen.[5] Miss Bassel would completely faint if she could see the service today!

Cornelia Bassel was not alone in her skepticism about foreign wives. Scrutinizing his guests at a staff dinner at the embassy residence in Moscow in the early 1930s, William C. Bullitt, ambassador to the Soviet Union, observed that none of his young officers had American wives. A close friend of President Franklin D. Roosevelt, Bullitt reputedly managed to have instituted the ruling that required a Foreign Service officer to submit his resignation before marrying a foreign woman, a ruling that remained in effect for four decades.

BRAZIL, CHINA, AND RUSSIA: THREE TALES

Three women from the Depression era exemplify the diversity of the Foreign Service spouse: Beatrice Berle, a medical doctor and spouse of the top-level, noncareer adviser Adolf Berle, an original member of President Roosevelt's brain trust; Caroline Service, a 1931 Phi Beta Kappa graduate of Oberlin College and spouse of the career officer and China expert John Stewart Service; and Fanny Chipman, introduced earlier in this chapter.

Beatrice Berle, in a 1989 interview, provided a good description of social life in the 1930s and 1940s at the top levels of the State Department. Her government years were spent primarily in Washington, D.C., beginning in 1938, and, near the end of World War II, abroad as spouse of the ambassador to Brazil. In Washington, the Berles first lived in Woodley, Henry Stimson's house, an imposing mansion that in the 1990s is the Maret School in northwest Washington. "Adolf and I were stuck with a great deal of entertaining because [Secretary of State Cordell] Hull didn't entertain. [Undersecretary of State] Sumner [Welles] lived out at Oxon Hill, Maryland, so he entertained the 'fancy' people out there," Beatrice Berle remembered, "and did it very grandly."

So we were the ones who were left with "other people," and we eventually had to do a great deal of entertaining.

There were tennis courts at Woodley when we lived there, and a croquet court at the bottom of the hill. [Secretary of Agriculture] Henry Wallace was among the prominent New Dealers who came to play tennis. Mr. Hull played croquet.

When Hull played croquet, the young, that is to say, my children, were supposed to be not seen and not heard. My daughters, Beatrice and Alice, climbed a tree one afternoon while the game was in progress. Beatrice sat on a branch where yellowjackets had nested. "Oh, ouch!" she cried out and screamed and screamed. Which therefore made her a "heard." Finally she jumped out of the tree—after being stung about eight times—and after I plastered her with bicarbonate of soda, we walked down to the tennis court to apologize to Mr. Hull for messing up the game and also to show, I guess, that we weren't into torturing children at the Berles' house.

Hull played croquet every single day, at five o'clock, I think it was, with three picked people from the State Department. He would designate who he wanted to play with. The best player was Stanley Hornbeck [a Far East adviser

In March 1961, Dr. Beatrice Berle visited the children's ward of Hospital dos Servi-dores do Estado in Rio de Janeiro, where she had worked as a volunteer when her husband, Adolph A. Berle, Jr., was ambassador to Brazil, 1945–46. *Courtesy of Beatrice Meyerson.*

and later ambassador to the Netherlands], another was [James Clement] Jimmy Dunn [later assistant secretary of state and ambassador to Italy, France, Spain, and Brazil]—the only people who ever beat him. Stanley Hornbeck had a large abdomen. The children would sit at the bottom of the hill and watch him. Most people shoot croquet sort of sideways, a few would shoot between their legs. Stanley Hornbeck was fascinating when he leaned down, you could see the tummy coming in between his legs. They (the children) had a worm's-eye view.

Hull always picked the weakest player to be his partner. And he always used a red ball. He would go around the whole course in one turn, because of course when you go through a wicket you get a free shot, and he kept going the whole way around. Before hitting the final stake, he would usually with his free shot go back, get his partner's ball, and hit it through all the wickets.

Even at Adolf Berle's rank, housing and transporting an active family became a problem in wartime Washington. As promised, the Berles relinquished Woodley to Henry Stimson (when he returned from a private-sector job in New York to government to become secretary of war), moving first to Single Oak on Cathedral Avenue and later to 4000 Nebraska Avenue. "My children were very, very impressed when I was commissioned a major in the Public Health Service," Beatrice Berle continued, "even though I didn't wear a uniform when I went off to work every day.

A uniform had been designed for us, but I had refused to wear it. I said, "I'm a doctor, and I'm sitting in an office. I wear a white coat." I was supposed to take care of minor ailments, like in an outpatient department. We had to make a survey for tuberculosis, and I also worked for the Office of War Information, evaluating the medical history of people they were considering sending on a mission.

The children, Adolf and I, in a carpool, would leave 4000 Nebraska Avenue en famille. The State Department didn't give anyone, except Mr. Hull perhaps, a car or extra gas. Adolf had an A ration card for one of our cars, which entitled him to three gallons a week. Because I was an M.D., I had a C ration card, which allowed me considerably more. I drove, Adolf got in, Alice and Beatrice were obliged to arrive at Potomac School by 7:50 A.M., along with their brother Peter. I dropped them off, then Adolf off, and I went down to Gallinger Hospital [now D.C. General] or to the office. By that time I was also on the teaching staff at Gallinger as well as working for the Public Health

Service. We're speaking now of 1942. The children and Adolf took a bus or taxi home.

Three years later, Adolf Berle was appointed ambassador to Brazil, and the family embarked for Rio de Janeiro. "And that," said Beatrice Berle, "is how we continued ever after to be happy with Brazilians."

By now we're in January 1945. I took a plane, Peter and Hagie, the au pair, with me; the two girls stayed in Washington to finish school. We were on a B-17, one of the heavy bombers.

The post report explained that the ambassador in that huge palace [the official residence] had to have his own sheets, silver, etc. I bought sheets for us and all the staff—there were at least 10 of them—and a hotel set of silver, but I probably took some of my own too because the dining table seated 60, 28 on each side. We took [the Department of State gold-rimmed] china, with the seal on it, but I felt we didn't want to eat breakfast on that, so I had to take more china. We weren't reimbursed for this expense. The hotel knives, somehow, survived, I still have them. I can't get rid of them! Before we arrived in Rio, we paid some of the staff's salary personally, to assure that they'd be there when we arrived. Otherwise, we'd have arrived to find no cook and the staff would have left. There was Dona Maria, the housekeeper, two young butlers, Wilson and Samuel, Francisca the laundress, and her helper.

Francisca, the black laundress, had a wonderful face. She did the laundry in a little house apart. Even though we had a washing machine, Francisca would build a fire outside the little house and boil Peter's jeans to get them clean. Of course, there was no dryer, so all the laundry was hung out in back, even though we were the embassy residence. And then at carnival time, Francisca absolutely filled the place with her lovely, big, starched white petticoats and white gown, a traditional carnival costume from Bahia in the northeast where many of the servants came from.

Then there was Lourdes, the chambermaid, and two chauffeurs. We had a wonderful, wonderful black cook. I'd go down to the kitchen and ask, "What'll we have today?" And she'd reply [she translates], "I'll think about it."

Soon after our arrival in Rio, the directors arranged for me to go into the ward of the Santa Casa, a combination asylum and acute hospital. There was a law against foreign physicians practicing, however I was allowed to help as long as it was a nonpaid affair. This was really a wonderful experience, because I gave the first penicillin. At that time penicillin was beginning, and I remember going in the evening to the Santa Casa and delivering penicillin to two people with pneumonia. I practiced in the sense that I took care of people on the ward, and I learned a great deal about the Brazilians who you don't meet at embassy cocktail parties; and also about parasitic diseases.

While she was working at Santa Casa, Beatrice Berle compiled The Book of Preventive Medicine, *a text on common diseases to be distributed in the interior of Brazil. She wrote the chapter on penicillin, a parasitologist compiled the chapter on tropical diseases—"one of those scientists who like to account for every microbe"—and a health expert drew up plans for a privy, "a really good innovation for the interior—to keep the people from getting amoebas and other parasites."*

Beatrice Berle's philanthropic work had a social side as well when she founded the Voluntarias (volunteers) to sew for children in the favelas (slums) that spill down the slopes of Rio's lush hills.

Adolf called it the equivalent of his mother's sewing circle when she was a minister's wife outside Boston. We set up a whole bunch of sewing machines in the ballroom and the Baronesa de Bonfim, a older woman of impeccable social standing, and others of her circle came one day a week and whirled away on their machines. They did have some concern for the poor, but it also became "the thing to do," coming to the residence to sew. We sewed mainly for the hospital—layettes for infants and so on. Singer gave us the sewing machines, and the project was financed by the women. The only refreshments served were *cafezinho* (coffee) and a few cookies, nothing else. This was serious business. And it still goes on.

The End of an Era

As the daughter of a West Point officer, Caroline Schulz Service was eminently suited to become a Foreign Service spouse. She had grown up with the mobility of military life—an amiable life at one post and conditions so appalling at another that her mother had a breakdown. When she graduated from Oberlin, where she had met her future husband, her father was commandant of Fort Humphreys in the countryside outside Washington. "When I graduated—

you won't believe this, but it's true—I went home," she said in a 1977 interview conducted for the oral history project of the Bancroft Library of the University of California at Berkeley.[6] "It never occurred to me to do anything but go home. I did not look for a job. I simply went home to Fort Humphreys, and I made my debut the next fall [1931] in Washington society, which is unbelievable to me today."

The memory of Caroline Service's social season in Washington contrasted with her transformation into a Foreign Service spouse in Kunming, China. John Stewart (Jack) Service had been born in China, where his parents were with the YMCA, and was fluent in spoken Chinese. "He passed the Foreign Service exams in 1933," Caroline Service recalled in a 1987 interview, "but there were no appointments made because of the Depression."

So, as we wanted very much to get married, Jack went out to China, where he had grown up, to get a job. He went into the consulate in Shanghai to see if there was anything that he could do. Before long there was a clerkship open in Kunming [then Yunnanfu]. He was overjoyed, as it would pay $1,800 a year and we could get married. I went out to Shanghai with Jack's mother, and from there I traveled to Haiphong [then in French Indochina, now Vietnam], on my own, by ship. This trip took about ten days by coastal steamer. We went through a typhoon and had to stay anchored at Hoihow, on the island of Hainan, for about three days.

The ship arrived at Haiphong shortly before four on the afternoon of November 9, which was a Thursday. Jack was waiting for me. We had to rush right up to the Hotel de Ville to be married by the mayor of Haiphong before 5 P.M. because a three-day holiday was starting the next day. The brief ceremony was in French, of which we understood little (we had an interpreter), and then we were handed our official marriage document, which had room for the names of 12 children! We shook hands all round and that was that.

The next morning, very early, Jack and I took the French train for the three-day trip to Yunnanfu. The train ran only during the day, which meant that we had to spend two nights in small, primitive railway hotels. The scenery, as we rose from the coastal flats of Indochina to the 6,000-foot altitude of Kunming, was spectacular. But as the train, a narrow-gauge, open-windowed, uncomfortable wooden vehicle, chugged slowly through and up and over the landscape, I'm afraid I didn't appreciate it as much as I should have. I thought I'd come to a wild, remote part of the world, and in many ways I had. We spent two years in Kunming, and then Jack was assigned to Peking [Beijing] for language study. Our daughter, Virginia, called Ginny, was born in Kunming.

Jack and I, the baby, and two Siamese cats arrived in Peking just before Christmas 1935. Living in Peking was an "Arabian Nights" experience. In retrospect, I realize that I never heard anyone mention that we might be at the end of an era. Nobody was worried. We all thought we were going to go on living in China forever. Bob was born in Peking, before the [Sino-]Japanese War started.

On the night of 6 July 1937, the Japanese attacked some Chinese troops at the Marco Polo Bridge near Peking, and the Sino-Japanese War had begun. We could hear the fighting going on outside Peking. Rather, we could hear guns and cannon being fired. And after a few days, those of us who lived outside the Legation Quarter were told we would have to move into the quarter. Shades of the Boxer Rebellion!

A year later, in the summer of 1938, the storm clouds of World War II were becoming increasingly hard to ignore, "so I left China in November 1940 with my two children," Caroline Service recalled.

By this time there was a feeling in the air that there was going to be terrible trouble with the Japanese. And I never got back there until 1971, when Jack and I went to China as guests of the Chinese government. We went back to Peking, and we stayed in the Peking Hotel, where Jack and I had gone dancing so many years ago. I felt as though I were in a dream.

Stalin's Moscow

Like Caroline Service, Fanny Chipman accompanied her husband to a remote post, in her case Moscow. Both Jack Service and Norris Chipman were totally absorbed in their work and were well schooled in the local customs and language. The women, by contrast, found themselves isolated from home, family, and all things familiar, and without a great deal to do because of cultural differences in China and the political situation in Moscow during the late 1930s, when Stalin's purges created a situation so dangerous that the American diplomatic corps looked inward for sustenance. Both posts were hardship posts for these spouses, but the small diplomatic communities' esprit de corps created a camaraderie among the different ranks that made these experiences memorable. "We knew our colleagues

41

*to an extent we never knew them at any other post," Fanny Chipman recalled in
1987.*

That was a charming part of our life there, that rank didn't exist. I don't
think it's so much that we were bored. There was a lot of entertaining,
and it was partly to counteract the lack of a relationship with the natives.
[Ambassador] Bullitt had accomplished a little bit of contact with ballerinas,
intellectuals, and so forth.

We were in Moscow from 1936 to 1939, so we were there when the
Stalinist purges were going on. I know my husband, Norris, went several
times with the ambassador, Joseph E. Davies, who was attending some of the
trials and wanted another officer with him. Chip Bohlen and Norris went with
him as translators.

It was a little difficult with Davies. I got along exceedingly well with Mrs.
Davies [the Post cereal heiress Marjorie Merriweather Post]. I was delegated
to go with her when she made official calls. She didn't speak French, so I went
with her and became very fond of her. This was not everyone's experience, but
for one thing, I appreciated her honesty. I was sorry to see Marjorie leave.
The staff were much relieved to see a man like Alexander Kirk arrive, whose
attitude was, let's say, thoroughly professional. This practice of appointing
political figures as ambassadors—sometimes it works out very well, but sometimes it doesn't.

When we arrived, the atmosphere was completely different. It was very,
very sick, I would say, and very tense. I think that as a reaction the diplomatic
corps entertained one another. I've never worn so many low-cut evening
dresses as I did in Moscow, that's the truth! White ties for the men, and at
one time there was a shortage of starched shirts because the laundry that did
them disappeared for some reason. The shirts had to be sent to Riga, Latvia,
to be done. It was a regular joke.

Ambassadors came to our *dacha*. The dacha, a Russian bungalow, had
already been rented when we arrived, so we took it over with the Bohlens and
Frank Hayne, the assistant military attaché. At first, I was rather opposed to
it because I thought, "Well, this is one more expense." Norris's salary wasn't
large, and I wasn't working any more. But they all persuaded me that it
wouldn't be such a big expense, and in fact it was not. All of our colleagues
were very generous. Everybody sort of contributed a little. Yes, I'll tell you,
it was a communistic organization!

Diplomats from the British and German embassies kept horses there. We
had a very old Soviet man, George, who looked after things and lived there.
So there was always someone to look after the horses. There was a tennis
court, which was flooded in winter and used for skating. Avis [Bohlen], who

loved flowers, kept a garden going. I took care of providing food when guests came out. All the diplomats, many of them ambassadors, came—the Germans, the Belgians, the French, the British—because there were so few places for relaxation. Life at the dacha was very gay, and very informal, and very relaxing, which we all needed. I don't think there were microphones, I don't know. The Russians must have heard plenty if there were.

The dacha was not a great distance from Moscow—we were there in half an hour. It was just a little shack, but a lot of American visitors also came out. Mary Pickford came with her second husband, Charles (Buddy) Rogers, a young, good-looking man; and, she kept her eye on him, I can tell you. Noel Coward, the British playwright, came, and John F. Kennedy. His father sent him on a tour of the major capitals when he graduated from Harvard. He was really a youngster. We were all very much taken with him, due to his youth, his friendliness, quickness of mind, and his undeniable charm. I remarked about that to Norris at the time, because being ourselves very different personalities in the dacha group, it was surprising how unanimous we were about JFK.

That was the agreeable side of Moscow—there was enough of the disagreeable side, because there was the constant terror: you couldn't help but feel it. I felt it so strongly that I had to go away after a while—the unhappiness, the people who had no shoes, their feet wrapped in newspaper. The only well-dressed people were the army wives, who had warm clothes, boots, berets. The others lacked food, lacked everything. Somebody like myself who had lived only in Paris and Washington was profoundly shocked by this state of affairs.

We were always under surveillance. We couldn't talk, really, except outside. I know Marjorie and Davies talked when they walked around the Kremlin, Red Square. We knew there were devices all over the place. One of the Marine guards at the embassy did nothing else but monitor what was happening with the telephones. We were well aware that we were watched, that our servants had to report on us. It was very annoying, I must say, the feeling that you had no privacy. I was shocked by all that I had seen and heard. I felt it was inhuman, and I was used to going where I wanted, doing what I wanted. I was harassed when I tried to paint outdoors, and had difficulty getting permission to copy a Van Gogh in the museum, even though the director had been a pupil of my uncle.

And there was nothing, you couldn't buy anything. We were eating out of cans most of the time. Later on, one of the big shops in Stockholm began sending things by plane. Then it was easier, because up to then we had to rely on the courier going to Riga. Can you imagine the courier bringing back meat and supplies that were supposed to last for 15 days? One of the newspapermen came to lunch one day and said, "Now the latest story is that the director of the zoo has been arrested. The reason is that he's been feeding nails to the animals." He'd barely said this when I burst in, "Where did he get the nails?" And the newsman burst out laughing. "I'm going to write this up," he said. There were no nails. They couldn't get needles, they couldn't get bread. They had some rather nice embroidered tablecloths in the shops, but they weren't for sale, they were just for show. In the shops there was nothing.

FIRST FLIGHT

In a quarter-century career that began in 1921, Elizabeth (Betty) Moffat White entered the service as a young spouse in Caracas, then, with short intervals in Washington, saw duty in Prague, Riga (capital of the Baltic republic of Latvia), Buenos Aires, Berlin, Calcutta, Kabul, Tangier, and Port-au-Prince, before retiring as an ambassador's wife from Lima to Washington in 1945. She was a descendant of the American founding father John Jay (hence her brother's given name of Jay Pierrepont Moffat), as well as Lilla Grew Moffat's sister-in-law. And when she married John (Jack) Campbell White, a distant cousin of her mother, she became the daughter-in-law of Henry White, who had been ambassador to Italy and France early in the century.

Her family background and what she called "a good classical education," which for the time might as well be termed progressive, prepared her for Foreign Service life. Betty White remembered growing up in New York City and attending Miss Chapin's School, from which she graduated in 1916 and where she had five years of Latin, a "help" when, on her own initiative, she studied Spanish, Russian, and German for the Foreign Service. The school also emphasized elocution, including Bible verse recitation, and "good Edwardian" posture, a difficult prospect when Irene Castle's dancing was the rage and the "debutante slouch" the preferred bearing of Betty's contemporaries, and herself.

After her marriage to John Campbell White, Betty White's fascination with the newly independent woman of the twenties continued. She recalled experimenting with the fashions of the time in Riga in 1924, and on entering Argentine society in 1927.

I didn't cut my hair until we got to Riga. There was a German woman who cut her hair, and it made her look so much better that I said, "Jack, I want to cut my hair." He said, "You can do exactly as you choose." And, of course, when I cut it, he was furious. . . . When I got to Argentina, I realized I had to use makeup, otherwise I looked too awful. It took me three days to get used to putting on lipstick! The only color available was orange, which suited the Argentine women's dark complexion. After a glass of wine, my cheeks would get purple. The mix of colors was awful.

Betty White's hands-on Foreign Service education began even before her marriage—when she and her mother visited her brother, Pierrepont, who was on diplomatic assignment in Warsaw, Poland, in 1920—and continued in Caracas, Venezuela, where she was a young diplomat's wife:

The first person I met in Warsaw was the wife of the dean of the diplomatic corps. She had a great influence on me. She couldn't bear the country she was in. She couldn't say anything bad enough about it, whereas the country she had lived in before was quite nice. And then I was told that while living in the previous country, she had been just as negative about it. And I said, if I am ever going to be married to a diplomat—and I don't think I will be— I am going to enjoy the country while I am in it.

The other woman who had a tremendous influence on me was an American woman who went to Venezuela with her husband, a businessman, for two weeks and stayed twenty-eight years. She never learned Spanish, she never settled in, she never lived. So I told myself, wherever I am, I am going to dig in immediately, I shall start learning a language immediately, I shall get my house and start making it attractive immediately. Because even if you are only going to stay two years, at least you will have lived those two years.

While the 1920s were a decade of great change for women in American society, they were less so for the spouses of Foreign Service officers. The writings and memories of diplomatic women of this period made little or no mention of the feminist upheavals in the United States: suffragists chained to the White House fence; President Woodrow Wilson's eventual capitulation on suffrage; and the ratification of the Nineteenth Amendment, which gave women the vote, on 26 August 1920.[7]

Betty White noted, "Actually, after I was married I could never vote until 1927, when we came home. I was never able to vote abroad because we didn't have absentee ballots then." In 1920, before her marriage, she had voted for the first time, and as she recalled with mock horror, "I voted for Warren G. Harding!" This disengagement from events in America was taken for granted and probably was of minor importance to the earlier generation. Yet there was an obvious commonality with Foreign Service spouses of the 1990s: both generations were removed from mainstream American events that were shaping women's lives.

The circumstances of her first flight were unusual, not because her husband had gone ahead to his new post as deputy chief of mission to Argentina, but because President-elect Herbert Hoover had decided on a tour of South America before his inauguration in March 1929. "I was following with [daughter] Marga-

*ret and the governess, sailing down the west coast of South America," Betty
White remembered in a 1989 interview.*

I took an earlier ship so as to get there before the Hoovers, as I didn't think
I should arrive in the middle of their visit.

When the ship got to Lima, some embassy friends came aboard to greet
me and urged me to stay over, as there was going to be an elegant party a few
days later. Earlier, one of my tablemates on the ship, a German, had warned
me that when the weather was rough it was not possible to debark at Mollendo, where I was thinking of leaving the ship to take the train over the
Andes to Buenos Aires in order to be there for the Hoovers. My friends told
me that there was an airline which flew from Lima to Mollendo. The airline
could get me to Mollendo in time to catch the train for Buenos Aires.

I flew on a very small airplane with room for only four passengers to
Mollendo, my very first time on an airplane. The trip was very exciting, the
landscape absolutely barren, but with the majestic Andes rising abruptly to
the east.

We did arrive in Mollendo in time for the train. It went up the Andes to
La Paz, where we overnighted. There I met an Englishman who was a director
of the railroad and was traveling on the same train in his own private car. He
invited me to join his group for the rest of the trip to Buenos Aires. I accepted
and the next day had the luxury of a bath in a full-size tub on the private train
carriage, arriving in Buenos Aires very refreshed.

Well, I did arrive a few hours before the Hoovers, and that evening I was
asked to take care of Mrs. Hoover. The president of Argentina at that time
was a bachelor, and so there was a stag dinner for Mr. Hoover that evening,
which Jack attended. Then there was a dinner for Mrs. Hoover, given by the
foreign minister's wife, who spoke no English, so I was to be Mrs. Hoover's
translator. And I had not used my Spanish since we left Caracas five years
before. Oh, I had had a few [Spanish lessons] at Berlitz before leaving home,
but it wasn't enough. At one point when I was translating, I turned to Mrs.
Hoover and said something in perfect Russian. She looked so astonished, I
realized immediately what I had done. Then she asked me to sing, and the
only thing I could think of was "I've Been Working on the Railroad."

Of course, the front page of the newspaper was devoted to the Hoover
visit. But there was a small article down in one corner about the American
counselor's wife who had flown over all the Andes.

*By 1933, 12 years into the service, Betty White had moved six times: from
Spanish-speaking to Russian-speaking countries, from the Northern Hemisphere*

to the Southern, from the never-ending social whirl of Buenos Aires, Argentina, to socially relaxed Riga, Latvia. In between, she stopped in Caracas, Prague, Riga again, and Washington, D.C., and finally she went from Argentina to Berlin. There was always adventure and exhaustion.

The thing [for me] to do when I get overtired is to go to bed. In fact, when in Argentina I was going socially morning, noon, and night, I [became] exhausted and began to deteriorate. So my ambassadress, Mrs. Robert Woods Bliss, said, "Now, you go to bed for two days." I was only too delighted and stayed in bed for two days and came back completely restored. The next year I found I began to get a little bit teary. This time I stayed in bed for a week and read. Otherwise, I had no time to read. The third year I was all ready to go to bed for a month when we were transferred, so there was no question of my doing it. But it makes me realize at some times that if you're always giving out, that you can't take in, you go to pieces.

In Berlin Betty White encountered early clues of the conflagration to come. "We got there in December 1933. Hitler had been there since the end of January."

The night after our arrival we attended a big concert in the Sportpalast, a tremendous place, as big as one of our armories. We were given special places. The concert was to raise funds for the *Winterhilfe* (the Winter Relief), which was the principal Nazi charity.

They were going to play the fanfares written by Frederick the Great, and the huge floor was absolutely crammed with people. Enormous klieg lights were playing all around. The music started, and a procession entered. Then with the klieg lights full on him, Hitler came forward alone, with everyone doing the Nazi salute and shouting "Heil, Hitler!" All very dramatic.

I actually met him when our ambassador went on home leave and Jack became chargé d'affaires. When Hitler had his first dinner as chancellor he asked Jack, asked us both. As you remember, in diplomatic circles the host can sit in the middle of the table and couples opposite each other. We were down at the far end, with the Haitian minister and his Belgian wife. They were very pleasant, but I don't remember their names. She asked, "What color are Hitler's eyes?" I said, "Well, he kissed my hand and then pushed it out of the way like a political handshake. I didn't notice."

So when we all filed out, saying good-bye, I was so intent on looking at Hitler's eyes that I completely forgot where I was. I said, "Good night," looking at his eyes, which were a beautiful blue-green, green-blue, not quite as dark as robin's egg, not quite so green. You know, with most of us the irises are puckered and they catch the light. His didn't seem to be so puckered. That was what was so extraordinary. I got an effect just of blue-green, like china. And when I said, in English, "Good night," I was aware of a look of fury. But as I was looking at his eyes and not looking into them, his fury didn't touch me.

My mother came out to visit us, and we had family friends for lunch, even though we had had a terrible time the night before getting home. There was a lot of traffic, but we had no real trouble—[Nazi leader Hermann] Goering's airmen seemed to be running the traffic, which seemed unusual. The next day they shut off Tiergartenstrasse entirely. I told Jack about this, so he immediately called up an American journalist and asked, "What's going on?" He replied, "Oh, Hitler has shot ['Brown Shirt' steel helmet organization leader Ernst] Roehm." We all discussed that, it was a great excitement.

That afternoon I . . . [learned] that [right-wing leader General Kurt] von Schleicher had also been killed. . . . He and his wife had been killed just an hour before I went to play tennis with some Jewish friends that afternoon. Roehm was to the left, so [we] couldn't believe that Hitler had gone both ways. But then it was confirmed [on the Czech radio].

The next day, we'd been invited to tea by some people that I'd only recently met, on the Wannsee, which was a lake just within the precincts of Berlin. I had trouble finding the house, but the lake was absolutely packed with little sailboats—"standing room only." And when we got to the door, finally, on a little peninsula, a man in a long coat came up to me and said, "You can't go any further." I replied that I was Mrs. White and I was invited to tea. Then he gave me a letter from my host saying he was very sorry that he couldn't receive me; . . . he was under house arrest, but was being very nicely treated; would I please give the letter back. Well, I hadn't thought of keeping the letter until then. I wanted to, but obviously I couldn't keep it because it would look as though he were passing a message on. So I gave the letter back.

Meanwhile, the Whites' daughter, Margaret White Bennett [spouse of former Ambassador and Assistant Secretary of State W. Tapley Bennett, Jr.], was gaining her own education about the Nazis' new world order. "I was 12," she recalled in a 1988 interview. "I was put in the Mommsenschule, which was the private school for girls run by the daughter or the niece of the German historian Theodor Mommsen."

Fraulein Mommsen wore a long gray flannel dress with her hair up in a bun and sort of a bib in front. Did you ever see that movie *Maedchen in Uniform?* [That] was very much the style of clothing she wore. [The school] catered to the lesser nobility, the Junkers, and the army. They did let foreigners in, and the daughter of our assistant military attaché was my best friend. She and I were in the same class of 13 girls. General von Schleicher's daughter—he was from the extreme right, and he and his wife were murdered on the thirtieth of June—attended the school, and she came back all dressed in black about a week after the event. We also had in my class a girl whose surname was von Spiegelberg, and she was definitely Jewish.

We were supposed to say, "Heil, Hitler," and do the salute and all that. I asked my father, "What do I do?" He said, "Do as they do, but don't go out of your way." And periodically Hitler would make a speech and we'd all have to listen to it on the radio. Boring!

Every time the teacher came in it was "Heil, Hitler." When I first got to the school, they were relatively relaxed about it. Then the powers that be started cracking down, and it was announced that we would all have to take an hour a week of Nazi indoctrination. I asked my father again, "Do I take this or not?" And he said, "Take it, but don't believe a word of it."

But then they began having more militant Nazi teachers. I remember we had one who I think was not naturally that way but felt she had to almost overplay her hand. She got rather firm about everybody doing their "Heil, Hitler" salute properly. In my class, we had one girl who was a Hitler *Maedel*, or, as they were called, *Bund Deutscher Maedel* I think it was. The BDM girl had apparently been told she must do something about the von Spiegelberg girl, the Jewish girl in our class. Well, I was not present when this scene occurred, and the reason I was not there is one that I think perfectly illustrated the German mentality. I was being hauled on the carpet for the misdeeds of my fellow Americans, some of them older students in other classes, because my father was the ranking American. And so I missed this great scene.

But apparently in the recess yard, Gerda, the BDM girl, went up to the von Spiegelberg girl and called her a couple of nasty names, "You something Jewess," something like that. And, interestingly enough, the Jewish girl burst into tears and the whole school rallied around her. When I got back to class, my American pal said, "We're not talking to Gerda anymore." One of her good friends stood by her, but for the rest of that year most of the class did not speak to her.

50

EVACUATION 1930s STYLE

An evacuation from Poland in 1939 initially seemed just a nuisance to Regina (Gene) Blake, a young Foreign Service wife in Warsaw who was "trying to do my job."

We went to an air raid precautions course, we wore masks and heard lectures. . . . There were rumblings in early 1939, but the summer was beautiful. Ambassador Anthony [Joseph Drexel (Tony)] Biddle, Jr., and his wife, Margaret, lived in a very lovely palace and entertained so much. There were gardens, even a platform outdoors where we danced. All kinds of celebrities came; I remember meeting Noel Coward. For a young Foreign Service wife, it was all very thrilling.

It was because of the beautiful summer weather that German tanks on dirt roads were able to go wherever they wished. On muddy roads rutted by cart wheels they could not have invaded so quickly.

Three days before the Germans attacked, all the American husbands came home and told their wives we were to be evacuated to Oslo. We all said we didn't want to go. They, in turn, said, "Well, so-and-so is going." We would have resisted going if we'd known that Mrs. Biddle was going to stay with her husband, who was still in Warsaw but who left later with the Polish government for Romania.

There were four of us wives, and our husbands saw us off on the train three days before the invasion. Our first stop was Riga, Latvia. We were there overnight, with our one small suitcase, which was all we were allowed to take, staying with Foreign Service friends.

Riga was a legation then, and our minister, John Cooper Wiley, and his wife Irena, who was Polish, had planned earlier a very large dinner party that evening. We four were invited and signed ourselves in the book "the not so merry wives of Warsaw." Somehow, even with our small suitcases, we had each taken one black-tie costume. I packed a sequined jacket that my husband called my "drum major dress."

After our overnight in Riga, we were to go by ferry across the Baltic to Stockholm, our next stop en route to Oslo. We spent the night in Stockholm and were then to go by train to Oslo. Discussing all this, we four wives decided, "This is ridiculous, why can't we go back to Warsaw? Before taking the train, we'll go early to the legation and say, 'We want to go back.'"

51

As we were walking along the street, we noticed big kiosks displaying news bulletins and crowds of people reading them. We asked some of the Swedes, "What is the news?" They said, "Warsaw has been bombed." We knew this was the beginning of a long, terrible thing.

3

WOMEN AT WAR

When we left New York, I carried a letter saying that if I fell into enemy hands, I was to be treated as a second lieutenant.

Doris Metcalf

I had no qualifications whatsoever because during the war I had no language. I could type, I had gotten my first job . . . and I was still studying shorthand. I got to "It was a gray day when Ted ran the great race," and I never got further than that. It would have been useful.

Julia Child

To Dorothy Hessman, the short article that appeared in the Minneapolis Tribune during the early fall of 1943 was appealing. For more than two years, she had been accounting officer for the Redwood County (Minnesota) Welfare Board in Redwood Falls, 100 miles southwest of Minneapolis. "Foreign Service Jobs Are Open for 300 Women," headlined the newspaper on 26 September. "Current need," she read, "is for trained stenographers, typists, accountants, and code clerks at starting salaries of $2,186, plus a $400 to $600 annual allowance for living and maintenance. To qualify, girls should have three years' experience and must pass the stenographer's examination of the United States civil service commission." The article also listed "immediate vacancies in Sicily, Italy, London, Cairo, and South American countries." [1]

That same afternoon, Hessman wrote for more information. The Foreign Service attracted her. In little more than a week, Hessman had sent the State Department recruiter a completed employment application that demonstrated her attention to one of the subtle requirements of State Department service for women: it was signed "(Miss) Dorothy M. Hessman." Miss Hessman was about to become a "Government Girl."

The State Department's search for staff to support its far-flung diplomatic and consular activities reflected the dramatic changes World War II had brought to American society. As men were drafted or volunteered for direct military service, women from all social classes increasingly filled the gaps— both in production of war matériel itself and in the expanding bureaucracy needed to get people and things to their destinations. Epitomized by "Rosie the Riveter," women were hired by the thousands to take men's places "for the duration" on aircraft production lines, in munitions factories, and on the docks. In Washington, women with stenographic, typing, and mathematical skills were recruited to keep the war machine operating at peak efficiency. They were called Government Girls.

Along with thousands of others who came to Washington from all parts of the United States, Hessman, Julia Child, and Doris Metcalf were alert to the possibility of serving abroad. Eventually, Julia Child went to the Office of Strategic Services and Doris Metcalf into the Foreign Service Auxiliary.

Dorothy Hessman's scrapbook preserved memorabilia of the time, including the paperwork that brought her to Washington. On 4 January 1944, the day she reported to work, Hessman received an "indefinite appointment not to extend beyond the duration of the present war and for six months thereafter." For these young women, this opportunity was an open door to an exciting life that offered the added advantage of service to the war effort.

While Hessman remained single, many others met their future husbands through wartime service. Julia Child, for example, would later prepare as a Foreign Service spouse for her career as television's "French Chef." She described in a 1991 interview one way that she and others were recruited. "I had no qualifications whatsoever," Julia recalled, "because during the war I had no languages."

I could type, I had gotten my first job . . . I was still studying shorthand. I got to "It was a gray day when Ted ran the great race," and I never got further than that. It would have been useful.

I started out [in Washington] at a place that we called "Mellett's Madhouse," which was across from the Willard Hotel [on Pennsylvania Avenue]. There was a little woman, a naval officer with feet that went like that [does a staccato tap-tap-tap with her fingers]. She was in charge, but very severe, you know. She never gave you a smile. I was typing little white cards, and I was so furious at my job that I typed them so hard that they had to get two people to replace me when I left. I thought I should get a job by myself without any pull, and that's what I landed, so. . . .

Just to be sure that I wasn't being disloyal to my country, I applied to both the WACS and the WAVES [the women's auxiliaries of the army and navy, respectively], standing to my full height, and I was an inch and a half too long. Thank heavens I didn't have to go in there, which I wouldn't have liked. But I did apply, so I was patriotic. Luckily I was tall. So Mellett's Madhouse I got all by myself. It just shows what you can do without any pull. And no talents.

I had friends in the OSS (Office of Strategic Services), so I applied for that, and I ended up in General [William J. (Wild Bill)] Donovan's [director of the OSS] file room, and he was a fascinating man. Kind of smallish and rumpled, piercing blue eyes. It was said that he could read by just turning the pages. People were just wonderfully loyal to him. I think that he took people very personally, was interested in them. It was fascinating being with Donovan. I saw everybody.

So I was in his files, and then they started an air-sea rescue equipment section, and I became the administrative assistant, that's the only time I really got out of the files. They started sending people overseas. I knew that I would eventually get to France [in peacetime], so I applied to the Far East.

Julia McWilliams's application for an overseas posting was soon approved, and in 1943 she was assigned to Kandy, Ceylon (now Sri Lanka), where she met her husband-to-be, Paul Child, an OSS visual presentations specialist. Before their marriage, the couple also served together in Kunming, China, from 1944 to 1945, and were there on 6 August when the United States dropped the atomic bomb on Hiroshima. They were married in 1946.

During Paul Child's USIS (United States Information Service) postings in Paris (1948–52) and Marseille (1953–54), Julia discovered the passionate avocation that would become her career. "My first French meal was in Rouen [en route to Paris], and I never turned back after that. I just fell in love with French food from the first bite."

Paris presented a marvelous opportunity for Julia. She promptly enrolled in Berlitz classes and in the professional course of the premier Parisian cooking school of that era, the Cordon Bleu. The only woman "with a group of GIs" on the GI Bill, she trained under chef Max Bugnard, who in turn had learned his craft from the most famous twentieth-century French chef, Auguste Escoffier. "I had been looking for a career all my life," she said. "I was passionately interested in it, the tremendous care that all the chefs and teachers took. It was art for art's sake. It made no difference how long it took; if it came out beautifully, that was it."

At a cocktail party, Julia Child met her two collaborators on Mastering the Art of French Cooking (1961), Simone Beck ("we literally embraced each other") and Louisette Bertholle; the two French women were already working on a cookbook for American audiences, but their American coauthor had died. "I never knew him," Julia Child said. But it was "good timing, so we started in on our book together."

Julia Child was able to continue collaboration on the book as Paul Child's assignments took them from France to Germany and Norway, where she recalled an encounter with "a typical American women's club luncheon."

They had a salad made out of jello, with bananas and grapes and marshmallows, and really it looked like a phallic symbol. It was sitting there on a little piece of lettuce. You couldn't hide it under anything.

The luncheon ended with one of those cake mixes with a white mountain of coconut frosting. Horrible! And some of us got together and said, "Never again!" and formed a cooking committee.

Paul Child's approach to his career allowed Julia Child an extraordinary amount of freedom to pursue her ambition in cooking. "We were always down around rank four, so we didn't have to do many embassy things," she said. "We had our French friends, and we lived a very, very nice life" in Paris, in a third-floor rue de l'Université apartment near the Chambre des Députés, where Paul could walk to work. But even keeping their heads down could not shelter the Childs from the strong political winds of anticommunism that buffeted the State Department during the 1950s.

McCarthyism brushed the Childs' lives abruptly when they were stationed in Bonn.

Paul suddenly got a cable, and it said, "Send Child at once to Washington." I said, I know why he is going—they are going to make him head of the department. It turned out to be an FBI examination.

They questioned him about colleagues and friends. He was furious! Because we knew a lot of fairly important people at that point, as soon as he got out that first day, he went howling to everybody he knew [and shortly the investigation was dropped].

The real object of the inquiry was an old friend of both Childs, from Kandy and Paris days, "who had turned out to be a Russian agent," said Julia Child. Paul Child retired from USIS in 1960. The following year, Alfred A. Knopf published

Julia and Paul Child, Oslo, Norway, 1959. *Courtesy of Julia Child.*

Mastering the Art of French Cooking, *changing forever the way Americans think about food.*

CASUAL RELEASE FROM SERVICE

Doris Metcalf was another Government Girl whose experiences revealed determination to contribute to the war effort—and to gain a coveted assignment overseas in the Foreign Service Auxiliary. She remembered a Washington much different, and much smaller, in the early 1940s than it is in the 1990s:

I loved that time in Washington, over 40 years ago. I would often walk down Connecticut Avenue to the State, War, and Navy building (now the Old Executive Office Building, next to the White House). There were very chic, beautiful shops, Ehrlbacher's, Rizik Brothers. I'd look at all the extravagant clothes. I just loved that walk, the broad sidewalk, with energetic men and women in and out of uniform, a "charged" atmosphere.

And when I drew the midnight shift in the code room, I walked down Connecticut Avenue, in the middle of the night, all by myself, if there wasn't transportation right there. It was still a town of streetcars and buses, too, but mostly streetcars at that corner of Pennsylvania Avenue and 17th Street, and I really never had any feeling of being afraid.

After training, Doris received orders to Istanbul, the place she most wanted to go. Her experiences reporting to her new post probably were typical of those faced by single women going overseas in the middle of the war. While transoceanic air travel was commonplace at the time, it was reserved for missions much more important than the transportation of new State Department support staff. She embarked from New York Harbor on the Mauretania, *after a short training in naval survival skills.*

There were 26 of us in a hotel ballroom, on cots in a row. We were told to paint our travel order number with white paint on our suitcase; we were allowed only one. Mine was IJ 909 LA.

We were taken to the Brooklyn Navy Yard and issued a helmet and a gas mask. And we had to go through a simulated gas room. The girl beside me put that gas mask on and had instant claustrophobia. Her hands and arms

58

were flailing, "I can't stand this, I can't stand this! I can't breathe!" I don't think we were ever subjected to any gas in this exercise, but we were told that this was the gas room and we did have to go through it with our gas mask on. I lost her in that melee, but I guess she got through it.

And then two or three days later we boarded buses that took us to our ship. There were 10,000 troops on board, also Red Cross women, and nurses.

We were on constant "alert," and we had lifeboat practice once or twice a day. Whistles would blow, and we would run to our lifeboat stations. I think at that station, except for one man, we were all women—I don't know who he was, perhaps a newspaper man, and he said, "God, what chance will I ever have with all these women piling into my lifeboat!"

We lined up at our battle stations with our panic bags, which held our K rations or C rations, and maybe a sweater. My father had given me two beautiful silver fox furs he'd gotten up at Churchill, on Hudson Bay. They were wild foxes, with very long hair—absolutely gorgeous. You remember how fabulous we thought fox furs were? In my one suitcase, I carried the two fox furs. If I were going to the battle station from my "stateroom," I always put those fox furs on. Of course, I got teased about it—some of the men asked me, "Are they going to swim?" But they were warm! I thought, "If I'm out there in that cold lifeboat, which looked awfully small to me, I wouldn't mind having my furs." I loved them anyway, two warm beautiful friends.

The *Mauretania* was for those times a fast ship, very maneuverable. It zigzagged all over the North Atlantic. We got almost up to Iceland, it was awfully cold. You could tell by the sun and early darkness. Then we came back down into the Mersey River and docked at Liverpool.

On the next leg of her journey to Istanbul, aboard the converted British cruise ship SS Orion, and with some excitement, Doris wended slowly down the coast of Europe and through the Mediterranean.

One day we were on deck when suddenly all the military people tensed up, and the gunners moved into position; everything started to move and turn. There were Nazi reconnaissance planes high overhead. I was with one of the Australians at the time, and I asked, "How do you know those are Nazi planes?" He answered, "You know the keys of your typewriter, don't you?" We later learned that the convoy ahead of ours had been attacked.

Doris survived the perils of convoy transit through the Mediterranean and went on from Egypt by train to Turkey, where she met her future husband, Lee Metcalf. But after a transfer to Romania, she became ill.

It was darn cold, that first winter in Bucharest. It was cold, and I had a cold. Actually, I think I caught my cold in the hotel in Naples, which was also cold. Once we left Cairo, everything and every place was cold, inside and outside. By now it was early spring 1945. We had been in Bucharest about six months. Six months in the cold. I finally realized that I was ill and took off a few days from the office. An American doctor who had come to see some American POWs came to see me. He could find nothing that he could diagnose; he thought I was run-down and tired. A few weeks later another American doctor came through and after listening to my chest said simply, "Home!"

I went into an army hospital in Naples. I still had no diagnosis but found there were GIs in the hospital with similar symptoms. After a week the hospital ship *Seminole* took on a boatload of patients; I was among them. By then I was considered contagious, so along with five GIs, six of us on litters, I was loaded into an ambulance, like bread in an oven, and taken to the dock.

On board we were put in isolation. Being the only woman in contagion, I was given a private room in the psychiatric ward, where I was very comfortable but feeling rotten. The *Seminole* was a narrow ship that had been built for coastal waters rather than ocean crossings. The trip took two weeks from Naples to Charleston, South Carolina, and it did a lot of rolling.

In the army hospital in Charleston, I was diagnosed as having a pleural effusion. My left lung had filled with fluid, and I was treated as if I had tuberculosis. I suppose my illness had been brought on by living in such cold, working long hours, and losing my immunity.

On discharge, I went to St. Paul to my parents' home. I was not completely well; I was still treated as though I had tuberculosis. TB was still such a scourge! There was no treatment except bed rest. I wasn't even supposed to raise my arm over my head, for that movement uses lung power.

When Lee [Metcalf] had home leave, he came to St. Paul to see me and to meet my family. He persuaded me to go down to El Paso with him to meet his parents and bask in the sunshine. We were married there in January 1946— not quite the country wedding in Yugoslavia we had talked about. I was feeling better and better, getting back my strength.

[My discharge from State was] all a bit hazy. It wasn't a medical discharge. There was no medical coverage in the Foreign Service then. We had sick leave, two days a month perhaps, which we could accumulate. [It was] just assumed that because Lee and I were getting married I would leave the office. At that time we were all "programmed" to accept such an idea. I don't recall when I left the service, but one day I wasn't "in" any longer. It must have happened while I was en route home, when my sick leave ran out. Later I did try to claim per diem; perhaps I got some before I was cut off, but I don't think so.

FROM EMPLOYEE TO SPOUSE

Government Girls were not the only women of the late 1930s and early 1940s who entered the U.S. Foreign Service, or for that matter participated in foreign affairs. To educated younger American women living in Europe in the days just before World War II, life was exhilarating and offered opportunity to perform the day-to-day diplomatic duties usually reserved for young men. For Margaret Jones Palmer, a Georgia native whose father had been American vice-consul in Glasgow, Scotland, several years before her birth in 1916, the lure of Europe was overpowering compared with her life as an undergraduate at the University of Georgia.

Margaret's experiences in Europe began in 1937. "In my senior year I was offered an exchange scholarship to Heidelberg University," she said in a 1992 interview. She was afraid her family wouldn't let her go. My mother said, "Of course you can go." This really threw me, because then I thought, "I don't know whether I want to go or not!"

I went, in June, and I meant to stay nine months. I ended up staying over two and a half years. By 1938 everything was brewing in Germany [and] I knew from being with the students that something was happening. I went to Vienna for spring break and was there when Hitler marched in.

The little student hotel where I was staying was turned into a barracks. Travel was frozen, money was frozen. I had to wait eight days in order to get out. I had no money, only German marks, which were useless. I thought, "I really should find an American embassy." They changed money for me and made sure I had enough to pay my hotel bill and eat while I was there.

During my studies in Heidelberg, Hitler came, and since I was in the school of journalism, I was able to get an interview with him—which turned out to be really a joke, because he interviewed me. I was very young and inexperienced. But it was a face-to-face meeting, which the *Atlanta Journal* published in 1938.

At the end of nine months, Margaret was reluctant to return to the University of Georgia. Her father suggested that, with fluent German, she try American consulates. She was offered several positions.

Assistant Secretary of State for African Affairs Joseph Palmer II and Margaret Palmer, 1966. *Courtesy of Margaret Palmer.*

I chose Hamburg. I thought, "That's a port city. Not if, but when, anything happens, that would be the place to be rather than Berlin or even Vienna." I had to sell my motorcycle in order to get there in September 1938. So I was in the consulate general in Hamburg for that whole winter. After *Kristall-nacht*, the "night of broken glass," when all the store windows of the Jewish shops were shattered, I was sent out the next day to report on it.

I was put in the visa section [of the consulate]. It was the time when huge numbers of Jews were trying to get out of Europe—Polish, Czechoslovakian, all came to the port cities. It was heartbreaking, there were thousands and thousands. The quota numbers were [such] that you knew they'd never make it, in spite of impassioned letters from their relatives in the States sending affidavits of support. There were a lot of suicides. I gave English lessons to people at night who were going over.

[Later] all American women were told to leave. I left on the last United

States Line ship from Hamburg, the *United States*, and the day we edged into Southampton on the way home, war was declared, September 3, 1939. And all the things that were important to me at that age, my books, my skis, I had left back in Hamburg because I thought "I will go back."

So I came back to the U.S. and went to Savannah, where my mother and father lived.

But Savannah, as beautiful and charming as it was, no longer attracted Margaret Jones. She soon discovered a way out, through Washington.

I'd been home about three weeks and had a letter from the State Department saying they had formed a special division to cope with people in the U.S. who were trying to find out what happened to their relatives in Europe, and that I could have a job there. My father said, "Go! It's your life." My mother said, "Please don't." But I said, "Let me go just for a little while."

And [the next spring] I thought, "I like this, but I really want to go abroad." So Senator Walter George of Georgia, who was on the Foreign Relations Committee and a dear friend of my father's, wrote George Messerschmidt—Cordell Hull was secretary of state—and found an opening in Mexico City. I thought, "It's not Germany, it's not Europe, but at least it's abroad!"

So Messerschmidt called me in, and he said, "Now, Miss Jones, we have an opening in Mexico City. They're combining the embassy and the consulate general and you can be useful. I have to ask you some personal questions" (which they wouldn't do any more). "Are you engaged to be married? You're not tied with anyone right now?" And I said, "No, to be perfectly honest, I'm not. Why?" And he said, "Because we have very bad luck with the girls we send out. We train them and instruct them and they go out, and the next thing you know they're married." And I said, "Oh no, no, I assure you."

So I went to Mexico.

But in Mexico City later that year Margaret became "discreetly" engaged to Joseph Palmer II.

I met Joe the very first day [in Mexico City], and I thought, "What will the State Department say?!" We became secretly engaged, and we thought nobody knew. One day the consul general came in to my desk, and he ripped out a pocket knife and he carved a notch in my desk. He said, "Didn't you see these notches on the desk?" And I said, yes, but I didn't know what they were. He said, "This is how many women I have lost." And he said, "Didn't you know that everybody knew that you and Joe were getting married?" So, I had to resign.

Yet Margaret Palmer's first posting as a spouse abroad in Nairobi, Kenya, where she and her husband were stranded "for the duration," showed beyond doubt that the old system—based on the unwritten rule that Foreign Service women were to resign when they married—was breaking down. Whether they had official status or not, spouses' participation in official, as opposed to representative, diplomatic affairs was becoming a necessity.

Nairobi, where as acting consul Joe Palmer earned $256 per month, was reached after a 27-day passage around Africa and "puddle-jumping" up the East African coast. They arrived on a Friday. The current consul greeted them by announcing, "I'm leaving Sunday," Margaret Palmer recalled.

We had one day for him to hand the reins to Joe. Joe was 26, and I was 24. The consul said, "Joe, your consular district is Keen-ya" (you didn't say Kenn-ya in those days), "Tanganyika, Zanzibar, Somalia, the lower part of Sudan, Seychelles and Madagascar."

The only thing we knew about East Africa was what I'd been able to find out in the D.C. public library.

Over the four years in East Africa, the Palmers adapted and grew. There was a maximum of four people at the post. Since Margaret had retained her security clearance ("nobody ever asked [for it back]"), she often worked as code clerk. In the 1992 interview, she described her days before their first child was born.

I spent them in a windowless crate about eight feet tall and four feet square, with a door and a lock. There was no way Joe could have done all the coding and decoding. So there I was.

We had brought the code books out from the State Department in a brown paper package tied up with string. They said, "Guard these with your life."

We slept with them, we carried them every place we went until we got on board the ship, and then we put them in the ship's safe. We corded them up and slept with them on the train. They were our honeymoon bedfellows, those code books. And we got [to Nairobi, and the consul] said, "They're out of date."

They sent out an absolutely terrible system called "the strip code." They were long strips of very bendable paper and a big board that you had to slide things in until it absolutely fit.

In spite of the challenges and rewards, four years in Nairobi left the Palmers wondering whether they had been forgotten by the State Department. They had a two-year-old child, and both families were very eager to get them back. (Margaret Palmer had never met her in-laws.) She told her husband, "I think it's time you wrote."

So he did, and we got a—it's almost like they said, "Oh my stars, the Palmers!" So we got a telegram to say that Joe was assigned back to the department. He was to go via Ethiopia, Asmara, and Cairo for consultations along the way. [Adding], almost, "you can just do the best you can with your wife and child."

And nobody wanted to take us. No ship would take us, there were no airplanes. [The war was not over.]

I said, "This is fine, you go back and be in Washington, and I'll still be in Nairobi!" Finally we complained a little bit. And they established a priority which was the lowest of the low, but they said that if I would take my chances on a C-37 transport, that I could take the child, provided I would put on trousers.

In those days women didn't really wear pants, so I went down to the tentmaker and had a pair of pants stitched up, and I had one suitcase, and in a string bag a ceramic pot, made for the baby, and also in the bag a body leash I had made for him, a little harness. I didn't know what I was getting into.

It took us ten days to get home. I had not changed drawers [underwear]. It was an ab-so-lute nightmare. I would be bumped, fly a little bit, and be bumped.

This little thing looked at me, like, "Mother, you took me out of that beautiful garden, where my ayah brought me my juice every morning at ten on the nose, and—what are we doing here?" We'd get on planes with bucket seats along the sides. We would be sitting up front, and he would say,

"Mommy, could I have some water," and I'd give him water, and ten minutes later, "Mommy, I have to pee-pee." So the men would just hand him all the way down to this big can in the back of the plane.

We got to [an airport] not too far from Accra, which was the big staging area in those days. But we had a crash takeoff, and I really wondered if I could get back on the plane. But I had to. In Accra I ran into one of my waffle-eaters [friends], as I used to call them, and I said, "Brad, is there anyone who can pull any strings to get me with this child any place?"

He said he was leaving the next morning to go to Ascension Island [in the South Atlantic], and he said, "I'll see what I can do. Stay in the Red Cross hut, and if you wake up in the morning at the normal time, you'll know I was not able to get you on. If somebody wakes you up at four, get up quickly." You had to sleep in your clothes anyway, you were always ready to go. So I woke up the next morning, and he had not wakened me. That plane crashed in Ascension, and everybody was killed. When Joe heard about this, he went to pieces thinking I was on it.

We finally got out of Accra and went to Brazil, to Natal. I never knew when I was going to get on the next stage of any flight, all I had was this child on a harness, plus a ceramic pot and a suitcase.

Natal was a huge area, and they said I would have to report to some place two miles away. I took this little baby on leash and the suitcase, which was getting heavier and heavier, although I didn't have too much in it, and I flagged down a jeep with two teenagers in it—you know, the very cocky kind. They said, "Lady, we can't take civilians," and I said, "Yes, you can, too, you can take me." So they did.

By then young Joe was running a temperature, and I thought, "This is just one more—I've got to get some help." So they took me to the medical unit, and I walked in, and this voice said, "Jonesy," my high school name, "Jonesy, what are you doing here?" It was a high school friend who'd gone on to Yale Medical School and was in the medical corps.

And I said, "Really, God is good." So he dosed little Joe up with an antibiotic and saw that I got on the next plane. We went from Natal to Puerto Rico and then to Miami, and I've never been so glad to get to any place in my life.

"THIS... IS LONDON"

During the war, when a woman became a Foreign Service spouse she was expected to relinquish her former life, regardless of her accomplishments. The most extreme example was Marvin Breckinridge Patterson, who in 1939 became the first woman CBS network radio broadcaster covering the war for American listeners. An accomplished filmmaker, photojournalist, and writer, Marvin Breckinridge had already spent a decade exploring both Appalachia and Africa for films and for publications like Vogue, Harper's Bazaar, Town and Country, Life, Collier's, National Geographic, *and* Look. *In 1932 she had made a photo safari from Capetown to Cairo, photographing the African landscape and tribal peoples.*

On 23 August 1939, the day the German-Russian pact was signed, Marvin arrived in Switzerland to cover the Lucerne Music Festival for Town and Country. *Things happened quickly. On 24 August the festival was canceled. On the twenty-sixth, a Nazi rally at Tannenberg, which she was to cover for* Life, *was canceled. On Friday, 1 September, Hitler marched into Poland and Marvin struck out for London. She traveled with Olive Barnett, a young English woman she had met in Lucerne. In her 1988 interview, she recalled, "I was delighted to have Olive with me."*

The trains were so crowded, and there was such confusion. You had to keep an eye on your belongings. When we got hungry, one of us would go for rolls and coffee and the other would guard the luggage. At Basel we managed to get sleepers on the overnight train to Paris.

At 11:50 on Saturday we were on the boat train to Calais. We had to stand or sit on our suitcases in the aisle. In our car there was a gang of young men. I gathered that they'd been called into the French army and were on their way to report for duty.

You could see that they weren't happy about it. They scowled at Olive and me, and we figured that they took both of us to be English, and in their minds it was England who was pushing their country into this mess.

I went over and spoke to them in their language. I told them I was an American and this wasn't my war. If only I could have foreseen what was coming. Soon they were quite friendly. There wasn't a crumb of food to be bought on the train, but they'd brought their lunches—hunks of bread and cheese and bottles of wine—and these they shared with us.

Marvin arrived in blacked-out London on Saturday night, 2 September, and went to the Savoy Hotel, where one of Olive's relatives was a director. On Sunday Britain declared war on Germany. At 2:30 Monday morning, she took part in the first London air raid, although on this occasion, no bombs fell.

We were herded into the Abraham Lincoln Room in the basement of the Savoy. The room had been sandbagged, and there were benches. People were in their nightclothes. One lady was accompanied by her maid—with a Pekingese in her arms—and her little husband beside her. I had brought my Rolleiflex with me, and I took photos of a group, pictures that later appeared in the pages of *Life*. They were the first photographs to be published of a shelter during a World War II air raid.

That afternoon Marvin went to the American Express office in Piccadilly to see about a ticket to the United States. She found the street leading to the offices, the Haymarket, jammed with Americans, many with children, trying to book passage home. She decided to remain in Europe.

I had brought along my camera and my typewriter and could continue my work as a photojournalist. I hurried to Fleet Street, to my photographic agency, Black Star. They were glad to see me . . . and within a few days I received a permit and was registered to photograph Britain in wartime.

From September to November, Marvin traveled around England, photographing and reporting on a country at war. In mid-November she received an invitation to dine in London with her friends Edward R. Murrow and his wife Janet. Murrow was director of CBS's recently established newscasting operations in Europe and was aware of Marvin's work in England.

Marvin had met Murrow when he arrived in New York, a penniless student, to work with the National Student Federation of America. While a student at Vassar, Marvin had been secretary of the organization. A mutual friend had asked her to take care of him, and she invited Murrow to stay at her parents' home in Manhattan. "We became good friends, but there was no romantic interest."

After their dinner in London, Murrow hired her, even though women broadcast-

ers were practically unheard of at the time. Murrow thought U.S. listeners would be interested in her report on the thousands of children evacuated to the English countryside from London, "where at any hour death might rain from the sky." Marvin's broadcast on 18 November 1939 from the BBC studios to an estimated 22 million people was a success. The only instructions she remembered receiving from Murrow were to "be neutral, be fair, keep your voice low, and cough if you have to." Her next report was on the activities of the Auxiliary Fire Service: 2,500 young women who had taken over in-station duties ranging from record keeping to telephone communication to relieve the men for fighting the fires resulting from the bombing of London.

A few days later Murrow signed her on as a regular broadcaster on the CBS news program "World News Roundup," a series of linked nightly reports to the United States from the capitals of Western Europe. She became one of "Murrow's boys," several of whom achieved fame, among them William L. Shirer and Eric Severeid. Marvin was assigned to Amsterdam, and on 7 December she flew to Holland in a blacked-out plane, all windows sealed, to take up her post.

When Murrow and Shirer were in Amsterdam for a broadcast on 19 January 1940, Murrow asked her to go to Berlin to relieve Shirer, who wanted to visit his wife and baby daughter in Switzerland. Shirer's diary noted:

Berlin, January 30—Marvin Breckinridge here and tomorrow I shall get off on a jaunt which Hitler's press chief and confidant, Dr. Diettrich, is organizing (to keep us in a friendly temper) to Garmisch. From there I hope to steal away to the Swiss mountains for a fortnight with Tess and Eileen. Hitler made an unexpected speech at the Sportpalast tonight on the occasion of the seventh anniversary of the Nazis taking over power. I had no burning desire to attend, so Marvin went off to cover it. She got a great kick out of watching the man.[2]

Her second day in Berlin Marvin renewed her acquaintance with Jefferson Patterson, first secretary of the American embassy, who had arranged for her to cover the Nazi Tannenberg rally that had been canceled in August. She had known him since the early 1930s in Washington, D.C., and theirs had been "a comfortable friendship."

Marvin Breckinridge and Jefferson Patterson were both from American families of long-standing wealth and distinction, families that were very formal and proper in the conduct of all their relationships. On the morning of 12 March 1940, after six weeks in Berlin, Marvin was booked on the 12:45 P.M. to return to Amsterdam. But just before she left, outside of her hotel, Jefferson Patterson had asked her to marry him.

Edward R. Murrow, Marvin Breckinridge, and William L. Shirer donning ice skates, Amsterdam, January 1940. *Photographer unknown, courtesy of Marvin Breckinridge Patterson collection.*

She accepted and in Amsterdam made a quick call to the CBS bureau in London. Sure that the telephone lines were tapped, she told Murrow obliquely, "I'm following Tom's example," referring to the recent marriage of Eric Sevareid's assistant Tom Grandin, adding, "It's an all-American affair."

That same day, in a confidential letter to his mother, Jefferson Patterson described the event.

"I feel that I should write this in the old-fashioned pen-and-ink—partly because you sometimes express a preference for what is, after all, a more personal means of expression, and partly because of the old and yet, for me, wholly novel message which I am about to surprise you with, which is that, as Marvin Breckinridge was about to leave by train today for Holland, I asked her to marry me. She pleasantly responded affirmatively (although I hesitated to urge her to decide at once) but asked that no public announcement be made at the moment.

"I have seen quite a good deal of Marvin, and find that, despite her keenness of perception, she appeals to me in a manner which I think will grow. She seems to be willing to cultivate domesticity and I feel that now or never is the time for me to make a home [Patterson was 49]."[3]

The wedding took place in Berlin, at the embassy, on 20 June 1940. In a talk delivered to the Society of Woman Geographers in 1986, Marvin described the scene. "We had to be rather careful since I was on both sides of the war," she recalled, "I had to move around."

But when I came back [to Berlin], having told Ed Murrow two or three months before I was leaving CBS to get married, I arrived and this time [Jeff] met me, of course. A few days later we were married in the ambassador's study, by the only American minister left in Germany. And there had been no ambassador since 1938, only a chargé d'affaires. I only invited six or eight of my journalist friends from abroad, and Jeff invited a few friends from the embassy.

My mother said it was the only wedding she ever heard of where the groom gave the wedding. Me with only a camera and a typewriter, and one suitcase, couldn't do very much about it. But Jeff, with connections, could bring in food from Denmark through our legation. . . . One of my best wedding presents was two pounds of butter, and with that we had a wedding cake made. The military attaché lent us his sword to cut the cake. And right after the ceremony, [Jeff] and I called our mothers in America. From four bachelor officers at the embassy we received a tandem bicycle as a wedding gift, which we rode to the Fourth of July reception a few weeks later. I had sent my dress on ahead.

But the one thing that disappointed me was that I was no longer allowed by the State Department to publish photographs, or to broadcast. In fact, the undersecretary of state said, "The less we hear from Foreign Service officers and their wives, the better we like it." That finished my career in broadcasting.[4]

Jefferson Patterson's Alter Ego

But for Marvin Patterson, the end of one career was the beginning of another: as a Foreign Service wife she became, in her words, "Jeff Patterson's professional alter ego." At the time of their marriage, Jefferson Patterson's work as a neutral U.S. diplomat included periodic inspection of the prisoner-of-war camps in Germany, Poland, and France. Marvin Patterson's new career began only a few hours after her marriage in Berlin. "They were driving down the autobahn heading for Weimar and points south when they spotted alongside the road the familiar lineaments of a stalag: the high barbed wire fence and the elevated observation posts at its angles," wrote the late Milton Lomask.

Here, only a few miles south of Berlin, was a camp Jeff had never heard of before. He stopped the car, suggesting that Marvin wait for him there. She shook her head. The journalist in her stirred at the prospect of seeing what went on in one of these grim cantonments. She tagged along. . . . [D]uring the next ten months she went with him into eighteen P.O.W. camps, obtaining permission from the commandant to talk to the prisoners while Jeff inspected barracks, showers, kitchens, and infirmaries.[5]

In one of Jeff's published reminiscences, he describes a visit by the two of them to a camp "in a fortress atop a high mesa-like hill" near Dresden where 97 French generals, four French admirals, and a body of privates to take care of them had been confined. "We had to leave the automobile half way up the hill," he wrote. "The tunneled entrance seemed like that to Dante's inferno. . . . Its stone-vaulted passageway through the walls seemed to lead into darkness. However, after turning, one came out into sunlight within the battlements."[6] The commanding officer objected to Marvin's presence, but with Jeff's help, she bluffed her way in and around the premises. After their departure, the commandant wrote to the Oberkommando der Wehrmacht, and six months later Jeff received a letter pointing out that a rule forbade the presence of women in the camps and asking him to refrain from taking his wife into them, this in spite of the fact that the Pattersons had made a trip to Hungary for Marvin to purchase a huge trunk full of essentials to be distributed among the needy prisoners: "underwear, socks, bath and laundry soap, tobacco and cigarette papers, tinned pineapple, etc." [7]

From Berlin, the Pattersons' career took them to Peru, Belgium, Egypt, Greece, and Uruguay, where Jefferson Patterson was ambassador from 1956 to 1958. After she had been in Montevideo for a year, Marvin Patterson was asked by Loy W. Henderson, then deputy undersecretary of state for management, to do a time study of her work as an ambassador's wife. The results were astonishing. "Over a period of six consecutive weeks in October and November 1957," she wrote, "I spent just over 70 hours per week on administrative work—40–50 hours (including five personal letters)—and representation—20–30 hours." A note on weekend activities included the entry, "Infrequent attendance at church (too tired)."

4

COLD WAR ADJUSTMENTS

I found it much harder to be an embassy wife than to be an employed woman in the United States.

Esther Peterson

Franklin Delano Roosevelt, in more than 12 years as president, held the reins of U.S. foreign policy tightly. His opinion of the "striped-pants" professionals in the State Department was low. But despite Roosevelt's misgivings, professional diplomats, and their spouses, were still essential to the conduct of foreign relations. By the middle of World War II, in 1943 and 1944 when defeat of the Axis governments became a realistic probability, senior State Department officials, both career and political appointees, turned their attention to the shape of the postwar world.

Their inevitable political disagreements, in a greatly expanded diplomatic establishment, contained the seeds of a conflict that would pervade the American government over the next several years. The professional diplomats, who had reliable reports on the holocaust Stalin had created in the prewar Soviet Union (see Fanny Chipman's testimony in chapter 2) and firsthand knowledge of the militarism of Japan's prewar society (described by Caroline Service in chapter 2), were vigorously opposed to postwar Soviet expansionism. Meanwhile, the Soviet government itself still was an active war ally, and a very touchy one. The resulting bureaucratic battle, pitting the old school against the New Dealers, was unprecedented in American diplomatic history. The prize was the direction of U.S. foreign policy in the postwar alignment, and control of an expanding policy establishment.

While reform had been attempted, and organizational charts shuffled, throughout the war, the outcomes were inconclusive as long as Roosevelt retained the final say on foreign policy. Thus the key event that signaled long-term change in American diplomacy was Roosevelt's death in April 1945. With his successor,

MARRIED TO THE FOREIGN SERVICE

Harry S. Truman, as president, State Department professionals once again played a primary role in setting policy.

As the devastation in Europe was revealed to diplomats and members of the press newly abroad in 1945, the case for a strong U.S. presence in world affairs seemed self-evident. Cornelia Lane, wife of Ambassador to Poland Arthur Bliss Lane, wrote to her sister on 3 August 1945 about conditions in Warsaw: "We had expected to see Warsaw in a very bad state but not as bad as it is. There is literally nothing left and Berlin is a joke compared to this."

"The old part of town is so ruined that one cannot find one's way around. We had to ask a man to direct us and he told us that seven members of his family had been killed there and that he was sad that he could not give them a Christian burial. Every other person one sees has a black band on his arm and every back yard is full of pathetic little crosses.

"The day before yesterday was the anniversary of the insurrection, so people visited the graves putting flowers and candles on them. We saw a crowd around one spot where 100 people were shot against the wall. While they held a short mass, the people were wiping their eyes. It is a most tragic story, hard to describe, but one should not forget that all this was done deliberately by the Germans, so let us not become sorry for the people of Germany.

"Before I finish this letter I want to tell you a story. On Pius IX Street there is still a burned out German tank. During the war, the Germans wanted to storm a big Red Cross hospital. The Polish insurgents closed in from the sides, so near that the gunners in the tank could not lower the guns enough to shoot them. The Germans took some women and tied them to the tank, hoping to rush through, but the crowd kept throwing Molotov cocktails (bottles filled with gasoline) into the back of the tank. The insurgents finally got near enough to free the women, and then beset the Germans in the tank by throwing the cocktails into the inside and then machine gunning them. The Germans took 100 people from the crowd, lined them up and shot them. Then they stormed the hospital, ordering the nurses to leave so that they could blow the place up, together with the wounded. The nurses refused and the German colonel decided to evacuate the wounded, saying in an undertone to his officer: 'I wish our nurses were as heroic as those girls are.'

"Columns and columns of Soviet soldiers, singing sad songs, are marching back to Russia, followed with carts piled high with their belongings and some women. They go by under our window every day."[1]

THE COMPETITION CONTINUES

The competition for control of America's foreign affairs activities persisted through the fall of 1945, showing President Truman's inexperience but also presaging the McCarthyite purge of government that began in earnest a few years later. Caroline Service, who was in Washington at the time, remembered one small thread of the story in a 1976 interview in Berkeley, California.

In late November [1945], the phone rang one noon—I had gotten very leery of phones and radios—and a friend said, "You better listen to the radio because [American Ambassador to China Patrick J.] Hurley has resigned, and he is saying that Jack [Service] and George Atcheson and John Davies . . . have lost China, and he's resigning because they were subversive and because they undermined him." I don't think Hurley used the word *subversive*, but . . . they ruined his mission to China, and he was resigning because of them, and they were terrible people and should be kicked out of the State Department. . . .

[T]his created an enormous storm. The Senate decided they would have hearings and look into Hurley's accusations. They did not call Jack and George Atcheson home. Nor did they call any of the others, but they got Secretary [of State James F.] Byrnes up there [Capitol Hill], and they got various other people. Of course, they got Hurley. . . . I went to some of the hearings when I could, but someone had to take care of the baby.

I had mixed feelings. I thought they'd bring Jack home from China, and that rather pleased me. But they didn't.

Hurley did not ever get good press except from the right-wing press. Actually, Jack and the others nearly always had good press except from the right wing and people who were violently opposed to our China policy, such as the China lobby. A lot of people just thought Hurley was a blowhard, which he was. . . . [H]e ruined careers. I never believed that anything he said was going to make much difference in our lives, but he did harm us greatly. I didn't feel that he was going to do this, because his accusations were so wild. If you read them in books today they sound absolutely haywire. . . .

He was surely one of the most egotistical men that ever appeared on the American political scene. . . .

I don't like to use the term, but I just felt he was crazy, crazy in terms of not knowing what he was talking about.[2]

This was a clue to the coming political storm in Washington. At the same time, it was becoming increasingly apparent to the American public and government that there was a pressing need to rehabilitate war-torn Europe and fight what would become known several years later as the cold war, as well as resolve the issues of military occupation in Japan.

A NEW ACTIVISM

Americans in the immediate postwar period, buoyed by military victory, were infected with a "can-do" spirit of optimism. The civil war in Greece, in particular, became an early focus of a new and activist foreign policy against Soviet expansion, leading eventually to the containment policy enunciated in the Truman Doctrine and the Marshall Plan to aid in the reconstruction of Europe. Spousal experiences in the forerunners of what became the outreach organizations of American foreign affairs during the cold war—in the Agency for International Development (AID), in particular—illustrated the trend.

AID TO GREECE

No domestic problem in 1990s America can be compared to the difficult conditions in Greece when the American Mission for Aid to Greece (AMAG) arrived. Retreating Nazi forces had destroyed everything in their path. Communist-backed guerrilla forces continued the devastation. Because of guerrilla activity in the hills behind Athens, American diplomats were not permitted to travel outside the city.

Legislation creating AMAG was signed into law by President Truman on 22 May 1947 and ratified by Greece the following month, in a historic decision to create "a program of assisting another country with its internal problems." [3] *It also was a historic moment for diplomatic wives: the women with the mission in Greece were to make a direct, hands-on contribution to U.S. foreign policy.*

Into this devastated country, now racked by civil war, a group of American women and children arrived to join members of AMAG. Priscilla De Angelis crossed on the Nea Hellas and chronicled her impressions of going abroad for the first time.

"We were from all over the country, and most of us were dependents of mission personnel. In general, most of the women were very well educated and committed to helping Greece recover. However, most of us had not traveled outside the United States before and were relatively naive. I was dismayed when I saw the size of the *Nea Hellas* at boarding time. Could we trust her to get us across the Atlantic? Her gross tonnage was 16,991 tons, compared to the *Queen Elizabeth*'s 85,000 tons."[4]

After sightseeing in Lisbon—"a landmark in the voyage"—docking in Italy gave the women a portent of conditions in Greece. Priscilla De Angelis wrote, "Our mood changed drastically when we arrived at Genoa and Naples."

"This was our first exposure to the devastation of war. We were tired of being cooped up on shipboard, and the novelty of sailing had worn off. The sight of entire blocks of Genoa gutted by bombing was shocking. Poor and

80

ragged Italians swarmed the docks carrying on a brisk trade in cigarettes and begging alms from travelers bold enough to venture ashore. Boats of hungry scavengers circled our ship—fishing out the refuse from the *Nea Hellas*. I decided that going ashore was more than I could face, and . . . [spent] the two days in port keeping the children happy on board. There would be better times to see Italy, I hoped.

"In October we sailed into Piraeus, each of us tense with the excitement of meeting our husbands. Although I looked forward to meeting Manny, my husband, I was also mad at him for having gone first, leaving me to cope with the children on shipboard. This one experience of traveling alone with small children has made me very sensitive to the plight of refugee mothers and children.

"The kids and I grabbed Manny as soon as he poked his head in the door of the cabin lounge. After 18 days on board in close confinement, we eyed the other spouses with curiosity. 'You mean that's her husband?' or, 'How did she ever land that gorgeous man?' Several enterprising husbands had rented a speedboat and were cruising around the *Nea Hellas* yelling, 'Yaaso!' [informal greeting, best translated as, 'Hi, how are ya!') and otherwise showing off their new Greek."[5]

The American families gradually moved from hotels, some with erratic dining hours, into housing as it became available. They steadily set about making an American home away from home in Athens, arranging schools for their children (after addressing some cultural differences in the British approach to education), establishing a church, and founding the American Women's Organization in Greece.

Evelyn Strachan faced difficult adjustments in both school and housing arrangements, in spite of her liberal background. Strachan's husband, Alan, a former labor unionist, went to Athens as deputy in the labor division of AMAG.

For a time, "home" was the Palace Hotel at Kifissia, a summer residence suburb about ten miles north of Athens . . . where early morning hot water was limited to a half cup delivered to our room for Alan's shaving. Our children were scheduled to attend the British Army school.

But after the first day of school, which had been greatly anticipated, my daughter, Heather, stormed home with "I'm not going back to that terrible school!" [Heather Strachan married Democratic Rep. Thomas Foley of Washington State, Speaker of the U.S. House of Representatives in the late 1980s and 1990s.]

"What's the matter?"

"The principal hit Dorothy Corfitzen's hands with a ruler, said she lied."

"Was it true?"

"Of course not. She never gave Dorothy a chance to explain. I'm never going back."

"There must be some mistake." Thirty-five thousand drachs, about five dollars, had disappeared on the school bus.

We all shared the big dining room at the hotel, and the next morning I felt every mother's eyes must be upon me as Heather declared again and again at the breakfast table, "I'm not going to school." But when the bus sounded its horn, I bravely walked my seven-year-old daughter to the bus, and she entered with the rest of the children.

There were several hot sessions over the use of corporal punishment during parent-teacher meetings. The British vigorously defended their point of view. British high military and foreign servants sent their children at about the age of seven back to England to 'public,' really private, boarding schools, and it was the children of sergeants on down who attended the British Army school. But so many American children attended as well that it became the British-American school, and finally the American school.

The housing situation also taxed Evelyn Strachan's liberal instincts to the limit:

After a month or so, we settled into a house with a large garden [and] a small cottage at the rear later rented by a hardy young British couple whose weekend treks and sleepings-out I envied. The landladies were the three Euclides sisters, one of whom had married and published an afternoon newspaper. The house had a deposit [water storage tank], it was true, but I shortly discovered that when the water came in two mornings a week at 6:00 A.M., it was a hassle between the gardener and me as to who was going to get the water. He would fill the huge reservoir at the bottom of the garden, and if I didn't run down and shut it off there would be none for the house. One always had to be careful of water. Don't flush the toilet except after serious business. I recall some of the office gals coming around for a bath or just a thorough wash. We paid water bills of $100 for three months, about 35 times what our U.S. bills would have been.

Then on Sundays, the three [landlady] sisters would arrive with small camp stools and shout instructions to the gardener. This deprived us of Sunday garden enjoyment.

I soon discovered that rental in Greece did not mean privacy for the renter. We did have an oil-operated furnace, which the sisters carefully had hidden during the [German] occupation, and Elaini, a somewhat buxom, determined woman of about 50, would enter the house, usually without knocking, pull at her heavy wool suit jacket, and cry out, "*Zesti, zesti!*" [Hot, hot!], and put down the thermostat even though we were footing the oil bill. The living room had a fireplace, which we burned most evenings, but I swore when we returned to the U.S. I would find a low-ceilinged living room that could be closed off so that I could feel warm and relaxed [in front of a fire].

It seemed we had only been in the house a few months when the sisters said we would have to move for the summer. This had not been mentioned when the contract was signed. We again scoured all sections of the city and suburbs but found no suitable house to rent as mission families kept pouring in from the States. Others were having the same problem of being asked to move.[6] Finally, the mission, in a conference within the Greek government, announced "that, due to aid being given to Greece by the U.S., American tenants were to remain in their houses."

This ruling made no impression on the three sisters, who believed they were special. They contacted someone in the States who they thought could rule in their favor, and who suggested we 'share' the house with the sisters. John Howard, chief lawyer for the mission, told Alan, "If you are so cowardly as to move out, we will replace you with another mission family. You do not have to let those people in the house."

But finally, to our great relief, a house several blocks away [and also] in Kifissia was brought to our attention, as the American occupant was returning to the States. It wasn't as charming a house, and it seemed to me the living room walls were of fake marble even in Greece, although they were cold to the touch, but the previous American had brought in a new oil burner, a beautiful electric stove with oven, and a large refrigerator, all of which he had sold to the owner. And what a different attitude on the part of the landlord, the Andresakises.

With the physical and educational needs of their families taken care of, the women of AMAG set out to nurture the spiritual needs of the American community. They reopened an abandoned church, built by the Nazi occupation forces but closed during the civil war. Soon afterward, they formed a church guild, the first organization of American women in Greece. Eventually AWOG, the American Women's Organization in Greece, took over the guild services, which included a wide variety of charitable and fund-raising activities.

In a Herculean effort, members of AWOG solicited, sorted, and distributed tons of used clothing from the United States. Ruth Redstrom recalled, "My personal contribution was in soliciting used (or new) clothing from the United States."

This we did through church groups, social and welfare groups, any group willing and able to collect and send much-needed clothing to Greece. As these boxes and crates arrived, we met and sorted the material for use by size, age group, sex, utility, and repacked it for distribution. Sometimes we worked in an empty hotel ballroom in Kifissia, once at least in an empty warehouse with a dirt floor, wherever we could find space. One consignment weighed one and a half tons. On my first trip to distribute clothing, four other American women and I, with our driver, brought 4,000 pieces of clothing to 275 families in a village in northern Greece. I think it was Lamia.

At this time, American women's clubs became support systems for wives shipped abroad, many of whom had never expected to leave the United States. The clubs provided an avenue into the local community and enabled women, usually on a volunteer basis, to put their interests and professional training to use. They provided outlets for the energies of educated women who, despite difficult living conditions in many countries, were freed from domestic tasks by willing, if not always competent, domestics.

With home, school, church, and charitable activities, these spouses established, to the best of their ability, an American atmosphere in which to nurture their children. Their activities often reinforced U.S. relations with the host country.

"GOOD MORNING, MRS. JONES"

Loretta Jones founded her own school. She used the home instruction courses offered by the Calvert School in Baltimore, a program that since 1906 has educated hundreds of Foreign Service children posted to faraway and isolated places. "Harold was on the faculty at Tennessee State University when he joined AID as an agriculture officer," she remembered.

He was assigned to Bhopal, India. We arrived there in 1956 with six daughters and no adequate schooling. Fortunately, I was a teacher and a musician. We later had another daughter for a total of seven—Burnetta, Christina, Carol, the twins Estrellita and Anita, Carlotta, and Loretta.

Our house in Bhopal was unbelievable, a Roman-style pavilion with Doric columns and marble floors. It had been a palace guest house for the last ruling royal family of the state of Bhopal but was a bit run-down by the time we arrived. It had six bedrooms, six dressing rooms, and six bathrooms around an enclosed courtyard, and a terrace overlooking a huge lake with the lights of Bhopal in the distance. There was no kitchen and no dining room—food had been brought in from a detached central kitchen. By constructing a cover from packing crates for the tub and toilet, Harold converted one of the bathrooms into a kitchen. A bedroom became a dining room. Another very large bedroom . . . became a schoolroom. Harold made desks from shipping crates, and he found a blackboard on the local market. The girls were my only pupils, and I taught first through eighth grade with the Calvert system and also used the University of Nebraska high school correspondence course.

We had a regular routine. The five school-age girls said goodbye to "Mama," "left home" at eight every morning, and "arrived at school" by walking around a huge roundabout in front of the house. When they entered the "classroom," they said, "Good morning, Mrs. Jones," and sang "The Star-Spangled Banner" or "America" before we began lessons. When school was over in the afternoon, they reversed the process. We had brought a piano, two violins, and a clarinet, and we had an ensemble, with the two younger ones singing along. We had a menagerie of pets: the usual cats and dogs and a rabbit, plus a rhesus monkey, a seven-foot python, and a tiger we later gave to a wildlife group.

When the temperatures were 100 or 120 degrees, we would sleep on the roof. Sometimes on starry nights, just before dawn, I would give lessons on

Greeted at school by "Mrs. Jones" (left to right), Bernetta, the twins Estrellita and Anita, Carol, and Christina, Bhopal, India, 1957. *Courtesy of Harold Jones.*

the constellations and lunar eclipses and other celestial phenomena. Other times the monsoon rains would send all of us scurrying downstairs.

During the week Harold was at his official post, a remote agricultural station in Budni, which was 60 bumpy, dusty miles from Bhopal. He came home on weekends, but for the other five days I was everything to the girls—mother, father, teacher, and nurse if necessary. I did this for four years and—after a break from 1960 to 1963 while we were in New Delhi—then again when Harold was transferred to northern Nigeria. By that time Burnetta was at Fisk in Tennessee, and Christina had gone to Vassar.

The girls have now attended nine universities and earned a total of twelve degrees—four from Vassar, two from Smith, and one each from Brown, the University of London, Harvard Law School, the Johns Hopkins School of International Studies, George Washington University, and the University of Maryland. Burnetta was married before she graduated from Fisk. Their adjustment to life in the United States has not been without problems: discrimination in the workplace, for instance, and being taken for foreigners because they didn't have American slang and mannerisms. But we were spared any drug or alcohol problems, and most of our disagreements have been over money management and male companions. With one or two exceptions, the girls are very poor housekeepers because, having had a housekeeper for 21 years in the Foreign Service, that is one area in which I am less than exemplary.[7]

A JOB TO BE DONE

While Loretta Jones's Foreign Service was unique, Edith Sebald, who accompanied her husband on his 1952 ambassadorial tour in Burma, experienced the apprehensions and anxieties common to virtually all spouses on arriving at a new post. In her unpublished memoirs, she wrote:

"It was 11 July 1952. The *Argonaut* was slowly circling Mingaladon airfield near Rangoon, attempting to land through turbid monsoon clouds. The noise of the engines vibrating in the inadequately insulated cabin made conversation difficult. I gazed silently through the rain-spattered windows at the flooded paddy fields below which stretched for unbroken miles into the misty distance. I had the impression that all of Burma was under water. Sometimes the whole landscape was blotted out by soupy clouds that boiled around us, and I felt a sense of near panic as we plowed into the dense screen of gray and threatening mass between us and the earth. . . .

"The rain was pouring down in a solid sheet when the plane finally came to a halt on the perforated steel mats left behind by our armed forces after World War II. No sooner were the propellers stilled, when a number of white-turbaned bare-footed Indians wheeled the landing steps to the plane. It had been comfortable in the air-conditioned cabin, but when the doors opened, we gasped. The steaming air was motionless and stifling. As we walked onto the steps, we saw a small group in light-colored clothes gathered under the eaves of the crude tinroofed waiting room, craning to obtain a glimpse of the new American ambassador and his wife. Most of the gathering, we discovered, were staff members of our embassy. Interspersed among the Americans were a number of Indian laborers wearing white dhoties, diaper-like loin cloths, chewing betel nuts, and impassively watching the scene.

"Twenty minutes after we had left the airfield, we entered white wooden gates, returned the Gurkha guard's salute, and, after a few minutes drive between mango trees towering fifty feet into the sky, we stopped beneath a large portico supported by massive white pillars."

This imposing, but moldering, marble mansion stood on seven acres of land overlooking a lake, and had been purchased by the U.S. government as the official residence from a Scottish teak king. The ambassador's wife lost little time in exploring her surroundings.

"That night, having finished our dinner, I decided to take a stroll in the garden which had looked so inviting earlier in the day, to escape the stifling heat of the residence. 'Mem-sahib, mem-sahib,' the head bearer called loudly. 'Please come back to the house. There are many bad snakes and scorpions in the garden and you should not come out alone after dark.' I quickly scuttled back. He was concerned about the venomous krait, for whose bite there was then no effective antidote.''

The following morning Edith Sebald inspected the servants' quarters and found "the grounds around the cabins [to be] in a shocking state of disorder. No effort had been made to keep the place clean or tidy. I glanced into one of the cabins and saw a debris-strewn concrete floor where children played, and whose mother sat like all the other mothers, idly smoking what Kipling called a 'smacking white cheroot,' as she lazily watched her offspring crawling around the unswept floor."

"Bluebottle flies buzzed around furiously. Under the one pump which provided water for the community, mounds of garbage had collected. After I had inspected the servants' quarters, I returned to the house to look at the kitchen. My mother had instilled into me the fact that one's life comes from the kitchen and it therefore must always be immaculately clean.

"I found the kitchen inadequately equipped, small and unbelievably dirty. Heavy exposed beams supported the ceiling and lizards and flies were crawling on them. I noticed the well-worn, cracked, and dirty sinks; grease stained, unscrubbed tables; and fly-specked wall. . . .

"When my husband returned from his first day at the office we exchanged stories. I told him about my inspection and of the many things that needed attention. He gave me his impressions of the city and of the six-mile drive to the embassy, impressions that were not exactly encouraging for the future.

"We went up to our living quarters immediately after dinner. The air was close and suffocating. Undressing, we stretched out on our beds under the white mosquito net almost as large as the room, and listened to the rain drops as they struck the tiled roof. We did not say much, but we both knew that our first day in Burma was not one which had filled us with great enthusiasm. And yet, we fully realized we were there to stay for two years, and that we had to remember that there was a job to be done."[8]

LABOR GOES ABROAD

"Labor's Role in World Affairs: A Memoir from a Socialist in the State Department"—the title of Morris Weisz's article in Horizons magazine in the summer of 1990 said it all.⁹ Weisz and his wife Yetta spent more than two decades in the Foreign Service: he first as a labor attaché and later as a senior instructor of young officers destined for posts with a need for organized labor experience; she as a traditional spouse, whose extensive teaching experience led to adventures of her own. Although a few labor officers were appointed during World War II, the labor attaché function quickly gained prominence after the war, owing to both the rapid expansion of foreign representation and the extensive changes taking place in world politics. "I would frequently meet old friends from our labor or socialist movement—or new friends in a foreign country—who expressed surprise that our government would appoint a person of my background to help carry out any aspects of its work abroad," Weisz wrote.

He explained by telling the story of the Potsdam Conference, where, in the midst of discussion about the shape of the postwar world, Winston Churchill was defeated as head of Britain's conservative government and replaced with Prime Minister Clement Atlee and a new Labor government. American diplomats had no contacts in the new government, except for a very junior member of London's American embassy staff.

With labor governments forming throughout Europe, there was an urgent need for labor experts in the expanding Foreign Service. Oliver Peterson was another of the first labor attachés, assigned to Sweden in 1948. His wife, Esther Peterson, in a 1989 interview maintained that she "found it much harder to be an embassy wife than to be an employed woman in the United States."

This is the same Esther Peterson who, before and after her Foreign Service life, had a distinguished career in labor, women's issues, and consumer affairs, serving as a top-level adviser to three presidents as well as to Eleanor Roosevelt when she was chair of the President's Commission on the Status of Women from 1961 to 1963. In the late 1950s Esther Peterson had been legislative representative of the industrial union department of the AFL-CIO, as well as the Amalgamated Clothing Workers legislative representative in the mid-1940s. She recalled that, in 1948,

[t]hey had no one in the Foreign Service who had any contact, or even understood the labor movement. My husband had that experience, and first

they offered us India. But I was afraid to take four little children there after I read the post report. Later we accepted the assignment to Sweden. I had to give up my work.

The embassy first put us up in Saltsjöbaden, this fancy hotel where we had to dress for dinner. So can you imagine taking these little [children, one a] two-year-old, and dressing for dinner, and, of course, he had to go to the bathroom—always in the middle. I'll never forget calling a Swedish friend who I met at the Bryn Mawr worldwide summer program for working women, saying that we couldn't manage this.

We had a rented house, but there was no furniture, nothing had come. My friend and the students from the Bryn Mawr group got together and got us some army cots, went to EPA [the equivalent of Woolworth's], and bought us enough plates and knives and forks, and got us some blankets, and we got a few things that we needed, and we camped in that house until our furniture came. I couldn't stand Saltsjöbaden; I couldn't stand dressing up for dinner every night, and with these children . . . ridiculous. Very ridiculous.

[Embassy activities also were] one of my objections because we had to participate in the afternoon, late, when I needed to be home with my children. I found it much harder to be an embassy wife than to be an employed woman in the United States.

The Petersons served under two experienced ambassadors, Freeman Matthews and Walton Butterworth. "I liked them both very much, and with 'Doc' Matthews we had a marvelous time," she recalled.

When we went—you see we didn't know anything about this [diplomatic] business. We had our cards printed, and we had to call on the ambassador and have the corners turned down. This was completely new coming from the labor movement. We had lived modest, not social, lives, you know. So we went to call, took the children, dressed them all up, and went to the door, and in came a great big Doberman pinscher, their dog Ben. And the first thing that dog did was jump up on my daughter, Karen. And Karen took her hand and swatted that dog and said, "You don't do that." And I thought, "Oh, here's where we lose our job." But that dog went over and licked Karen, and the ambassador was so impressed that Karen became the person who trained the dog, and they gave us the pick of the litter.

The point is, I was scared to death . . . but he liked us immediately, and we became very good friends.

The second year I was there I did a study for the Women's Bureau [of the

U.S. Labor Department]. I got very interested in the [Swedish] labor laws when we were invited to a number of parties and the [American] hostess would say, "You have to come at such-and-such an hour because we don't want to pay overtime." And I thought, "Overtime for domestic workers?" So I talked with people here at home. I'd been adviser to the Women's Bureau, and they asked me if I would do a study on domestic employment. That was my only gainful employment during our time in Sweden.

It opened doors for me and, I think, opened doors for my husband, too. We had no problem at all, with the labor movement.

While I was in Stockholm, I got a call from Philip Murray, the president of the CIO, saying, "Esther, we need you badly." It was when the Taft-Hartley Act was up [for repeal], and they felt I was the only one who could get into certain senators' offices. I said, "I can't possibly come. I have a two-year-old child." But I telephoned, and I got [our former housekeeper], and, of course, she would take care of Lars.

So I called Murray back and said the only way I could do it would be if I could bring Lars back to the U.S. with me. And Oliver thought I should do it. So I did come back [for two months]. And there was another advantage, because at that time Oliver was negotiating a trip for Swedish officials to come [to the United States] on a visit under the USIA. So I was here at that time and therefore could help from this end. And I shan't forget going to LaGuardia to meet them when they came, and thank heavens I was there. Because our immigration service had a red flag on Axel Strands, and they didn't want to let him in. The president of the Swedish Federation! I didn't let him see it, I negotiated, I called people in Washington. If I hadn't been there he might have been sent home.

We do some of the sloppiest things! I thought, "Thank God I was there, it was worth the whole thing." I took them around the Hill; I had them meet with everybody. They told Oliver they appreciated that very much. They accepted me completely as a woman.

A decade later Yetta Weisz, whose husband was assigned to New Delhi in 1965 as counselor for labor affairs, arrived in India, where she promptly was drafted to be president of the American Women's Club.

At the end of the first week, the American Women's Club nominating committee telephoned. They wanted to nominate me as president of the club. One week in India, and having been a simple schoolteacher I'd never belonged to a women's club. And I said, "Are you sure you've come to the right wife?

(Left to right) Coretta Scott King, Dorothy Stebbins (Steb) (Mrs. Chester B.) Bowles, and Yetta Weisz at Roosevelt House, the official U.S. embassy residence, New Delhi, 1969. *Courtesy of Yetta Weisz.*

Mary Lou Weiss lives here, too, and she's an old-timer, and I just came last week. They left, thinking maybe they did come to the wrong wife. Then I got a telephone call, "No, you're the right Mrs. Weisz." There I was, president of the American Women's Club.

As ambassador's wife, [Dorothy Stebbins] Steb [Mrs. Chester B.] Bowles was very supportive. She actively participated in several committees, and she insisted that our meetings be held at Roosevelt House, the most beautiful ambassador's residence in the world. Our club library was given a room there, and the house was always open to American women.

Not long into her presidency, Yetta Weisz found herself seated on a stage with a group of Indian women and faced with a cultural dilemma that she solved in a very practical manner. "Remember, this was the sixties, when our hemlines were above our knees. I was the only American, and I felt absolutely naked on that stage. I couldn't get that miniskirt to cover my knees, and I felt like a burlesque queen." The other women were in long, graceful saris, and from then on she frequently wore a sari.

94

Mrs. Bowles also wore saris. She had close friends among the All-India Women's Conference, women who had been freedom fighters close to Gandhi, Nehru, and Shastri, who were very proud to have her wear the sari. But we were both criticized by Americans who didn't understand that in the Indian culture saris were appropriate, comfortable, and, equally important, didn't have to be ordered from the U.S.

It was through her job as president that Yetta found rewarding work in her field.

The second week I was in Delhi, the American Women's Club received a letter from Jagat Singh, the principal of the Child Guidance School for Difficult Children, who asked, "Is there any American teacher who could come and assist our teachers in methods?" The children in his school were physically, some of them mentally, handicapped children and were called "difficult."

I answered that letter because here I was, a ready-made schoolteacher who had just left the Sharpe Health School in Washington, D.C., a school similar to Jagat Singh's, where I soon found myself. He wanted to know who I was before he would allow an American into his school, what I believed, what direction I would take, why I wanted to work at his school. I said, "You invited, so I came, that's why." He said, "Come, I'll show you one of the classrooms."

We left his office, which was a cheerful, beautiful room, and he took me into a room that had no windows, had a naked bulb hanging from the middle of the ceiling, the walls seemed to be painted black. I said, "This is a classroom? Jagat Singh, you may never want to see me again, but this I must tell you: you have a very beautiful office, the sun is shining, you've got flowers on the windowsill. You take me into a classroom where the children are, and it's the black hole of Calcutta transferred here to the Child Guidance School." And he said, "What are you talking about?" I said, "Go and look, you haven't ever seen." He went back, then he returned and said, "Oh, my God. You come back next week."

The next week that black hole was gone. The room was whitewashed, it did have windows, and the sun was streaming in. I could see children—I hadn't seen any on the first visit. He said, "What other suggestions do you have?" I said, "Would you be happy to tell somebody you went to a school for difficult children?" He said, "Well, they are difficult." I said, "Yes, but you don't have to say it. You have to work with the difficult, but you don't say it." He changed the name.

ADJUSTMENTS IN ASIA

Nearby, in Afghanistan, Clemence Jandrey (Boyd) got off to a shaky start with a new ambassador's wife, but in time the women developed a mutual respect. Clemence spent more than 20 years as a Foreign Service spouse, beginning in Naples in 1938, and spending the World War II years in Australia. In 1949 she and her husband, Frederick William (Fritz) Jandrey, who left the Foreign Service in 1959 as deputy assistant secretary of state for European affairs, were assigned to Kabul, Afghanistan. They arrived, with some difficulty, just before the new American ambassador, Louis G. Dreyfus, and his wife Grace, who was a demanding yet fascinating and supportive woman of the Foreign Service's old school.

In letters to her mother in 1949, Clemence Jandrey wrote:

"Our ambassador and his wife have now arrived in Kabul. Yesterday afternoon we drove, with our military attaché and his wife, out to the small town of Bagrami. It is about four miles out of town, where there is a small rest house which the Afghan king uses for shooting and the officials for greeting foreigners of note, since they consider it courteous to come out from Kabul and greet the VIPs as they finish their hard drive from Peshawar [Pakistan]. The chief of Afghan protocol was already there when we arrived, and on the lawn, under the huge silver poplar trees two tea tables were set up on oriental carpets. The tables were covered with fruit, flowers and cakes. I was all dressed up in hat and gloves; quite correct, ready for any kind of ambassador's wife, formal or informal, though hats and gloves are NEVER worn here, even by ambassador's wives.

"Meanwhile, constant messages were arriving to keep us in touch with [new Ambassador Louis G. Dreyfus and his wife's] progress from Peshawar, and after awhile we became somewhat dismayed by the apparent delay, for dark was approaching, and the Afghans wanted to greet them in daylight and give them tea. It got darker and darker as we waited from 5:15 to 8:15, while I sat in an automobile to keep warm in my light dress. It was pitch dark when we at last saw the lights of their car. Mr. Dreyfus got out of the car and shook hands all around, and was most charming and courteous, but Mrs. Dreyfus chose not to appear. She sat in their automobile without stirring, and did not wish to be spoken to or to even have us introduced through the window of the car. My hat and gloves were so sadly wasted! Mr. Dreyfus said she was ill

96

with a cough and bad throat (one swallows gallons of dust on the drive up). We followed their automobiles into town, as they were guided in by the chief of protocol, who went with them in their car. . . .

"When we arrived at the embassy residence, Mrs. Dreyfus sent for me, and though she obviously felt terrible, was very good-natured and full of jokes. I was pleased that I had a chance to show off my respectful hat and gloves. Meanwhile, I felt that in her place, holding myself upright with one hand on a chair-back and coping with throat and chest full of dust and a convulsive cough, I would hardly have been game enough to smile and be vivacious. She said she must rest for two weeks, and asked me to explain to people and help her to maintain this plan.

"My present job is to keep people from calling on her for a couple of weeks, until she feels better, but without giving the impression that she is really ill or reluctant to meet people. . . .

"I made a very unfortunate move with Mrs. Dreyfus, owing to having sat at home and worried about her being ill alone in her house. With no desire to intrude on her, I relieved my feeling of guilt by dropping her a little note in which I told her that I had no desire to break in on her two weeks of R& R [rest and recuperation], but that I just wanted her to know that if she needed anything, I was there. I received a note back implying that since I seemed set upon seeing her sooner than the two-week deadline, it must be so, and that I might call on her alone, on such-and-such a day. So I did go to call, this time most foolishly not wearing a hat and gloves, since in this part of the world complete informality is the keynote.

"When I arrived at the embassy I did not notice that Mrs. Dreyfus was upset until we had seated ourselves, at which time she said, with that smoothness which sometimes has a worse impact than rebuke, 'I see you are not wearing a hat to make your call. I assume that is because your head is so swollen that you cannot get a hat on.' I was so appalled that I sat speechless. Her mind was obviously set on the protocol of the great capitals of Europe; and I later learned that she was very upset over the treatment her husband had received from the State Department. She was very devoted to him, and felt badly that he had been sent away from a legation in a European country just as it was about to be made into an embassy.

"She then turned to the subject of the inevitable dust in the oriental carpets, dust which she did not feel was necessary, and partly blamed me for it, since I had stayed in the residence for a few days before they arrived. I left the embassy after this call, rather disenchanted. Two things have made my relations with Mrs. Dreyfus rather difficult. First, her deafness had made it hard for me to communicate with her and to be on a comfortable basis, or to develop any intimacy or affection, if she was to be so severe. Secondly, it is our first post at an embassy, and I have no experience. Our assignments to consulates do not count with her, and I am sure she would much prefer a wife who has had considerable embassy experience already.

"Also, I freely admit that she could have fallen heir to a more tactful handmaiden than I—I know several of the younger Foreign Service wives who could doubtless have won her over in ten seconds flat. I am willing and eager, but hopelessly ignorant, slow to pick up the nuances. Mrs. Dreyfus interprets this as stubbornness and unwillingness on my part; and I am sure that she thinks I am working against her and trying to be queen of a clique of the younger American women, fomenting rebellion. I had not dreamed of having ambitions of that sort."

In a later letter, Clemence Jandrey recalled that Mrs. Dreyfus had proven herself to be a real force in Iran when her husband was minister there: she started a hospital and an orphanage and went out herself to nurse the poor, while at the same time both she and her husband were great friends of the shah. "She had great energy and endless love and kindness to be bestowed wherever it was needed," Clemence wrote.

"Mrs. Dreyfus soon earned the respect and admiration of everyone in Kabul, that of the Afghan officials and of the various ambassadors and their wives. She became really the big figure of the entire diplomatic corps; and I also learned in time that though she might be severe and even demanding, she always stood by her embassy people, a characteristic which aroused my eternal respect and gratitude. . . .

"Parties can be difficult if one does not speak several languages. At our ambassador's party yesterday [written 18 January 1950], most of the guests were Russians, and the Russians they send here don't seem to be accomplished linguists. (Not that the Americans are either!) On my left at the table yesterday was the Czech minister, who thank God has been studying English; but on my right was the Russian first secretary, who spoke no English or French, and of course no Italian: my 100 Farsi words were quickly exhausted, and I would soon have sunk without a bubble had it not been for a nearby Italian who speaks all those languages and many more, so he kept the two of us afloat. Mrs. Dreyfus got along tolerably well with two Russians, by means of speaking French to one, who translated into Russian for the other, and back again for her. She is an extraordinary woman. Though she was dressed all in black, only our military attaché and I happened to know that she had just received a telegram telling her of the death of her mother, to whom she was most deeply attached. She did not cancel the luncheon; she wore dark glasses, because her eyes kept filling with tears, but she did not make her guests suffer with her. She can do that sort of thing—she's a monument of character and personality."[10]

The change in their relationship over time was a tribute to both women. After gaining her own footing in Kabul, Grace Dreyfus became more sensitive to Clemence Jandrey's needs. She added impetus to the younger woman's interest in crafts—by making a gift to Jandrey of "an antique string of 'worry beads' made of delightful old melon-cut corals," which the younger woman had considered too extravagant—and teaching her to appreciate the region's luxurious carpets, which Grace Dreyfus avidly collected during tours in Iran and Afghanistan.

Clemence Jandrey's positive experience in Afghanistan demonstrated the value of steady, evenhanded, involved leadership on the part of wives of senior officials. Grace Dreyfus was a towering intellectual personality at post, epitomizing the adage that "rank has its privileges, but also its responsibilities." There were other senior wives, however, who became legends in the grapevine of Foreign Service spouses.

THE DRAGON LADIES

No study of Foreign Service women in the twentieth century would be complete without an examination of the "dragon ladies," the spouses of senior officials who made unreasonable, and at times capricious, demands upon subordinate wives. Before adoption of the 1972 directive, the "Policy on Wives," failure to please a superior's spouse could have an adverse effect on an officer's career path. And regardless of the 1972 directive's "declaration of independence" for spouses, the world of international diplomacy remained strongly dependent on its hard-earned and hard-learned systems of rank and protocol.

The key observation that successful high-ranking spouses made, regardless of their official position within the State Department hierarchy, was that they were going to be accorded a social rank derived from their husbands' positions at post, and that consequently, rewarded or not, they had an opportunity to positively shape that role.

Morale came from the top. It suffered when the ambassador's wife was "not at all interested in her husband's job," as one of the most infamous dragon ladies put it; or when a young, first-tour wife of a ranking officer accepted the perquisites but not the responsibilities of rank; or when a foreign-born spouse was overwhelmed by the demands of functioning in a third culture.

Embassies are small, enclosed worlds. In this fertile ground for innuendo and gossip, dragon lady stories flourished. And although some of them were apocryphal, they were all grounded in the experiences of Foreign Service officers and spouses. There was the newly arrived spouse making her initial "duty" call at post and kept waiting 45 minutes by an imperious, thoughtless "first lady." There was the dutiful young officer, kneeling by a pond in the residence garden to swirl in blue coloring while an impatient ambassador's wife shrieked from a balcony that the water "still isn't blue enough" to create the desired ambience for an impending reception. There were the junior wives ordered to the embassy residence to help set tables for a luncheon to which they were not invited. And then there was the first lady who issued an edict that mission wives were not to wear pink to an official function because her own gown would be of that delicate color. The effects of all these actions were magnified in the feudal microcosms that constitute life in a mission abroad. Whether or not these stories are true, they still circulate among Foreign Service couples in the 1990s.

In the years since the 1972 directive, and with the growth of two-income families, the senior spouse has often remained at home in the United States— where she could receive both an income from her professional career and a separate maintenance allowance—while her officer husband served at post. Consequently, the absent spouse's occasional appearances at post have sometimes engendered resentment because, in her absence, and with the demands of protocol, a subordinate spouse had assumed her senior role by default. One spouse reported that with the spouses of both the deputy chief of mission and the ambassador absent from a Central American embassy, it was assumed that she would accept responsibility for women's affairs. Yet, the official residence, the government-provided domestic staff, and the silver tea service and official china were all off-limits to her in her attempts to fulfill that role.

THE WRISTON WIFE

The final chapter in the expansion of the Foreign Service that began in the later stages of World War II began in 1954 with the adoption of Secretary John Foster Dulles's personnel integration program, announced on 8 September in Department Circular 115 and published in the Department of State Bulletin *on 27 September. In essence, it solved two problems: first, it incorporated experienced civil service and other government employees into the Foreign Service, requiring them to take overseas duty where the expansion of U.S. government responsibilities had created severe shortages of personnel; and second, it consolidated the control of foreign affairs policy and the policy implementation apparatus into the hands of professional diplomats.*

The process was called "Wristonization," after Dr. Henry M. Wriston, president of Brown University, who chaired Secretary Dulles's Public Committee on Personnel. Before the adoption of the Wriston reforms, the foreign affairs bureaucracy had been divided into four separate personnel systems, of which the formal Foreign Service comprised around 10 percent. Wristonization brought high- and midlevel civil servants into the Foreign Service through what was called lateral entry. (The Foreign Service was traditionally staffed from the bottom up, with career officers serving apprenticeships abroad.)

Spouses, many of whom had put down strong roots in Washington, were not consulted. But Secretary Dulles's circular did acknowledge them, if only in its final substantive paragraph: "[I]n making assignments of new lateral entrants to overseas posts, care will be exercised to avoid undue disruption of Departmental operations and undue personal or family hardship to the officer concerned. It is not expected, therefore, that Departmental officers will be assigned to overseas posts immediately upon, or even shortly after, their acceptance of FSO [Foreign Service officer] appointments." [11] *Here was a clear demand that spouses go abroad, although some spouses and their husbands did successfully challenge the requirement, and some resigned.*

Many couples had reservations about joining the diplomatic mainstream. Mary Louise Weiss and her husband Len, like many other Wristonized couples, weighed their choices: to remain in the department or to go abroad. "I had been overseas with the American Red Cross during World War II, a very patriotic and exciting time," recalled Mary Louise Weiss.

Our Red Cross team traveled with sealed orders which couldn't be opened until we had been at sea for 24 hours. That's when I found out I had been

Mary Louise Barker as an American Red Cross staff assistant bound for Brisbane, Australia, 1943. *Courtesy of Mary Louise B. Weiss.*

assigned to Brisbane, Australia! Many ships would not take women, but the captain of a Swedish freighter, a neutral ship carrying contraband of war, finally agreed to take our group. There were unassembled bombers on deck and no protection—no railings or anything—and we sailed a zig-zag route to Sydney. Fourteen years later, making the decision to go abroad with small children was more stressful!

We had just moved into a new house in the suburbs, in Arlington. We had a new baby, and a little child, and we weren't prepared for this sudden decision. We had about a year to decide. Every night or so we would make a different decision. But we had always thought that, perhaps in the future, we would be interested in the Foreign Service.

Our friends were having to make decisions, too. I remember long conversations on the phone with friends who were in the same position, with little children. Then we finally bit the bullet and said yes. Being brand-new at all this, we had to learn about a lot of things, and our sense of adventure developed along the way: getting shots and passports, renting the house, buying a three-year supply of clothing for two growing children.

It was a jolt, but as I look back, it seems to me that it was no more of an adjustment than any Foreign Service wife has going to a first post. It was just that we were a little bit older, a little more settled at home. But you adapt.

Before we left, I felt some difference between the Wristonee wives and the traditional Foreign Service wives. I remember going to a luncheon—the [precursor of the] Association of American Foreign Service Women had luncheons at Fort McNair, and they were mostly social. And I remember the new Wriston wives were asked to sit at tables where there would be at least one senior Foreign Service wife, maybe an ambassador's wife, so we could ask questions. I found one person I talked to a bit condescending. She had been in the service a long time. I think it was just the natural feeling that here comes a new crowd, and they are going to change everything, and we're used to the way it used to be.

We arrived in Belgrade at a time when the [Foreign Service] inspectors were there, and we learned that the morale among the women in the embassy was very low. Wives had been reporting to the inspectors how bad things were. Yugoslavia was a communist country, and there were a lot of isolating factors: language, the cultural and political problems, etc. I soon found that most of the senior wives were foreign-born Europeans who spent a great deal of time away from post. For instance, if the ambassador's wife had to go to the dentist, she went back to Holland where her family lived. The deputy chief of mission's wife was French and frequently in Paris, the agricultural attaché's wife was Italian and she spent a lot of time in Bologna. The AID director's wife was French, and she almost never came to post. So the top-level women who you would expect to be leaders were not there a lot of the time and therefore were not all that aware that the situation in Belgrade was not easy for wives.

We got clues from experienced women who were more our level. Since it was my first time abroad in the Foreign Service, I had nothing to compare Belgrade with, and I think that was an advantage. I just sort of took everything as it came along. We quickly felt that we had made the right decision: our children may have been deprived of fresh, pasteurized milk, but there were many other rewards in the years to come!

Carolyn Dorsey's decision to go abroad as a Wriston spouse was more easily made. To ease the transition from Washington, D.C., to Beirut, the Dorseys asked their African-American domestic, Wilhelmina Bolling, from Lynchburg, Virginia, to accompany them. She did and remained with the Dorseys for 33 years. "Wilhelmina was accepted by the American communities," Carolyn Dorsey remembered, "and, with the exception of Sudan, was permitted by the local authorities to accompany us." In the Middle East, Wilhelmina's social life gave Carolyn Dorsey a crash course in the marital mores of married Muslim men.

Steve and I discussed "Wristonizing," and I said, "What better opportunity to see the world and be paid for it, too." I'd been abroad before but never lived there. Steve agreed, he had not been overseas. He became a sort of Middle East specialist and took a lot of trips: to Bahrain, to Dhahran, to Kuwait, Saudi Arabia, all these Middle East countries. I didn't go with him.

Well, eventually Steve was assigned to Beirut, and I thought it was rather exciting. We had a wonderful maid who we took with us. She came to me when my daughter, Lyn, was six months old. We told her, "We're going a long ways off, to the Middle East, a place called Beirut, Lebanon. But we'd love to have you come." She was a marvelous cook as well as a housekeeper, baby-sitter, and everything else. Steve told her, "The government does not pay your fare, so I will have to pay it. If you come, you'd stay for six months, and then if you [don't] like it, I'll send you home." She just jumped at the chance.

In Beirut everybody was nice to Wilhelmina. Ambassador Donald Heath was so nice—[his family] went to the American Community Church, we went to the Anglican Church. They'd come and pick Wilhelmina up and take her to church, and after the service people would come up to her and say, "Mrs. Bolling, would you like a ride home?" and she'd say, "Thank you very much, but the ambassador is taking me home."

When we had parties we called on a sort of pool of men who were mostly drivers who spoke English and wanted extra income. They made all kinds of passes at Wilhelmina! Her social life was quite busy, but she was always very particular—she would say, "Are you married?" Most of them were, a few were not. One of them who liked her very much said, "Yes, I'm married," and she said, "Then I won't go out with you." "Why not?" he asked. "My wife doesn't work, I keep her very well, buy all her clothes, and it's none of her business who I go out with." Of course, they were all Muslims. She said, "Well, if that's the way you feel, all right, but I don't want to be upsetting your family household." There were several others who wanted to marry Wilhelmina, looking for a U.S. passport. She knew that.

She's still living, down in Lynchburg, Virginia. A wonderful person.

I remember one time when [Deputy Undersecretary of State for Management] Loy [W.] Henderson was coming through Khartoum. He'd been to South Africa and had a crew of seven or eight men. He called Steve and said they were coming through Khartoum and would not be there for lunch but would land, be there maybe an hour, then leave, around 3:00 P.M. The morning of the day they were due, Steve had an appointment and was away from the embassy. The embassy called me about 9:30 A.M. and told me that Ambassador Henderson had changed his mind, they now wanted lunch on the ground and would arrive about 1:00 P.M. This was 1959–60, and there just wasn't any place to take him.

It was on a Friday, and my cook, or *saffragi*, was off. I panicked. There would be members of the embassy, seven or eight with Henderson, about twenty-five people. I'm no cook. I sent our driver Hussein out and told him, "See if you can find the cook, I've got to have him with all these people coming." So he went out looking for him. About eleven o'clock he came back and said, "I found him, he was at the mosque, and he said, 'Not to worry, Mrs. Dorsey.'" So he came back in turban and *gallabiyeh* (robe). Meanwhile, I got out some frozen chickens we'd ordered from Beirut because food in Khartoum wasn't all that easy to come by. I had planned to play bridge with Mrs. Moose, our ambassador's wife, and two other women. The women said, "We'll bake an angel food cake!"

Furthermore, two inspectors were there at the time. They came over to see the house when I was putting up bridge tables and other things, and asked, "How's everything going?" And I said, "I guess all right." The airport was only five minutes from our house. At 1:05 P.M. Ambassador Henderson arrived with his gang. We sat down and had lunch—the chickens and salad the cook had made. About 1:45, the men left to return to the plane. Ambassador Henderson came up to me and said, "Mrs. Dorsey, I know I've put you to a terrible inconvenience to do this, but I just want you to know this is the best meal we've had since we've been away!" So that was worth it.

5

PARTNERS IN CATASTROPHE

*McCarthy frightened Americans. He frightened the public. I was frightened.
I wasn't frightened in China. I wasn't frightened the year I spent alone
in India. I wasn't frightened traveling around the world. But I was
frightened by McCarthy. I thought, "What is he going to do to us?
What is he going to do to our children?"*

Caroline Service

*The unprecedented growth of America's Foreign Service during and after
World War II reflected a new confidence and new sense of responsibility for
participation in international events as a world power. It affected the lives, to a
greater or lesser degree, of all Foreign Service spouses and became for many one
of the defining experiences of their careers. But for a few of these spouses, the
upheaval that accompanied the U.S. rise to superpower status also brought with
it an unforgettable and very personal exposure to one of the darkest chapters of
American political history.*

*The phenomenon later known as McCarthyism had its origins in several widely
disparate facets of American political life. In an immediate sense, for the spouses
concerned, the rapid institutional growth of U.S. foreign affairs agencies created
bureaucratic power vacuums and bottlenecks in the machinery of diplomatic
representation and, ideologies aside, fostered intense competition among officers
for control of the policymaking apparatus. More importantly, and more broadly,
in the flush of World War II victory Americans' expectations for the future were
raised to an impossibly high level, and when these expectations were not fulfilled,
the competition between left and right in the country's politics slowly assumed
a new and bitter cast.*

*By March 1947, seeking to head off criticism, President Truman had by
executive order implemented loyalty investigations of government employees. But
when the Communists led by Mao Ze-dong proclaimed the People's Republic of
China in October 1949, the days of a practical bipartisan American political*

consensus on foreign policy were numbered. Julia Child, Susanne Newberry, Esther Peterson, Mildred Ringwalt, Caroline Service, and other Foreign Service spouses would soon feel the effects of this cataclysmic split, which combined outrageous scapegoating with reasoned, sometimes eloquent appeals to the nation's democratic principles. This was power politics practiced at its nastiest level, and to their misfortune, the State Department's most experienced personnel in the always delicate relationship with China, the so-called "China Hands," became its primary target.

After the "fall" of China, American domestic politics wasted little time in heating up. On 9 February 1950, in a speech before the Women's Republican Club of Wheeling, West Virginia, Republican Senator Joseph McCarthy of Wisconsin launched his opening salvo. "I have here in my hand a list of two hundred and five [names] known to the Secretary of State as being members of the Communist Party and who nevertheless are still working and shaping the policy of the State Department," he reportedly said (no transcript was made).[1]

Ironically, one of McCarthy's targets, John K. Emmerson, reported more than 25 years later that the senator got his original idea from a traditional center of training for the Foreign Service, Washington's Georgetown University. "The idea of Communism as a profitable political issue was suggested to the senator by my old Georgetown mentor, Father Edmund A. Walsh. At a dinner at the Colony Club in Washington, McCarthy was searching for a dramatic issue for the 1952 election campaign. Father Walsh suggested Communism, its power in the world, and its capacity for subversion. McCarthy jumped at the idea, 'The government is full of Communists. We can hammer away at them.'"[2]

"It was as though the country were facing a great outside menace which was inside the country," Caroline Service recalled in 1987. "It just drove people nuts to think that China was not pro-American anymore. But we were at fault, too. We did not want to have diplomatic relations with China except on our own terms. It was an internal public relations business. It was like a red flag to a bull to mention China except in pejorative terms."

While the personal futures of these officers, and their spouses, seemed ominous in retrospect, at the time they generally viewed it as normal to the vagaries of diplomatic representation abroad. The China Hands themselves had attempted to report the facts as they saw them and undoubtedly would have been replaced had they not done so during the prewar and war years. But by 1950, what a Foreign Service officer had reported a decade before could easily come back to haunt him and be reinterpreted in an entirely different fashion. What actually happened to America's experts on China was serendipitous, depending on where they were stationed when accused, on how much high-level support they could muster at home, and even on personal factors. This itself was circumstantial proof of their essential position as pawns in a high-stakes game of domestic power politics.

Caroline Service's experiences during the McCarthy persecutions offered the most comprehensive account. Looking back, she counted herself lucky to have spent a year in India, with her children and without her husband, during the worst of the period. Her trials lasted from McCarthy's initial West Virginia speech in 1950 until 17 June 1957, when the U.S. Supreme Court ruled that her husband John Stewart Service had been illegally fired from the Foreign Service.

Her personal story began with the posting to India early in 1950:

"[T]he department suddenly decided to get Jack out of Washington, and in January [1950] we were given orders to go to India. . . .

"Jack would be consul-general in Calcutta. The department couldn't make him consul-general because that would need Congressional approval. Even though he'd be the chief officer, as they called it, he was only to have the rank of consul. They wouldn't try to push this through the Senate right now.

"When [McCarthy's] speech hit the headlines Jack called up the State Department because McCarthy had a list, he said. Nobody quite knew how many. There were different numbers. There were no names, but each number was described.

"None of these descriptions applied to Jack whatsoever. So, when Jack called the State Department and said, 'What shall I do? Shall I go on to India or come back to Washington?' they said, 'Go on, because you're not one of McCarthy's numbers.'

"We spent a month here in Berkeley. Nothing more happened. McCarthy was making speeches. He made another in Nevada. But they never seemed to pinpoint Jack. It was just rather general, 'The State Department is full of Communists.'

"We went to Seattle and took an American freighter bound for Tokyo. We were going to Madras.

"One night the radio operator came down and he said, 'Say, they're talking about a guy named Service on the radio. Is it you by any chance?' Jack said, 'Why, I don't know. What are they saying?' Then the operator said, 'McCarthy was making a speech about Service—that he had undermined the State Department, he had lost China, and that he was a Communist.' So, Jack went up and listened.

"Also, the radio operator was in contact with a ham operator in Los Angeles, who had been in China and had known Jack or knew about Jack. So he was willing to relay anything that he heard at other times when our 'Sparks' was busy with his regular work. . . .

"I think the next day we got a radio to the ship from the State Department saying, 'Come back,' to Jack. 'At Tokyo, come back to Washington.' But in this telegram which was quite long it gave an option about the family. It said the family could either stay in Tokyo, come back to Washington, or go on to India."[3]

But their destination was changed to New Delhi, presumably with the hope that being a subordinate in the embassy would be less conspicuous than being in charge in Calcutta. The Services decided that Jack would return to Washington while Caroline, with three school-age children, the household goods, and an automobile, would continue on to New Delhi. Thus began her year as a single head-of-household in India. "I was in a very strange position. I had no official position whatsoever. I was a lone woman without a husband, part of the American embassy, but not officially part of it. But, pretty soon people began inviting me to all the things because there I was."[4]

When the Service family parted in Japan, it was assumed that their separation would be reasonably short, that Jack would answer questions by the State Department's Loyalty-Security Board, and perhaps the Tydings committee of the Senate, and then join his family in New Delhi. But McCarthy had aroused the country, and settling cases like Jack's had proved more complicated than anyone expected. Loyalty standards were changed, and new accusations and "evidence" required repeated reexaminations of cases already thought to be cleared.

Jack in Washington was heavily engaged in preparing his defense and appearing at hearings. Besides, he was continually moving as various friends were able to offer hospitality. Caroline, far away in India, found her best Washington contact and source of information to be Lispenard Green, who was the daughter of an American ambassador and, later, the spouse of one. They had become great friends, despite a 15-year age difference, when the two families served together in Wellington, New Zealand, in 1946 and 1947. Caroline Service recalled the development of an unusual Foreign Service relationship.

"When Lisa and Marshall [Green] left [New Zealand], we gave a cocktail party for them. Lisa wrote back to thank me, but it was more than that. It was a chatty, amusing, warm letter. So, after a while, I answered it because I wanted to tell her about everybody in Wellington and what they were doing. Soon I got another letter from Lisa. I like to write letters so pretty soon I answered it. Well, I don't think either of us thought that we were starting a correspondence which was to go on for years and years and years. But, by the time Jack and I left New Zealand a year later, Lisa and I had started a real correspondence.

"[When I went to India in 1950] we started our letters again. . . . I actually used the Greens' house as a mailing address for Jack, who was going around living with various friends . . . and Lisa would always deliver any mail to him. And Lisa went to the Senate hearings and wrote me all the details of those and any other information she was able to glean. And she wrote how Jack was bearing it all.

"In India I began keeping Lisa's letters. . . . Every six months or year now, we ship our letters back to each other, which is why I have my letters to Lisa and she has her letters to me."[5]

With her youngest child, Philip, Caroline Service left New Delhi for Washington on 30 March 1951, to be reunited with her husband after a separation of 13 months. As the summer and fall continued, their two older children returned safely from India, and loyalty investigations of Jack Service, as well as Edmund Clubb, John Paton Davies, John Carter Vincent, and many others ground on. "It became evident at this point," Caroline Service recalled, "that this was a real attack on the China people per se."

"They would have attacked Jack too regardless of anything else. Anybody connected with China at that period who had in any way given a favorable picture of the Communists would have been attacked, because by this time the country was in quite a state of, not hysteria, but of fear, well hysteria too.

"McCarthy was riding high. The Tydings committee [a subcommittee of the Senate Foreign Relations Committee set up under Maryland's Millard Tydings to investigate McCarthy's charges] was trying to investigate things, and they did give Jack a clean bill of health. But, there was a kind of miasma— I think that's the word I want—in Washington. You really didn't know from day to day who would be the next to be attacked and for what reasons."[6]

By November, the search for someone to blame for America's reversals in China reached a fever pitch, Caroline remembered.

"Jack was going through endless hearings again. Although Jack had been cleared, they decided that they would set up another board, an outside board. . . .

"This was under [former Senator Hiram] Bingham . . . [who] was not on Jack's board himself, but he had much to do with it. [As a senator in 1929,

Bingham had been censured by the Senate for bringing a lobbyist into a closed session of the Finance Committee. The next senator to be censured was Joseph McCarthy.[7] My personal opinion now is that Jack never had a chance, that once the Loyalty Review Board got hold of it, they were determined to fire somebody—Jack—from the State Department. I may be doing Bingham a great injustice, but I feel this very strongly. . . .

"Jack was their easiest target. . . . If they could fire Jack, they could go after others. I'm not trying to say there was a plot. I do not think somebody sat down and wrote all this out. I think that there was just this feeling that something had to be done, some victim had to be given to the public. After all, the whole public in this country had been aroused by 'Communists in the State Department,' or by nefarious people, or 'Who lost China?' Somebody had to be produced. . . .

"They had aroused a great deal of fear and apprehension in the American public. People were frightened. But, you can't go on forever saying these things and not producing something, unless you just want to admit it was all a red herring."[8]

The Services met their greatest challenge as a couple beginning on 13 December 1951:

"We were having two couples to dinner. . . . My mother was there. I was going to have baked beans, homemade baked beans for supper.

"About one o'clock in the afternoon the phone rang and it was Jack saying that the board's decision had come in. He was to be fired the next day for 'reasonable doubt of his loyalty to the United States.' He was calling from [Jack Service's attorney Ed] Rhetts's office.

"I can hardly describe my feelings. He said it would be on the evening news. In those days there wasn't much television. I said that I would come down to Rhetts's office. I asked my poor mother, who was seventy-five years old, to please tell the children because I wouldn't be there when they came home from school.

"She said, 'What about dinner?' I said, 'Somebody's got to eat this dinner. Don't say anything. They'll just come. We've got to have dinner. We might as well have the guests that we have asked.'

"So I went down to Ed Rhetts's office, and I wept, of course, a great deal. Jack and Ed Rhetts were just sitting there looking at each other. I said, 'Well, what are you going to do?'

"Jack . . . was to be fired; he was to be terminated on the next day at the

Accuser and Accused

John Stewart (Jack) Service and Lisa Green at U.S. Senate Tydings subcommittee loyalty hearings. Right (arrow), Senator Joseph McCarthy, 23 June 1950. *From the* Washington Daily News, *courtesy of Lisa Green.*

end of work, on the fourteenth . . . they said they were going to appeal. We talked about it. The processes are very complicated and long. First you appeal to the White House to override the Loyalty Review Board and if that doesn't work then you must go to court. You have to start with the lowest court because the upper courts, of course, won't take you. . . .

"I must have stayed about an hour, maybe not that long. I kept thinking of Hiram Bingham. So, when I left Ed Rhetts's office I went to where I knew the Loyalty Review Board held its meetings, down on Pennsylvania Avenue in an old building. I had never been there before. I walked in. There were no guards or anything. I saw where the offices were and I went upstairs to the offices and I saw a secretary. I said, 'I'm Mrs. John Service and I'd like to see Senator Hiram Bingham.'

"If I'd come from another planet she couldn't have been more shocked. She looked at me. I have to laugh. I looked at her. The woman didn't know what to say. She finally said, 'Just wait a minute.'

"So, pretty soon a man came out. I think his name was Malloy. He said that Senator Bingham was in a conference and could not see me. The old ploy.

"So, I said, 'You know'—this must have been about three o'clock in the afternoon—'I don't know why the Senator can't see me. He spent a lot of time on my husband's case and I think that he can give me a few minutes of his time.' I said, 'I have nothing I have to do, and I will just sit here. The conference must be over sometime. I will just stay here till Senator Bingham is free.'

"Mr. Malloy, if that's who it was, looked at me and disappeared. In about five minutes he came back and said Senator Bingham would see me. I was ushered into a handsome office. Senator Bingham was a very handsome man, tall, good looking; he took me by the hand and said, 'What can I do for you little lady?' I could have screamed. 'Little lady.' Awful.

"So, I said that I thought he had done a great injustice to a very worthy man. His reply, which I will never forget, was that many people have had grave injustices done to them."[9]

For more than a decade, through Jack Service's difficult yet successful experiences as an international salesman, through his eventual exoneration by the Supreme Court, and through their happy years in the U.S. consulate in Liverpool, England, Senator Bingham's judgment echoed in Caroline Service's memory. While they had been honorably restored to the Foreign Service, the State Department seemed adverse to the risk of using Jack Service's talents in understanding the Chinese character and nation. In the early 1960s they retired to Berkeley, California.

"In 1962, when we retired we came back here to Berkeley. Jack's father and mother were both the class of 1902, the University of California. One of their classmates was a Miss Lila McKinne. She was a maiden lady who lived in San Francisco on Nob Hill. She had been a dear friend of my mother-in-law, Grace [Boggs] Service, all her college days, and afterwards they kept up the friendship.

"I had luncheon with an old friend of mine who knew Miss McKinne, and she said, 'Did Miss McKinne ever tell you that Hiram Bingham was in love with your mother-in-law?'

"I said, 'This is impossible. Where would they ever have had any chance to meet? Hiram Bingham went to Yale. My mother- and father-in-law went to the University of California.' She said, 'You ask her sometime.'

"So I asked Lila McKinne about this. She said, 'Hiram Bingham came out to the University of California in 1900 after he had graduated from Yale and did graduate work here.' Lila McKinne's exact words were that, 'Everybody knew that Hiram Bingham was crazy about Grace Boggs.'

"I said, 'But she was in love with Roy Service.' Everybody knew that too. The university in those days was a small place. But, the fact is . . . whether he was in love with Grace Boggs or not, he had admired her, he knew her, he knew that Jack was her son. He never, never should have had anything to do with the board that was having anything to do with Jack's loyalty case."[10]

The intervening years—between Jack's firing and his rehabilitation by the Supreme Court—proved both arduous and exhilarating to the Services. In the political atmosphere of the early 1950s, Jack Service was nearly unemployable, with his life work as an expert in Chinese affairs having been discredited. From the close of business on 14 December 1951, the family was on its own, with few prospects for an income, Caroline Service recalled in a 1987 interview.

We had no money, we had no outside resources at all. We were paid back what Jack had put into the pension fund.

But early in January Jack got a letter from a man in New York, a Mr. Clement Wells, who had a steam trap business [the Sarco Company], and he offered Jack a job. It was a miracle to receive this letter.

We moved to New York, to Kew Gardens in Queens. Actually the children and I stayed in Washington until the end of summer. Mr. Wells had Jack go to Bethlehem, Pennsylvania, for a few weeks to work on an assembly line to see how steam traps are put together. There's a steam trap on the floor there. We use it as a door stop. After Bethlehem Jack moved to New York and went to work for Mr. Wells in the export side of the business. Mr. Wells was English and had come to this country long ago, and Sarco was his own company.

When it came time for the family to join him, Jack rented an apartment in the Bronx. It was owned by the Equitable Life Insurance Company. When the company found out who Jack was they returned the deposit check because they would not rent to us.

It was awful. I then knew how people felt who are dispossessed, or who face discrimination.

Jack was then able to rent an apartment in Kew Gardens. The Sarco office was in the Empire State Building and Jack rode the subway in to 34th Street. He claims that in all the years he made this trip he never sat down on the subway when he was going to work.

In the meantime, his lawyer Ed Rhetts had determined on the day Jack was fired that he'd take Jack's case through the courts to try to win a reversal.

Finally the case reached the Supreme Court, which accepted it. With our children we went to Washington in April 1957 to hear Ed Rhetts argue the case before the Supreme Court. It was a solemn and moving occasion.

The decision was handed down on 17 June 1957, a Monday. Ginny was going to the dentist to have a wisdom tooth out at two o'clock. About twenty minutes to two, just as we were leaving the apartment, the phone rang and some newspaper man said, "Your husband has just won his case in the Supreme Court. A unanimous decision." "What!?" I screamed. The man wanted to know how to get hold of Jack, and I gave him the number at Sarco. And then I hung up and Ginny and I just looked at each other. I guess we must have hugged each other. Then I called Jack and I phoned my family. How I wish that my father and Jack's mother had been alive. Jack came home by subway—it was a very hot June night—and the phone never stopped ringing all evening. The phone just rang and rang and rang.

And then people wondered if Jack would really go back to the State Department. Actually, the Supreme Court decision stated that Jack had never been out of the Foreign Service—never had been out—never should have been out.

Jack never had any intention of doing anything other than returning to the Foreign Service if he could. Not only for our good name, but because we loved the Foreign Service. I loved the Foreign Service, I think it was a marvelous life. And I think that, well, it was just the only thing we would ever have considered doing.

TARGETS OF OPPORTUNITY

*The witch-hunts of the McCarthy era went through the Foreign Service commu-
nity just as a tornado might have, touching down here and there to devastate a
family, yet skipping others, who wondered at their good fortune in later years.*

*Like many others of her generation, Esther Peterson remained reluctant even
in the late 1980s to discuss her husband's inclusion in the McCarthy hearings.
McCarthy, as chairman of the Senate Government Operations Subcommittee on
Investigations, had a broad mandate to subpoena government employees before
his panel. "Well, it touched us deeply. I don't know whether I should talk about
it or not," Peterson remembered in a 1989 interview.*

He was on the McCarthy list, my husband, because of my work as much
as his. In fact, in the hearing it came out that Communists were known to
meet in my office. I was doing it for Phil Murray [Murray then and later was
engaged in a struggle with Communists in the CIO (Congress of Industrial
Organizations), which later merged with the American Federation of Labor
to form the AFL-CIO], under his instruction, and, of course, we did go
through a hearing and Oliver was cleared completely by it. But we went
through hell. We went through hell. It was one of the things that killed Oliver.
He could not stand it. . . . He wouldn't let me talk about it, I couldn't tell
the children about it because, "They'll say there's something about Dad. . . ."
And how can you explain?

We were then in Brussels. We had just moved at Christmastime, and there
was an "eyes only" thing to the ambassador that Oliver was to be called
home. . . . It was the McCarthy thing. Everybody was on the list. I think
McCarthy said he had a list of probably 200.

So Oliver had to come home for consultations, which he did, and left me
with the children there not knowing what, and he had to come home and
build up his case. Of course he won, but we had to get a lawyer and had to
go through all that. Which was a great drain on us financially. It was a cruel
period.

One of the things that came up in Oliver's hearing was that we had
entertained the Deep River Boys, a group of blacks who were on a concert
tour. One of them was apparently a Communist, and it was in Oliver's record
that he entertained Communists in his home. It was the Deep River Boys.
One of them happened to be . . . whether he was or wasn't, who knows, we

117

never asked these questions. I try to not think about it because I get very emotional about it because it hurt my husband. It hurt me. It hurt my children. I can't talk about it, and Oliver wanted me not to talk about it.

McCarthy's scattershot approach did not work in all cases, however. In her memoirs, Mildred Ringwalt wrote of being shielded from McCarthyism by her husband, and by Julius Holmes, who was minister in London, where Arthur Ringwalt was assigned during the McCarthy-inspired persecutions. He was one of the few China Hands, even if only peripherally involved, to escape unscathed. It is worth noting, however, that Mildred Ringwalt was a cousin of Edith Bolling Wilson, President Wilson's widow, who at that time was a grand dame of Washington society.[11]

A VIEW FROM THE BOTTOM UP

Susanne Newberry had a unique view of the McCarthy phenomenon. As a student, she had studied in Paris, and her overriding consideration in joining the Foreign Service as a secretary was just to get back there. But eventually her disgust with the seemingly interminable loyalty investigations led to her resignation. As a journalist at the United Nations in New York, she met her diplomat husband-to-be and later rejoined the service as a spouse. In Paris in the early 1950s, Newberry had a safe front-row seat on the effects the McCarthy search for Communist sympathizers was having on the workings of the Foreign Service abroad. She recalled her experiences in a 1989 interview:

In the material they sent me, the Foreign Service exam was described as being so very difficult. I'm wondering why I was put off by that, because I was an A student in high school. I just felt I couldn't pass it. So I went to USIS [United States Information Service] as a secretary in the regional public affairs office in Paris, which was separate from the public affairs office. It had responsibility for programs in all Western European countries.

Toward 1953 and 1954, the McCarthy era really heated up. McCarthy had two young men in their midtwenties working for him, Roy Cohn and David Schine. The newspapers called them "the gumshoe boys," and one weekend—one Easter weekend—when almost everybody was out of town, these two slipped into Paris. They didn't tell anybody at the embassy they were coming. They just appeared, and they found people who were disgruntled, and they interviewed them. They got all kinds of dirt, and then they disappeared out of Paris.

Well, from that time on, every time my bosses got together, they closed the door. They never talked where anyone could hear their comments about the action telegrams about putting books into the USIS library, taking books out of the library, Dashiell Hammett out, Dashiell Hammett in, Dashiell Hammett out. [Hammett was the groundbreaking U.S. writer of hard-boiled detective fiction, including *The Maltese Falcon*.] This was a weekly, sometimes a daily occurrence.

I began to get very disgruntled with this whole thing because here all these USIS people were fighting Communism all day long with everything they had, and Senator McCarthy and these two boys were trying to prove that the USIS people were crypto-Communists.

My own brush with the seamy side of government service came when two Senate investigators, a man-and-wife team, came to our office and were very interested in what the Voice of America was doing. The VOA man in the regional public affairs office refused to let them look at the files. They knew that I was the secretary and that I had access to those files, so they turned up at my church one Sunday. They invited me out to lunch afterwards at one of the very nicest restaurants in Paris, and we had a beautiful lunch and a nice Sunday afternoon. But at the end of it they told me that they were employees of the U.S. Senate, and the Voice of America man in Paris was blocking the intentions of the Senate, and that they very much wanted to see those files. At that point I think my stomach turned upside down, and I said, "Absolutely no!" and I walked out of that restaurant. I think that's what really made up my mind that I didn't want anything more to do with the government.

Also there were no promotions coming at this time, so after two years I decided this was not for me and I left. But I had a fabulous two years in Paris. It was just a wonderful time to be there. The Foreign Service salary enabled secretaries to do anything we wanted, as the dollar was so high against the franc. It was a wonderful experience, and also a learning experience in the way government can work.

SPOUSES ON THE RUN

Meanwhile, halfway around the globe, a catastrophe of another sort was brewing. These were the 1950s, long remembered by many Americans as a decade of quietly increasing prosperity, when June Cleaver ruled in the kitchen. In fact, the Eisenhower years, initially perceived as "boring," were not a return to the pre–World War II status quo. It was a decade of profound transformation: televisions slowly appeared in most households, and a new suburbia and an interstate highway system spread across the land. Women had returned to home and hearth after the war, some pushed out of their wartime positions and others happy to leave them.

While the early 1950s seemed bucolic at home and, as Susanne Newberry noted, a strong postwar dollar made assignment abroad attractive, the world at large was still troubled. Foreign Service spouses were caught up in several ways, most dramatically in the sudden evacuations from post required by the flaring of brushfire insurrections and coups and, in Korea, a full-scale war. The intensification of the cold war, the Soviet Union's repression in Hungary, the Suez crisis, and evacuations from Korea and Laos were not isolated incidents, but symptomatic of turbulent times.

The expanding post–World War II Foreign Service brought new twists to the age-old diplomatic problem of evacuation from post. Rather than a few dozen personnel as before, these embassies and legations, and their dependents, could now involve hundreds of people.

Patricia Bartz's description of the infamous evacuation of women and children from Seoul on 25 June 1950 tells one such story. One man and 682 women and children took part in the journey on a small freighter with room for a crew of 12 and a partial cargo of 100-pound fertilizer bags that threatened to shift when the ship, destined for the nearest port in Japan, ran into heavy seas.

We had no guidelines for evacuation. It was the beginning of the war, a Sunday. My husband and I were downtown, and when we were going home, we saw some Koreans angrily shouting. The Armed Forces Radio did say there had been an attack across the border. We lived in a military compound, and the Korean Military Advisory Group men got word back to their wives that this was bad. By noon the military wives had begun to pack. There had been no word from the embassy whatsoever.

During the afternoon it happened that we had some guests, and as we were

121

seeing them to the gate, planes came over flying at treetop level and sprayed the compound. Nobody got killed, but that was just lucky. I started to think about what I might take.

In the latter part of the day, the Armed Forces Radio announced that this was "Sunset for Dependents." We had no idea what it meant, we had not been advised of any code words. We blacked out [windows] and packed some things we thought necessary for an emergency.

During the night military police knocked on our door saying buses were there to evacuate dependents. I took a small suitcase and blankets and got on the bus with other women and children. The bus drove without lights to a military airport halfway between Seoul and the port of Inchon. Vehicles from other places gathered all American dependents—military, missionary, business as well as embassy—at this collection point. No one had been advised to bring food, and the children were very hungry. The next afternoon we were evacuated to a ship that had been delivering fertilizer for ECA [Economic Cooperation Administration], as it was called in those days, now AID. We were poled out in barges and frequently strafed.

After we got on board, there was no control of the situation at all. One senior wife commandeered the only cabin with her friends. The crew had done what they could, they had [hard-] boiled eggs and bread and lard. People were to line up on deck to get some of this. Standing behind me was a UNICEF nurse who said, "This is going to be a disaster unless we get organized." There were over 600 people on that little ship. The wife of one of the KMAG people, a nurse, had broken into the embassy dispensary with an open suitcase and just swept the drugs into her suitcase. That was all she brought on board. It was vital.

A crane finally came with a net of food. There was a mad and uncontrolled and vicious scramble. People were doing it not for themselves but for their crying kids. A very brave military woman seeing this pandemonium stood up with great personal courage and told them off. She succeeded in stopping the riot. The food was then used collectively. Adults got one meal a day. It took a great deal of effort to organize.

In the meantime, the UNICEF nurse was given a little pantry to organize food for the babies and the children under two. I was her helper. We sterilized and filled bottles. To control access to the sole refrigerator, the door was locked, mothers had to knock to get a bottle.

As we got out to sea and weather got rough, the wall of fertilizer bags in the hold threatened to topple. The women had to go down and rearrange the cargo. We needed a work brigade. And of course the toilet situation was very difficult. Maintaining order in that was another problem. The military woman leader organized a latrine detail, a food detail.

People slept in the holds. They didn't have blankets or sleeping bags. It was a sunny day when we were evacuated, and many were in summer dresses.

As we got to sea it got very cold and rained. There were four women who were in labor. We got to Japan without either a birth or a death, and it was a miracle that we got there without a death. We had elderly people, we had an epileptic who threw a fit, we had unsupervised children who had accidents, a broken finger, this and that, and we had one child who was sickening with polio. The nurse I mentioned, who got one or two other women with nursing experience to help her, just didn't stop working the entire trip. The medication she had brought along saved that trip. I remember her wearily walking down the gangplank carrying this terribly sick little child in her arms when we finally got to Japan. And I did hear subsequently that the child had polio.

It was something like the morning of the fourth day when we pulled up off a harbor in the southern part of Japan. The Red Cross were there with coffee and doughnuts, and also Kotex and bandages and other things that were necessary. I was so weary at that point, I remember our joy in seeing them, and learning our husbands had been safely evacuated by air.

We were taken in buses to a military camp, where the poor youngsters who had joined the peacetime army and had not really thought they were due for war duty were packing up. We were in their barracks, so we helped them get ready to go off to war. Got the names and addresses of their mothers and parents and said we would write. And there were young boys who had been in the occupation forces in a sort of idyllic situation in southern Japan and we saw them off, back to war.

After her arrival in Japan, Patricia Bartz, a trained geographer, was quickly summoned to general headquarters in Tokyo, where she assisted in making maps for the U.S. pilots who bombed and strafed military targets in the parts of South Korea occupied by the North Koreans. "In General [Douglas] MacArthur's headquarters in Tokyo, we were handicapped by the fact that up-to-date statistical information and maps had not been brought out [of Korea]. They were destroyed instead of being brought out," she said. "I hope they were destroyed, that I don't know. The lack handicapped the war effort. I'm not saying anything I shouldn't say. I'm sure that anyone who worked in intelligence would tell you that." At the time of the Korean War, Patricia Bartz was a first-tour USIS spouse, 29 years old and pregnant. In 1967, when her husband was again assigned to Seoul, she wrote a geography textbook, South Korea, *which was published by Oxford University Press in 1972.*

6

REINVENTING THE WHEEL

I did draw the conclusion over the years that a really good man was never affected in any way by the kind of wife he had. I did notice that a man who was perhaps not especially gifted was greatly helped by a wife who was friendly and who was interested in what was going on and who was helpful both in personal and professional ways.

Lucy Briggs

In the early 1930s Cornelia Bassel, the assistant to the director of the recently established Foreign Service Officers Training School, had undertaken the social training of a new kind of young diplomat—young men whose professional and educational credentials were excellent but whose pedigrees did not necessarily include the social skills (or wealth) of earlier generations. Informally, as well, she took on the task of social mentor to their spouses and fiancées.

In the small Foreign Service of the time, with classes of 20 or so new officers, and in a society with much more intense social strictures, this individual contact helped many new wives understand what was expected of them, particularly those slated for European posts, where Bassel had a broad familiarity with society.

But with the all-out mobilization of World War II and its aftermath, the foreign representation of the U.S. government expanded more than twentyfold. There was a clear need for spouse training, and in much more than social etiquette. But formal training for spouses was not established in the Foreign Service Institute (now the National Foreign Affairs Training Center) on a permanent basis until 1962. In 15 years, three different spouse training programs were established in the State Department—by Romaine Alling, Regina Blake, and Mary Vance Trent. As these courses evolved from the one-on-one communication of Cornelia Bassel, and as the Foreign Service grew, rapidly increasing emphasis was placed on what to expect in the destination country, beginning with what questions to expect about American culture. At the same time, the conventions of social usage, while still covered, occupied a smaller and smaller portion of the curriculum.

SPOUSE TRAINING GOES FORMAL

The beginnings of organized spouse training in the State Department evolved slowly out of Bassel's tailored advice to wives and new officers. It was further complicated because three separate approaches were made to the subject, each succeeding effort walled off from the previous one by a combination of bureaucratic turf-building and, until 1962, a lack of congressional authorization.

The early courses and counseling for senior Foreign Service spouses began when Romaine Alling, widow of Foreign Service Officer Paul Alling, was hired in 1949. Records of this period are sketchy at best, but instructions were apparently suspended two years later when Romaine Alling remarried. They continued in 1955 when Ambassador Harold B. Hoskins, then director of the Foreign Service Institute, commissioned Regina Blake, also a Foreign Service widow, to undertake spouse training on a part-time basis; he instructed her, however, to begin the program from scratch, and not to utilize Alling's earlier efforts. This program ran into difficulty before a House appropriations subcommittee in 1960. It was shut down, and because Blake was a part-time hourly employee, the files she had built up over the years went with her. In 1962, when Foreign Service Officer Mary Vance Trent was asked to set up a course for wives in the Foreign Service Institute, no institutional memory remained of the earlier attempts.

Few details of Romaine Alling's instruction survived into the 1990s, owing in part to her unexpected death in an automobile accident. She was, however, a good friend of Cornelia Bassel's and known to be the epitome of "Mrs. Foreign Service," according to her daughter Anne Alling Long. She was never seen in anything but a skirt, no slacks, and was always very proper with hats, calling cards, and gloves. Romaine Alling's spouse training, which began in 1949, remained in large degree informal, as had Cornelia Bassel's. But she was a paid employee of the State Department and began in a rudimentary way to expand spouse training beyond social usage into the special aspects and responsibilities of diplomatic life. She also developed a small series of informational reports on what could be expected at several different posts, and she introduced a semblance of formality into spouse training through two lectures that she called "Problems of the First Post" and "Customs and Social Usage."

"SOMETHING NEW IN THE DEPARTMENT'S MUSTY HIERARCHY"

Romaine Alling was the first to face the dilemma of formally training a group of young women from State who were not going abroad in a diplomatic capacity. They were the spouses of Kreis (a unit of German local government) Resident Officers (ROs), young men—some of whom went as Foreign Service staff and later became officers—who were assigned to Germany to work with HICOG (High Commissioner, Germany) during the Allied occupation after World War II. "Mrs. Alling had a very difficult time trying to tell us what to do," remembered Elsa Kormann. "We weren't going as diplomats, and she felt we needed to know something more than how to pour tea. She said, 'I don't really know what to tell you,' but we had a couple of lovely meetings with her."

A Kreis is not unlike a county, and the ROs were in charge of one or even several of them, "trying to sell democracy and goodwill in a tough territory." Elsa Kormann reminisced in 1993.

My husband, John, was officially assigned to Frankfurt in 1950, but we spent our two years in Neumarkt, which was an hour and a half north of Munich, in central Bavaria. The town had been 90 percent destroyed by the Allies. John was in charge of three Kreise with 100,000 people under him, and we were the only Americans in 600 square miles, the sole U.S. representatives. John had 15 or 20 Germans working for him, some of whom were considerably older and with professional titles. This was his first Foreign Service assignment, and he was totally his own boss. He loved it, always said it was the best job he ever had and that he went backwards from there. Our house was the finest in town, up on a hill; we had competent German servants, a fleet of automobiles, and our own uniformed driver. John was 27 and I was 22, just out of college, and all of this was pretty heady.

Most of our entertaining was for Germans, but being so close to Munich, we also had a lot of visiting firemen from the United States. As a new spouse, I was completely on my own, no training, no older diplomatic wives as role models. It wasn't always easy.

Her evacuation from Warsaw to Oslo (see chapter 2) was just one of the experiences that qualified Regina (Gene) Blake to be the next woman, in 1955, to lead State Department spouse training. Like Romaine Alling, she became involved after the death of her husband, Monroe Williams Blake. Several months after he died, she heard Ambassador Harold B. Hoskins, the new director of the Foreign Service Institute, speak to the Foreign Service Wives' Group at a luncheon in Chevy Chase, Maryland. Ambassador Hoskins was eager to begin a new training program, "a course for wives." Gene Blake, who had known him "when he was in Iraq and we were in Iran," offered to help.

Gene Blake was an ideal choice for Hoskins's ambitious plans: she had education credentials and had taught school. For 16 years, her Foreign Service posts had been varied and wide-ranging: pre- and postwar Poland, Norway, Switzerland, Mexico, Iran, Italy, Senegal, and, very briefly, Manchester, England. She accepted the job as a temporary WAE ("while actually employed") position, as what in the 1990s would be called a contractor. Harold Hoskins was financing this term of spouse training out of unauthorized "broom closet" funds. Her salary was $4 per hour.

In 1990 Gene Blake's files from the Foreign Service Institute—forgotten for 28 years in the far reaches of her storage locker—documented the development of the monthly, two-week M-112 course. The training began officially on 5 December 1955, and 394 women registered during the next 11 months. They were wives new to the service and going abroad for the first time. Although a number of men's courses were available to them, the women usually opted only for the social usage courses. Gene Blake's most innovative session was a panel of experienced Foreign Service wives—"properly dressed, with hats"—who spent an afternoon fielding questions.

The Wriston wives—whose civil service husbands had been drafted into the Foreign Service in the mid-1950s—complicated matters and made Gene Blake's work "quite a bit harder." They were going to high-level positions with no previous experience abroad, and training had to be adapted to their needs. From 1956 to 1960 the curriculum began to include crash courses in American architecture and art, commerce, labor, and education, as well as sessions such as "Communist Propaganda and Tactics," "Intercultural Transfer of Techniques and Values," and "Fundamental Concepts of American Foreign Policy." In addition to broadening the curriculum, Gene Blake raised the visibility of the program in three other ways: with speaking engagements, interviews, and the handbook she assembled and pushed through to publication on her own initiative, "Social Usage in the Foreign Service." The department resisted the handbook, fearing it would further a "cookie pusher" image. But Gene Blake organized the Wives' Advisory Committee to help move her project through the bureaucracy. Committee members were wives of high-ranking department officials and included Caroline Simmons, whose husband was chief of protocol.

Despite, or perhaps because of, the success of her program, Gene Blake's training efforts became vulnerable to the vagaries of Capitol Hill. The technical issue that drew congressional ire was the use of government funds to train nongovernment *personnel—wives—without legislative authority. As New York Congressman John Rooney put it to Ambassador Hoskins before an appropriations subcommittee in early 1960, "But you still think it would be perfectly all right to use government funds to instruct wives, even though it is illegal?" In spite of Hoskins's affirmative answer, spouse training in Washington, as well as spouse and dependent educational efforts at posts worldwide, was quickly suspended by an airgram on 14 April.*

For the next two years, the letter of the congressional stricture was observed: Gene Blake directed her talks to entering Foreign Service officers and staff personnel, but not to wives. Returning from a self-financed fact-finding trip abroad in the spring of 1962, Gene Blake learned she had been subjected to the worst sort of bureaucratic maneuvering: Harold Hoskins had left the Foreign Service Institute; rumors circulated that, by congressional mandate, the director of spouse training was to be a Foreign Service officer. Gene Blake has no memory of official notice that her contract position had been terminated.

SETTING THE RECORD STRAIGHT

The final, and ultimately successful, beginning of formal spouse training in the State Department began with congressional authorization for a program in 1962. Even this program started with reinventing the wheel, once again. When Congress authorized spouse and dependent training in 1962, Gene Blake was informed that a Foreign Service officer would lead the effort. Officer Mary Vance Trent was invited by the Foreign Service Institute's new director, George A. Morgan, to assume the position, which she essentially developed from scratch. But the broad philosophical grounding of Trent's spouse training sounded remarkably similar to Blake's aims, although Trent was unaware of the former's five-year effort. "I am not interested in running a sort of 'etiquette school' for Foreign Service women," Trent wrote to Morgan on 19 July 1962. "An American woman going out to reside abroad [should] be conversant with the principal elements of American life and have at least the interested beginning of an acquaintance with the country, people, and language where she is to make her home." [1]

The newly formed Association of American Foreign Service Women also had played a key role in obtaining congressional authorization for spouse training, so it was with special irony that 20 years later, in December 1982, the AAFSW News celebrated the anniversary of what it called the first wives' course. Marvin Patterson (see chapter 3), who had collaborated with Regina Blake in the late 1950s, wrote to set the record straight. [2] But even so, when the newsletter published two articles on earlier spouse training, it made no mention of Romaine Alling or Cornelia Bassel. The lack of institutional memory, always a problem in a far-flung, rapid-transfer organization like the State Department, extended to spouses as well.

EMPHASIS ON THE SUBSTANTIAL

"I do approve a lady's knowing what fork to use at dinner and whether or not she keeps her gloves on at a reception," Mary Vance Trent's 1962 letter to Morgan continued, "but in one half of the world there aren't any forks, and nobody wears gloves! In this world of many civilizations and races and cultures, in which Americans are necessarily conspicuous, I would want to help American women (who are already remarkably well-adapted for their demanding and unprecedented roles overseas) to meet their new neighbors abroad with the friendly and open thought that is, after all, one of our best American traditions. Their personal reward will be inestimable, and their country will be well served." [3]

By 1965 spouse training was firmly established in law. Amendments to the Foreign Service Act of 1946 had virtually adopted Mary Vance Trent's rationale for training and authorized the secretary of state to "provide appropriate orientation and language training to members of family of officers and employees of the government in anticipation of the assignment abroad of such officers and employees or while abroad." At the time, the department's official policy pronouncement on the subject went even further: "While living overseas a wife is expected to contribute to the realization of our foreign policy objectives: by creating a home environment which enables her husband to do his work most effectively; by representing the best in America through her home and her children; by fostering a friendly team spirit in the official American community; by cultivating personal contacts in both the local and American community; by participating in community activities; and by assisting in other representational duties." [4]

Mary Vance Trent was a career Foreign Service officer with 15 years' experience when she received the call to set up a training program for wives. One of the few woman officers at the time, she had joined the State Department in 1944 and, three years later, in 1947, took the exams and entered the Foreign Service. She brought extensive overseas experience to the task, most recently having served a tour as political officer at the American embassy in Djakarta, Indonesia. As Trent told the New York Times Magazine, "We try to help women get rid of normal or neurotic fears, to open new doors for them intellectually and help them realize that there are important roles for them to play abroad—maybe not big, but important." [5] *Trainees also came from agencies other than State, women whose husbands held Foreign Service–related positions in the departments of Agriculture, Defense, Justice, and Treasury and in AID. AID provided Trent's capable assistant, Jeanne Shallow.*

Trent described her experiences and intentions in setting up the course in a 1988 interview.

I note that you're referring to our subject as "spouse training," as it is known today. It is perhaps a sign of the changes in our society over the past 28 years that the course I set up in 1962 was called "the wives' course." At that time, the only active career officers who had spouses were male. A female officer was expected to resign on marriage, and "tandem couples" had never even been thought of.

From the point of view of a woman Foreign Service officer, I had admired the work of the Foreign Service wife at post, beginning with early postwar years in London, in Paris, in Oslo, Prague, and in Djakarta. I'd seen these wives performing under some difficult circumstances—friendly but austere in Norway, unfriendly and very austere in Czechoslovakia, somewhat glamorous but also quite demanding in Paris. And in Djakarta—well, the problems and the challenges, and the joys, too, of serving in a Third World post that was beginning to feel the roots of its recent independence. Over this wide span of time, space, and conditions, I'd seen the Foreign Service wives under the guns. And in my view, they had performed magnificently.

The program was organized in an old red brick building called Arlington Towers. And there I was presented with a barren room with sort of worn linoleum on the floor, one metal table, one old typewriter, a pad of paper, and a pencil. So we started from that.

The first thing that I did was to go around and talk to people. I saw an interview with Mrs. Lyndon Johnson, then the wife of the vice president, after she and the vice president had come back from a trip to Turkey. According to this story, she was very much impressed by the assistance which she received from wives of embassy officials in Ankara, and particularly from a Foreign Service woman officer who was a good friend of mine fluent in Turkish. Mrs. Johnson took this occasion in the press to state her admiration for the work of Foreign Service wives. So I decided to start almost at the top—number two anyway—and go talk with Mrs. Johnson about the beginning of this program. I felt it was important that we should get very high-level backing for it. If we started down in the lower echelons, that would be fine and we needed that support, but we also needed a little bit of PR, frankly, and also the staunchness of women whose opinion would be more publicly recognized than others.

So I went through the channels and got an appointment with Mrs. Johnson. She was very supportive. Then I went to Mrs. Rusk. I knew I had the secretary's support or the program would never have been launched in the first place. The secretary was splendid. He said that there's no profession, with the exception of the ministry, which requires such close cooperation between the husband and wife in giving the service that the profession called for. A lot has changed in our society, but I've often thought of those wise words of the secretary, which perhaps seem a little bit dated, but there's something very fundamental about them.

I also felt we must have the cooperation of the various departments of the government involved in foreign affairs. I talked with the secretary of the army, who, of course, later became secretary of state, Cyrus Vance. In fact, we had a little joke about his name and my middle name (there's no relationship in particular). Through him we were able to set up a care facility for children of our wives who were to come to the course. This sounds utopian as we talk about it 25 years later, but our pitch was, "If we're going to train your wives on our budget, how about you taking care of our children on your budget?" Secretary Vance set this up with army nurses, and there was a playroom, made available nearby, and it helped us tremendously in those early days.

Trent's first spouse training course began in November 1962, just two months after she began working on it. "I found it was the right idea at the right time," she recalled. "We found wonderful support. One of them was an outstanding American historian, Elspeth Rostow, whose husband Walt Rostow was a Kennedy adviser in the White House. She kicked off each course with a survey of American history, which we felt was a very good background." But as far as earlier spouse training efforts were concerned, including Regina Blake's, Trent was in the dark. "I had been [an officer] abroad and didn't even know about that course until several years later," she remembered. "I didn't realize there had been one."

The content of State Department spouse training, even though it evolved and became more sophisticated, remained driven by the needs of spouses overseas. As Trent put it in 1988, the two weeks of training were divided in half, the first devoted to the subject of "what's going on in American life?" and the second aimed at "how do you fit into someone else's community?"

THE TIP OF THE ICEBERG

Although officially constituted and recognized, spouse training touched only a small portion of the spouses—women and men—who could have benefited from it. Joan Wilson, who served with her husband in Paris, Madrid, Bangkok, and Manila, as well as Washington, and who went on in the mid and late 1970s to become an instructor for spouse training at the Foreign Service Institute, recalled in 1989 that she received no instruction until after her fourth and final overseas posting.

When we came home from Manila, it was a dreadful first year because we all had reentry shock going from seven servants to mother doing everything, and children saying, "Why isn't my underwear ironed?" It was a difficult transition. We weathered it, but I reached the point one day, embracing the washing machine, when I said, "This is not what life is meant to be forever," and marched out that very afternoon for a job interview. It was at that time that I first heard about the Foreign Service Institute course for wives which had been going on, and I'd never been able to attend, mostly because I didn't even know it was there. So I decided to indulge myself and leave the great washing machine and take the course. It was so stimulating, so gratifying, so important in helping one process the feelings, the memories, the experiences, that I was just 100 percent intoxicated with my two weeks there.

A week later I got a phone call asking if I would like to come work at the wives' seminar—this out of the blue while I was poring through the help wanted ads. I nearly fell through the telephone.

Wilson's sensitivity to the problems of spouses going into the field without orientation had been hard-won. "I had absolutely no training," she remembered.

I don't think I saw the State Department protocol handbook until our second post. I had no idea what was expected of the diplomatic wife, of me individually. I imagine I did everything wrong and was forgiven just because the general morale in the first post was so warm and friendly. I harbor a very deep resentment that anyone is put in a position of such ignorance when it could have been corrected with one day of classes.

Wilson's eight-year affiliation with spouse training in the department also led directly to the establishment of the Overseas Briefing Center of the Foreign Service Institute, a repository, or "depot," as Wilson called it, of printed and visual materials on conditions likely to be encountered at different posts. Wilson was inspired to push for its creation by her encounter, during a conference in Canada, with a briefing center established by the Canadian government "for its technical assistance employees going overseas," Wilson recalled in 1989. "It was so apparent that if you could have pictures of housing at a post, information on the school, the medical situation, what's available in the stores, etc., at hand as you pack, it would save you a great deal of worry, and many mistakes."

The first videotape made for the Overseas Briefing Center was done by an AID photographer who was given free range to use his own creative ability to make a videotape of what life was like in Afghanistan for Americans stationed there. It was so well done, so useful, that when it was shown to ambassadors going out to other missions, they felt they had to do as well in order to serve their own staffs. As a result, it began to snowball.

I take pleasure also in the fact that the cultural surveys were started—short papers summarizing what one needs to know as an American about social customs when one arrives at post. This whole thing grew out of the fact that we had so many brilliant women serving overseas who were good writers, or were good social anthropologists. They were good cultural observers who learned a lot about how to behave successfully as a foreigner in that country, and there was no way to get their wisdom to the next person going out there. So a contract system was developed to pay small sums to some of these women to write a 30- to 50-page paper about customs at their post.

But the male attitude was very exasperating, and I'm glad to see it has changed with the advancement of women. The recognition of these cultural studies is one strand of evidence. There was a sort of pooh-poohing that this was all going to be about "wear your little white gloves, little lady." Then when these studies came in that touched on matters of importance for political reporting and economic understanding and general deportment at post, there was a total reversal of opinion.

One of my most painful moments occurred when I was on a trip to Central America and I persuaded the Peace Corps director to allow an embassy employee or dependent to participate in the training that was given on-site

135

to Peace Corps volunteers. I hastened back to the embassy, waving aloft this proud news, to be told by the senior official of a post that will be nameless, "It is ridiculous for anyone in the embassy to bother with Peace Corps training, because embassy people don't need to know that sort of thing about the country. They deal on a very different level."

I don't know how we overcome a mind-set—which I think is fortunately crumbling, but it prevailed for a long period—that the embassy official is a political scientist, a diplomat, a scholar, who would use purely cognitive powers to analyze the activity taking place in a foreign country. I think the ideal diplomat was viewed as such a brilliant linguist, and so witty, that he would automatically find entrée anywhere. And the ideal officer's wife was beautiful, elegant, well-groomed, a linguist, witty, deferential to her husband, and a superb cook. There was no recognition of possibly different underlying assumptions, hypotheses, value systems, religious beliefs, not to mention surface behaviors, that were resistant to this approach.

THE AMBASSADORS' SPOUSES

Over the years, spouse training moved through the ranks both from the top and the bottom. Cornelia Bassel's counseling of young wives gave way to Romaine Alling's one-on-one consultations with spouses of soon-to-be ambassadors. Gene Blake's more formalized efforts were replaced with officially sanctioned courses. Throughout this growth of training in Washington, the role of senior spouses continued to be important, even vital, to the successful functioning of a post. Whether recognized by the State Department or not, they set an irreplaceable example for younger wives.

Lucy Briggs served overseas in 11 countries from 1928 to 1962 as the wife of Ellis O. Briggs, who began as a vice-consul and later served as ambassador in seven posts (a Foreign Service record). She gained through experience perhaps the widest view of the changes that were coming in the lives of Foreign Service spouses. "Before the professional service," she remembered in 1989 from her home in New Hampshire, "as everyone knows, it was impossible to be at the top of the service without a considerable private fortune."

The salaries were extremely small, and it was necessary, if you went to any big post, to pay a great deal out of your own pocket. My husband also said later on that it was quite interesting and remarkable how very many excellent ambassadors there had been in the service, even with that particular consideration.

Lucy Briggs's posts, including Washington from time to time, began in Lima in 1928, continued with Havana (twice); Santiago; Santo Domingo; China; Montevideo; Prague; Pusan/Seoul; Lima again (in 1955); Rio de Janeiro; and Athens. Separation from her spouse was part of the territory, she said.

I think it was very good for me that at the very first post I knew navy wives, because separation to them was just part of their profession. And I realized this could happen and it wasn't that important. That was your way of life, and you managed. We had a lot of family separations.

Our second assignment was in Washington, and my husband got a job going to Liberia with the judge advocate general of the army. The League of Nations had accused Liberia of practices analogous to slavery. So the general was sent out to check on what was going on in Liberia, and my husband went along with him. That was a very interesting adventure for them, but I stayed behind.

They left the very day before the [stock market] crash in 1929. And I found myself in Washington with no bank to go to. Happily, an uncle was visiting me and gave me $10.

Lucy Briggs's life in the Foreign Service spanned nearly four decades, with a geographical range of residence that was unprecedented. Her experiences gave her a uniquely perceptive view of how life for the spouse had changed.

When I married, the Foreign Service wife expected to be part of her husband's life. That was not always true in the lives of women whose husbands were businessmen and who were involved [in] bringing up their children, or as volunteers, or active in clubs. Some of them, occasionally, had professions which they followed. But on the whole I think most Foreign Service wives looked forward to a life that was going to be full of adventure and possibly excitement and possibly hardship, although I doubt if we thought of that very much.

In those days, when a man's efficiency report was written, his wife was also commented on. And if she added to his social position, or if she was helpful, that was always noted. Or if she was something of a handicap, that was put down, too. I did draw the conclusion over the years that a really good man was never affected in any way by the kind of wife he had. I did notice that a man who was perhaps not especially gifted was greatly helped by a wife who was friendly and who was interested in what was going on and who was helpful both in personal and professional ways. That was the part that was interesting to me, that it was a professional career.

"This is the climax of a long adventure that began many years ago," said Judith Smith in a 1990 interview, one week before departing to Conakry, Guinea, as the spouse of the new American ambassador. But the Smiths' rise to the top of the Foreign Service profession did not sway her intense commitment,

developed over 20 years in the service, to productive involvement in the local culture.

The Foreign Service was, for us, a shared decision in 1965. We were Peace Corps volunteers in Ethiopia. Right after we were married and I had graduated from college, Dane and I went to Ethiopia. We were teaching in Asmara, Eritrea. Dane had planned to return to seminary and have a career as a minister, and I fully expected to be a minister's wife when we were married and joined the Peace Corps. But when we went to Ethiopia and were living overseas for the first time, we found that we liked getting to know the people of another culture.

Dane decided then to take the Foreign Service exam and to make the service his career. It was a decision in which I concurred. Our commitment was to work and serve in less developed countries—trying to be of help in them—and all of our career has been in developing countries, most of them in Africa, Pakistan being the one exception. They have all been hardship posts. Going to Guinea is, I think, quite appropriate for us. We're looking forward to the challenge. Having left Khartoum, Sudan, a year ago, after serving three years there at a difficult time, I doubt that Guinea will be any more of a challenge. We're looking forward to going back to French-speaking West Africa because our first Foreign Service post was Dakar, Senegal.

I have been thinking quite a bit about the differences in me after 20 years, in returning to the same part of the world. I found our first post very difficult. Perhaps because our only other experience abroad was as Peace Corps volunteers, and I had myself been a teacher and enjoyed a very important independent role, I found it difficult then to be a Foreign Service spouse. In Dakar I went through a lot of soul-searching, identity crisis, and even depression. I'm hoping that in returning after 20 years of maturing and of working out my own identity and my own role, that I'll be able to return to French West Africa with a different outlook. I think finding a role is very important for a Foreign Service wife, and I think it's the most difficult thing for her.

When we arrived in Dakar, we had two young children and a baby. I had grown up in a very self-sufficient family; we had no servants [and] did everything for ourselves, as most Americans do. In the Peace Corps that was also the work ethic, and I felt worthwhile and very useful. In the Foreign Service, for the first time, I was put in an environment where I did not have what I considered any "useful role," because I had someone to clean my house, to cook my food, to take care of my children. In a way I resented this help because it left me with a problem of what to do with the extra time. At the same time, I couldn't refuse this help: serving in a developing country, in Africa, we needed that help for cleaning house and cooking food and to employ the Senegalese, who needed work. So I decided then that I had to create a role of my own other than just being a hostess.

My husband was very supportive. Dane said, "If you're finding it so difficult, if you think this is not the profession for us, I'll leave the Foreign Service. My life with you and my marriage to you is more important to me than being a Foreign Service officer." So I've always sort of held that in reserve. It's been very helpful to know that he wanted me more than the Foreign Service.

It was after this first tour in Dakar that I went back to graduate school and got a master of arts degree in teaching English. This is a portable profession, which I enjoy immensely, but it is also very important to me as a Foreign Service wife.

We've just come from Khartoum, where I found teaching Sudanese University students very satisfying and fulfilling. It added an element of contact which my husband wasn't able to have in the diplomatic field—he had one level of contacts, government officials and diplomats, and I knew the university professors and intellectuals. So, together, it made our life very rich, even though Khartoum was our most difficult post from a security point of view, as there was a threat of terrorism.

The only way we could communicate was by our radios, telephones didn't work, and we had a whole communication network via radio. Even when I was teaching across the river in Omdurman, I could radio the embassy and find out what was happening. From time to time there were demonstrations—when there was no bread, or no transportation when bus and taxi fares went up because gasoline was scarce. Every day I would drive my trusty Landcruiser across the Nile to the university, and one day on returning I got caught in a rock-throwing demonstration. I guess that was the scariest thing that happened to me. I didn't really know what to do—I thought if I just explained to them that I just wanted to get by, of course they would let me by. I was ready to get out of the car and try to explain, but the teacher who was with me said, "No, gun it, let's get out of here." The windshield was broken, and there were holes in the Landcruiser from rocks, but I was safe and everything worked out okay. I recrossed the Nile to go to school the next day.

Judy Motley, wife of Langhorne A. (Tony) Motley, noncareer ambassador to Brazil (1981–83) and assistant secretary of state for inter-American affairs (1983–85), reminisced about her introduction to diplomatic life in the Brazilian capital, Brasilia:

I had to learn a lot very quickly. We arrived in Brasilia in September 1981. Two weeks later Vice President and Mrs. [George] Bush came for a state visit.

Chief of Protocol Lenore Annenberg; Judy Motley and daughters, Valerie and Allison; and Langhorne A. (Tony) Motley, at his swearing-in ceremony as ambassador to Brazil. *U.S. Department of State, courtesy Judy Motley.*

We only had a family cook, no one to handle huge formal affairs, and the embassy had already scheduled three parties at our house. Then we learned that [Brazilian] President Figueiredo was ill, had a heart attack, and his cook was not busy. So we asked the president's office if we could borrow the cook for our vice president's visit, and they said, "Certainly." So things worked out well. I could not have done this without Frida Mauger [a Brazilian employee], who became my closest friend and adviser.

George and Barbara Bush were the best house guests anyone could have. They made sure that they had two hours to themselves in the afternoons to relax. They write their own thank-you notes. Barbara Bush played tennis with my daughters, and George Bush went jogging. They visited three or four Latin American countries, and the schedule was just horrendous.

I always said that their visit was baptism by fire and ignorance was bliss. The children had to sleep with us while the Bushes were there because the entourage took over all the other bedrooms. He had brought four men with him: his military adviser, his doctor, and two advisers. And the men who ran the communications, and the Secret Service men, who stood shifts all night in the hallway outside their bedroom. The visit really made us jump into the community. We wanted to be good hosts in showing the Bushes around.

I had a luncheon for the spouses of the country team the third day I was there. That helped me figure out what a country team was: the economic counselor, the political counselor—the senior officers in those positions—the deputy chief of mission (or DCM), the "admin" counselor, the defense attaché, USIS. Their wives gave me tips about where to take Barbara Bush and what would be a good program for her. The country team wives also lent wonderful knickknacks because the only things we had with us had been brought in our suitcases. We had enormous bookshelves and étagères that were empty; there was nothing on the coffee and end tables. I was nervous. All the beautiful things that people insisted I borrow. But that was a great help.

Which brings to mind another impression of our two years in Brasilia. There are so many things that you do as a team in a job like that. It was the first time since we'd been married that we worked together so closely. Being an ambassador and his wife is wonderful teamwork. There are those who probably wouldn't agree with me, but we had a good time.

It didn't occur to me that I should be paid. The things that I got to do were enough compensation for me. However, through the 11 years we've now been associated loosely and closely with the Foreign Service, I can understand the career spouse who gets a little exasperated. But it was fun for us because almost every day there was some new eye-opening situation.

The Bush visit was important, but the most momentous occasion was the [President Ronald] Reagan visit. He didn't bring Mrs. Reagan because it was a working trip. I had been waiting a year and a half for my living room drapes, which were sitting in a workroom somewhere in New York. I called the workroom myself and said, "I understand you have some fabric that you're going to make into draperies for the residence in Brasilia." "Oh yes, we'll get around to it soon." And I said, "President Reagan is coming to Brazil next week. I'd like to have them in my house before he arrives." They said, "How can we get them to you?" I said, "There's an advance plane coming tomorrow, leaving Washington tomorrow night." They said, "We'll have them there." I didn't tell them that I didn't really expect Ronald Reagan to come to our house. He was staying at the [Brazilian] presidential palace because Figueiredo didn't live there. I didn't exactly lie, but I was able to expedite the draperies.

The visit was successful, but chaotic. There was a stag working dinner given by President Figueiredo—I think it was stag, because just the working officers and Brazilian diplomats and diplomats from other countries attended. The group that travels with the president—I'm not even counting the press—is enormous. There was the White House staff, and Secretary of State [George] Shultz, and his staff, too. While Tony was at the dinner at the presidential palace, I had a buffet supper at the house for the support groups. We had a great time.

Stuart Marshall Bloch, husband of noncareer Ambassador to Nepal Julia Chang Bloch, was a Washington-based, separated spouse during his wife's tenure from 1989 to 1993. An attorney and well-known philanthropist, Bloch recalled the difficulties of a long-distance marriage during a 1992 interview.

I've been to Nepal 11 times. I've got to be setting a world record for commuter marriages, I should be in the *Guinness Book of Records*, anybody who's been around the world 11 times in three years. People say, "You're not together," but when we're together, it's great quality time, we're really seriously together.

If I lived in Katmandu, the ambassador would be concerned about my not being kept in a substantive way busy and engaged. I do things over there while I'm here. We have started a Katmandu Valley Preservation League, small projects, for instance, where there's a monument and there's a problem with the roof, we fix the roof. We've worked on maybe a dozen monuments so far.

The ambassador is interested in the women's cooperatives there, and I've been helping on this side trying to get them in touch with cooperative retail operations here in the States. I try to do whatever I can here to support whatever she's doing over there. It would be very difficult for me to disengage from my law practice and investment holdings.

I do things for the ambassador here which I couldn't do over there, and she would worry more about me being there. I think that we've reached a balance between my own activities and my visits to Katmandu.

We also started the first Harvard Club in Nepal. There are actually quite a few Nepalese that have attended Harvard and went back to Nepal. We have a golf tournament every year, the Ambassador's Cup tournament. It was started by our predecessor, but we continue it because it's quite an athletic and social event. That's my bailiwick.

Regarding this business about compensating spouses, the ambassador and the spouse, you're on call full-time. When I was over there in April 1990, when they had the democratization movement, I was very much engaged in helping communication with Americans that were there, in going with the ambassador to visit the Americans who were trapped in hotels, just in trying to help maintain communication and calm during this difficult period. So far as I was concerned, I was as important as the Marines!

I wouldn't expect myself to get paid because I'm not living over there. But I really think spouses should get paid. My wife, the ambassador, always says, "What I need is a wife," and what she has instead is a manager of the house. He gets paid, and he serves a lot of the functions that a spouse would serve in a similar situation.

I think it is archaic and infantile for the State Department not to recognize the contribution of spouses—all that entertaining and the management of the household, and all of the volunteer activities with the local schools, or the clubs.

The whole attitude of our government to the way that they take care of Foreign Service people, particularly the kind of money that they make available, is laughable! Other countries understand that foreign representation is important and you have to have proper resources for representation. We don't provide the kind of resources for entertaining and lodging and transportation compared to the Japanese, even the Chinese, who have a much poorer country. Australia, Germany, even the Russians spend a lot of money on their foreign representation.

Spouses should be paid based on the time that they spend doing certain things they wouldn't ordinarily do. It might add up to $50,000 a year, or $25,000, or $5,000, depending. The whole Foreign Service apparatus should be better funded. To me, it's as important as the Pentagon, so they ought to be treated with the same kind of support. They shouldn't take advantage of people's goodwill. There's also being uprooted, the dangers you face, the diseases.

People say to me, "How can you let your wife go off for three years to be an ambassador some place?" I say, "Suppose it was World War II and it was the opposite, and I was a general or a captain or sergeant and she was my wife? She'd send me off for my country." You do these things, for your country.

We complement each other, we're very yin and yang. I think it's been a team effort. I take a lot of pride in her success.

7

ROCKING THE SHIP OF STATE

There was a suggestion box at one of the lunches, and I put in that suggestion box a strong statement that we should have a formal organization with elected officers. And this was read out at our next meeting. The jaws dropped, I mean, there was just hushed silence. It was heretical.

So I just stood up and said, yes, I had written that, and I felt that it was important for us to investigate the possibility of developing an organization.

June Byrne (Spencer)

In the opening days of the Kennedy administration, Foreign Service spouses were not immune to the resurgent optimism and confidence then sweeping the broader American society. During the summer of 1961, the trauma of assassinations, the walk on the moon, the civil rights movement, the Great Society, still lay ahead. Vietnam and the Six-Day War were challenges of the future. At home, a new, youthful president and his wife held great promise for an America led by a new generation. Abroad, the receding tide of colonialism brought dozens of newly independent countries into existence, particularly in Africa, and created new opportunities for American Foreign Service officers and their spouses.

The beginning of the modern women's movement, signified by publication of Betty Friedan's The Feminine Mystique *(1963), was close at hand. And although the winds of change were beginning to blow—as evidenced by the founding of the Association of American Foreign Service Women in 1960—typically, Foreign Service women's muted protests about the ways in which diplomacy was practiced were published anonymously or under pseudonyms. One spouse, Eleanore Lee, who published a number of critical articles in the* Foreign Service Journal *during this period, wrote under the nom de plume of Mary Stuart, after the sixteenth-century Scottish monarch who was beheaded by England's Queen Elizabeth I. The tone of Eleanore Lee's column, called "Department of Dissent," is revealed particularly well by one that appeared in February 1964, "Belling the Cat":*

"The vast majority [of Foreign Service wives] spend their hours thinking about food, clothing, and protocol. After ten years of exposure to these problems even the most splendidly intellectual of us is prone to conversation somewhat lacking in substance. It is difficult for Foreign Service wives to 'consider the lilies of the field.' Hordes of people must be provided with mountains of edibles. We fix and arrange these edibles all afternoon. We may have a Ph.D. in Modern European History, but unless we also have a private income, we spend a great deal of time posing artfully sculptured cucumbers on toasted bread squares, with dainty little dabs on top of them. And in those countries—alas, growing larger in number—which have progressed beyond the feudal system, we hand round the hors d'oeuvres and do the dishes after dinner."[1]

At the same time, there was a sense of glamour to the period, one that affected both the spouses who participated directly and those who watched from a distance. The state visit of John and Jacqueline Kennedy to Paris in May and June of 1961 was one of the high points of the phenomenon that became known as Camelot.

CAMELOT ABROAD

The purpose of the visit to Paris, less than five months after Kennedy's inaugura-
tion, was to strengthen relations with President Charles de Gaulle, who had
returned to power in France three years earlier. It was a whirlwind stopover to
confer with an important European ally on the way to the trip's true destination:
Kennedy's first meeting with Soviet Premier Nikita Khrushchev.

Kennedy's meetings with de Gaulle went well. But perhaps the real impact of
the trip could be seen in the hundreds of thousands of Parisians who lined the
boulevards for a glimpse of the young American president and, just as important,
his young, beautiful, and French-speaking wife. The visit had terrific impact on
the French. The world was dazzled, too.

Elizabeth (Elsie) Grew Lyon's husband, Cecil, was deputy chief of mission at
the American embassy in Paris at the time of the trip. Her impressions, recalled
in a contemporaneous letter to her father, retired Ambassador Joseph C. Grew,
were of a magical and unforgettable two days.

"We were lucky enough to be included in the intimate luncheon at the Elysee [French equivalent of the White House], and were touched that the French had put us on the list. I started very early to meet Cecil at the embassy. The streets and bridges were decked with French and American flags. At the Rond Point des Champs Elysees, there was a tribune with flags and bunting, and at the Place de la Concorde [across from the embassy], there were the most enormous flags I had ever seen.

"The dejeuner intime [intimate luncheon] consisted of forty guests, but as so many of the men with President Kennedy had come from Washington without their wives, I was placed very high, being next but one to Jackie, with Prime Minister Debre between us. On my other side was Herve Alphand, French ambassador to Washington, and other officials from the Department [of State]. It was a lovely, warm sunny day, and there were throngs of people waiting to see the Kennedys drive up through the Grille d'Honneur, which brings one straight across the Champs Elysees and into the lovely garden of the Elysee.

"As soon as the de Gaulles and the Kennedys were lined up, we were allowed to file through and shake their hands. Jackie looked lovely in a pale yellow suit and a yellow straw pill box hat and lovely jewels. She has a most winning smile. I had forgotten that she is as tall as she is. She is apparently 1

Elizabeth (Elsie) Grew Lyon, Hancock, New Hampshire, 20 August 1987. *Courtesy of Mary Brown Lawrence.*

meter 65 (5 feet 6 inches) and weighs 60 kilos (132 pounds), my present weight! I was so proud of her. At lunch she was speaking such beautiful French with de Gaulle, and what a pleasure it must have been for him to have someone like her beside him, someone with intelligence and esprit, with fluent, beautiful French.

"Two interpreters were placed, one between de Gaulle and Mrs. Gavin, the other between Madame de Gaulle and President Kennedy. The French were very critical of the interpreters during the visit, saying that neither of these two caught the nuances. But imagine having to take notes as the speaker goes along and then reproduce it in flawless French. Kennedy's speeches could never be interpreted in advance because he changed them as he delivered them and never stuck to a prepared text. But he spoke very well.

"After lunch de Gaulle presented Jackie with a beautiful gold minaudiere [token of friendship and affection] and she looked starry-eyed, like a child opening a birthday present. He gave a beautiful Louis XVI commode to the president. All of the members of the White House party got presents, I believe. Beautiful brief cases from Hermes for some, but there was only one present that made me envious. That was a framed photograph of de Gaulle, with the nicest possible message in his own handwriting.

"The next night was one I shall never forget as long as I live. No words could do it justice. We had been asked to fill in at the last minute at Versailles. The top members of the embassy staff had been divided between the two dinners, one group dining at the Elysee the previous night and the other at Versailles. Originally we were scheduled to come to Versailles only for a theater performance after dinner. But, with the change in plans, we set forth for Versailles; our driver, unfortunately, took the worst possible route and got into a terrible emboutillage (traffic jam). Once we were solidly packed among cars on all sides, and hadn't been able to budge for several light changes. The driver asked the police if they couldn't free us or we would be late for the dinner. This they did, getting cars to back up and let us through, and it was only as we sailed past that we realized the traffic was being deliberately held at a standstill to keep the approach to the Autoroute free for the Kennedys, who weren't due to pass for another half hour. Very unfair!

"When we arrived at Versailles, we assembled in one of the large halls to await the arrival of the presidential party. It seemed almost a sacrilege to have cocktails served in the old world atmosphere among beautiful paintings and tapestries. We could also look across the park and the fountains to the large étang [pond] around which we so often walked. It was a gray, misty evening, and the outlook had an other world quality. It made me feel as if I were dreaming. After three-quarters of an hour a line formed, and we were marshalled through, one by one, or two by two to shake hands with the de Gaulles and the Kennedys. Jackie very sweetly said, 'Enchantee, Madame,' to me, so obviously didn't recognize me this time, but I should think that she would have been numb by then.

"She looked perfectly lovely in a Givenchy gown, with flowers embroidered in beads on a bodice fitted to a full skirt. Her hair was in a 17th century style, with large diamond clips holding a large noeud [dome of hair] on top of her head. She really looked like a fairy princess, perfectly enchanting. When the 200 dinner guests had filed through, we were taken into the famous hall of mirrors, and that was an incredible sight.

"Try and picture a table long enough to seat 200, with no guests facing the de Gaulles and the Kennedys, so they would have an unobstructed view of the park, and the entire table lighted with candles in large gold candelabra, and decorated with masses and masses of deep rose roses and matching sweet peas. The effect was breathtaking. The only other light came from the wall fixtures, which looked like candles and were so cleverly done that they flickered. Four Louis XIV pillars were decorated entirely in flowers, with masses of carnations, peonies and greens.

"Imagine the trouble they had given themselves. The long, long tablecloth, which seemed to be all one piece but couldn't have been, was decorated in gold thread with stars, and the napkins were embroidered in gold thread. I wondered how they could ever be washed! The china was entirely Sèvres, and

I was told that each dessert place cost $140.00, and the entire flatware was vermeil [gold-plated silver]. I tried to picture it as it used to be in the days of Louis XIV!

"When dinner was over we proceeded through endless galleries, each more beautiful than the last, past the chapel where the magnificent organ was being played. It was all so incredibly beautiful that it was almost more than one could bear. Down endless halls, with statues of the Kings of France, to the Louis XV theatre, restored as it used to be, the blue and gold curtain having taken seven years to embroider. The orchestra, in costume and powdered wigs, playing music by Mozart, Rameau, and Lully.

"After the performance, the presidential party—consisting of many, many cars—drove through the park, past the fountains, while the andante of Haydn's Clock Symphony played over loud speakers. I think I shall always associate that symphony, which I love, with that misty evening, with a fine rain falling on the illuminated chateau and the park, with the lighted fountains and statuary, and all the pomp and pageantry. It was unforgettable."[2]

A SENTIMENTAL JOURNEY

For Kristie Miller (Twaddell), the romance of the early 1960s took a different, and unexpected, form, one that later would foreshadow her experiences as a Foreign Service spouse. The occasion was a visit to Japan with her longtime friend Joanna Sturm. They were "tagging along" with Sturm's grandmother, Alice Roosevelt Longworth, daughter of President Theodore Roosevelt and widow of former Speaker of the House Nicholas Longworth, and were retracing Alice Longworth's 1905 journey to "show the flag" to the Japanese when then-president Roosevelt was negotiating an end to the Russo-Japanese War.

"We were two slightly bohemian college students of the turbulent 1960s when we went to Japan with 'Mrs. L.' (as everybody called her)," Kristie Miller said in a 1989 interview about the 1965 trip. Upon arrival in Tokyo, the three were taken under the wing of Dorothy Emmerson, wife of Deputy Chief of Mission John K. Emmerson. But ironically, Kristie Miller, who had no inkling that she would soon become a Foreign Service spouse (see chapter 9), did not notice that special preparations had been made to ensure the success and enjoyment of their visit.

We had no idea that Mrs. Emmerson had been delegated by the embassy to entertain Mrs. L.'s party. Joanna remembers that Mrs. Emmerson was with us almost all the time, but she seemed so glad to see Mrs. L. that we assumed they must be old friends. We had met other old friends of Mrs. L.'s who had sponsored some special entertainments for us, too, including tours of local art emporia, a Japanese ghost movie, and a bath Japanese-style, which Mrs. Longworth, of course, declined. So the idea that Mrs. Emmerson was just another of her wide circle of friends was a reasonable one.

One of the many things she arranged for us was a trip to Nikko, which Joanna and I considered the high point of the trip. We would have been horrified to think that the establishment in the shape of Mrs. Emmerson had been put in charge of us. In fact, at Nikko, Joanna and I escaped from the official party and went hiking in the forest up behind the temples, which was much more to our liking than the elaborate embassy dinner, which we attended with a solemn sense of doing our duty. I had absolutely no idea that a year later I would be married to Bill Twaddell and that he would go into the Foreign Service and that a day would come when it would be my responsibility to host visiting VIPs, taking them on tours and struggling to serve them dinners.

Alice Roosevelt Longworth was famous as a Washington hostess, with a sharp wit and irreverent sense of humor. In a 1987 interview, Dorothy Emmerson remembered the visit fondly, and from a different perspective:

I kept Mrs. Longworth for myself. She was my most treasured memory of a VIP. At one point in Nikko I found her on the verandah of a temple in the lotus position, in her signature wide-brimmed hat. Mrs. Longworth explained that her father had taught her yoga, and she had been interested in it ever since. And I never thought of Teddy Roosevelt as being a devotee of yoga. But that's what his daughter said.

And then going back on the train, she and I were sitting, talking, and she fingered her pearls, and she said, "People don't really appreciate pearls anymore, do they?" And I said, well, in Japan I thought they did. And she said, "No, not really. These were given to me when Nicholas and I went to Cuba on our honeymoon, and the Cuban government gave me these pearls as a gift, and they are real pearls." And then I realized that she meant pearls that come out of oysters by chance, and will match up or not, as the case may be.

When we got back to Tokyo, Joanna wanted to go to see the Daibutsu [great Buddha] in Kamakura [south of Tokyo], and I said [to Mrs. Longworth], "Do you want to go with her?" She said, "No, of course not, I've seen it." This remark was made because she and Longworth had been [in the group that came] to Japan in 1905, before she married Longworth. When you asked her about it, she'd say, "Oh, yes, that was just a junket." But that was her first trip to Japan, and she had not been back for 60 years.

Well, then, the crowning blow was when my husband had gotten the emperor's household to research books on the earlier visit so she could go back and look at them, and my husband gleefully would escort her. So he told her about this—that the emperor and empress would like to receive her and reminisce about the other visit.

And her reply was, "Well, I have reservations, I think I'll just go on to Hong Kong. I met the emperor the last time I was here."

OUT TO AFRICA

Also in the early 1960s, and half a world away, Alice McIlvaine, a new bride, almost 40, and a career woman in her own right, arrived at her first post, as spouse of the U.S. ambassador to Dahomey (now Benin). Not only was Robinson McIlvaine the first U.S. envoy to Benin, he was the first ambassador ever to the newly independent country. And while Cotonou was not quite ready for the McIlvaines—construction on their cinder-block residence was just beginning when they arrived—Alice quickly learned that the "establishment" at State had not been quite ready for the situations she and others would confront in West Africa. As she recalled in a 1988 interview:

There was no regular briefing program for spouses in 1961, so some of the experienced wives got together and arranged interviews for me before we set off for Dahomey. I had two sessions with several ambassadors' wives who briefed me on protocol, rather old school manners and the like—which side of the car to get in, where to sit, on the right-hand side of the sofa only, when to stand up, and other advice, such as, "Whatever you do, my dear, please don't go around with hairdressers. Please focus your attention only on the wives of senior officials."

Of course, Africa south of the Sahara in those days was almost a new continent for Americans—until the new countries started becoming independent in the late 1950s, early 1960s. There were no post reports, few books if any written on Dahomey, and we could find only one man in the department who had actually been to Dahomey, so he kindly told me all he knew.

No one could tell me what to take. Nobody could tell me what the weather was like. I got married and headed off the next day for West Africa, armed with a few items as advised: the leather guest book and the leather seating charts, both of which mildewed in the tropical humidity, linen tablecloths, and such.

The next thing I knew, we were landing in Ghana. Then Bob and I got into our little Peugeot station wagon and headed out for Dahomey. We drove, and we drove, and we drove, and it was bush, and it was sparse, and it was an endless, red dirt road, and there was nothing to be seen until a few palm trees appeared along the coast just before we arrived in Cotonou. The department had managed to rent a tiny cement bungalow, which had become the chan-

cery, and behind it, in a sandpit, was the beginning of a cinder-block bungalow, which was going to be our official residence.

We drove through the town, which was very simple, very plain, but it did
have the palm trees, and it was on the coast. We drove up to the funny little
old French hotel on the beach where we would stay, and it turned out that
the French manager absolutely despised Americans. He had given us the worst
possible room in the hotel. It was in the back, over the kitchen, and on a
street. One window opened onto a courtyard where they held nightly open-
air movies, with the crowds roaring over Marilyn Monroe, or cowboy antics,
with all of the films dubbed in French.

The walls of our room were painted the Dahomean national colors—
orange, green, and black. We had a sagging bed, a table, and no closet. The
lovely ambassadorial trousseau was hung on the shower curtain rod, and each
time we took a shower, which was often in the intense heat and high humidity,
we had to take all the dresses off so they wouldn't get wet. The air conditioning
would stagger on periodically. There was no toilet. One had to go out and
down the hall to the public one, which had cockroaches and salamanders all
over the place.

The embassy was about as small as one could have, and when we arrived,
almost all of the staff was sick. The deputy chief of mission's wife had terrible
pneumonia and the AID director's wife was in bed with dysentery; the com-
municator and the administrative officer had hepatitis and were evacuated;
and the USIS officer had had a heart attack. There was one junior officer who
had been educated in Paris and knew the local scene, the government officials.
But she was vague, and as I remember, when we arrived she'd misplaced the
Great Seal in the brief period she had been at post. [The Great Seal, the
embossed seal for official documents, is carefully secured at every mission.]
Because the others were ill, the junior officer was the only one sitting on the
terrace of the hotel waiting for us to arrive.

We lived in that little hotel for three months, entertaining out of it. We'd
have the staff over for an after-hours swim, and they'd sit in their wet bathing
suits on our sagging bed, and we'd drink warm beer. It really wasn't what the
senior wives at State had pictured as the life of an ambassador's wife!

There was practically no protocol, and it was months before I made my
first call, even though I had arrived armed with boxes and boxes of calling
cards. And then, when I would go to call on, say, the foreign minister's wife,
I would be received by someone I had never seen before. It would turn out
not to be the wife I expected, but wife number 5, the youngest wife, who
had been educated and learned French and was therefore sent out to meet
me. Then a tray would follow with champagne, cognac, and cassis at ten in
the morning, and I would have to sit through that, struggling with French in
the deadly heat.

The wonderful instructions not to "make friends with your hairdresser" were particularly inappropriate because mine happened to be the niece of the president and was married to a very fine old Swiss family. She was a powerhouse in Dahomey, being a favorite of the president, and was someone you definitely wanted to befriend. She was better informed than anybody.

Eventually we moved into our bungalow, which, though small, was adequate. Actually, I think an elaborate, lavish residence would have been inappropriate in Dahomey. We had wonderful parties out on our terrace and in the garden, the kind of parties the Dahomeans enjoyed, which involved barbecues, music, and dancing. I wrote to Washington and asked for plastic plates, stainless steel, ice chests, and such for the kind of entertaining we were doing and was told quite firmly that ambassadors were to use the white and gold-crested china only.

We were trying to be very careful with the embassy budget, and it was only after considerable effort that I managed to inveigle my husband into allowing me to spend money to buy pebbles to cover the muddy driveway. I am not sure anyone had told me in Washington that I could order such things as rugs and draperies, but it was much too hot and humid to want them anyway, so we made do with black tile floors, wooden shutters, and iron grillwork, which were fine. For Bob's office, I went to the marketplace and bought some local fabric and then carefully made pleats, which I fastened up with thumbtacks. When the [Department of State] inspectors finally came to post, they did comment that the ambassador has been abstemious to the point of starkness. I found out later, to my dismay, that all the money we had saved by our frugality had been turned over to our embassy in Paris for further beautification of that already magnificent residence.

The McIlvaines' situation rapidly declined from merely bad to ridiculous, she told another interviewer in 1990.

"Then I was pregnant. This had caused concern in the department, which didn't expect an ambassador's wife to get pregnant. They were supposed to be too old for that. And for an ambassador's wife to be almost 40 and pregnant, and to be stationed in a small, remote African post—this was too much. A doctor was quickly dispatched from the department to check on me and to look into the available medical facilities. When he saw the delivery room, he suggested that I either go to Ghana or that I leave three months in advance and fly to Germany or the United States. We settled on Ghana, but by the next month Ghana had had a quarrel with her neighbor, Togo, and the border between the two countries was closed. Finally we decided that we'd just stay put and have the baby in Dahomey, despite the inadequate facilities. Bob found a copy of *Birth without Fear*, and we read it word by word and started exercises. We settled back, relieved that we'd made our decision. Now that I was large with child, the Africans thought better of me and became much more friendly and open. At long last, in their eyes, I was fulfilling my wifely duty.

"About a month before the baby was due, Washington insisted that Bob return to serve on an important promotion board. We were stunned. Bob certainly didn't want to go off and leave me alone in Dahomey, and the airlines wouldn't allow me to fly. Finally we called our local doctor, and he solved it calmly by saying, 'No problem. I'll order that you be evacuated. Then the airlines will be forced to take you.' My worries were over, or so I thought.

"By late afternoon the next day, we were both on a plane headed for Washington. We stopped in Paris to change planes, and we checked into a hotel. Feeling too keyed up to sleep, we slipped into the famous *Herald-Tribune* bar for a nightcap, and while we were sitting there, something happened. Floods of water started pouring out of me. It was the start of labor. The excitement and the plane trip must have brought it on. Off into the night we rattled, to the American [military] hospital.

"The doctor arrived. He started questioning me and had gotten to 'How do you spell McIlvaine?' when I gasped, 'Doctor!' He looked at me and ordered the cart brought. The time had come. The doctor was calm, helpful, and I was grateful we were all speaking English. After a few bad moments, Ian was delivered.

"Later, my mind raced, thinking of problems. I had nothing with me, as I'd planned to have the baby in Washington. The baby had nothing. No diapers. No shirts. Nothing. But I needn't have worried. Word had already reached the American embassy, and the following day the 'club' went into action. One wife had met me only once, in Africa, but she immediately called and took down a list of necessities, which she promptly purchased. I fully realized then what a wonderful extended family the Foreign Service is!"[3]

Alice McIlvaine went on to spend 12 years as a Foreign Service spouse in Africa, a career that in 1966 included being held hostage in Conraky, Guinea, while a rioting mob trashed the ambassador's residence.[4]

BLACK POWER

"I coined the term 'Black Power,' but its origins are not what you think," Ruth Bond said in a 1992 interview. [Her nephew is the former Georgia legislator and early black activist Julian Bond.] "I meant the economic power that Tennessee Valley Authority electricity was bringing to the lives of poor black women." It was much earlier in her career as a government spouse, in the midst of the Great Depression, while her husband, J. Max Bond, was employed by the TVA, that the term got its start. Ruth Bond was working with the "country women at the dam site, sharecroppers really," when she got interested in their quilts.

The women were beautiful quilters because the slave quilting tradition had been handed down to them. Their grandmothers had made the quilts for the "big house." I designed new patterns for them, I would design the colors, and cut out the pieces. One of the quilts became famous, but unfortunately the original is now lost. It was known as the "Black Power" quilt.

The design was a strong black figure, with one hand grasping a bolt of electricity, like lightning. . . . In the 1960s I was told by some of the civil rights activists, who had been TVA student interns, that my quilt was the beginning of the term "Black Power."

I always had a sense of community service wherever we went: Haiti, with the Good Neighbor Policy; Liberia, where Max established the University of Liberia at President William Tubman's request; and then with the State Department to Afghanistan, Tunis, Sierra Leone, and Malawai. What did I do in all those places? I tutored in Haiti. In Liberia I was head of the English department at the university. In Kabul, in 1955, I was the only American woman invited into an Afghan home at that time, and I was permitted to work with a group of Afghan women who were learning household skills under the direction of one of the ministries, headed, of course, by a male.

In Tunis I organized a group to sew for underprivileged Tunisian children. Our committee found out that along the border between Tunisia and Algeria there were a lot of Algerian refugees who had crossed the border into Tunisia and needed food. Our government was sending food up to them. But the refugees sent word back that the food was making them sick. We were sending them canned goods, but the thing was, they would mix it with their brackish water, and they were also putting that water in the milk. We were sending

157

lots of milk because there were babies up there. So, as the community affairs committee, we organized five carloads of women to go to the border, to take sterno stoves, canned milk, food—everybody donated, and we took clothes, little jackets and things like that, and took them up to the refugees on the border. We showed those people how to use the stoves and told them not to add any of their water to the cans of food. If they had to use water, they were to boil it first on the little sterno stoves. The U.S. government official who was supposed to be sending the food up to the refugees didn't organize the caravan, didn't do anything to help, but afterwards he bragged about what the mission had done for the Algerian refugees. But the women didn't mind. I can truthfully say that wherever my husband was assigned, I made a contribution by helping the underprivileged.

GETTING ORGANIZED: THE ASSOCIATION OF AMERICAN FOREIGN SERVICE WOMEN

"*I do want to impress upon you,*" *Secretary of State Dean Rusk told an early AAFSW meeting on 4 October 1961,* "*that we are determined to do everything we can to insure that the women of the Foreign Service get every possible opportunity for the exciting and exhilarating experiences and service which are there, and to make it possible for them to show their professional talents and skills in every possible way.*" *This was a succinct, if awkward, expression of the aims of the new organization, which the women who founded it, including the first president, June Byrne, saw being honored more often in the breach than in the reality by the State Department of the late 1950s and early 1960s. Foreign Service spouses had been meeting regularly, in a social way, for a quarter-century before they decided that a more organized representation of their interests at the State Department was needed.*

The Foreign Service Wives' Group, as it was called, had been established by Edith Carr; her husband, Wilbur J. Carr, had marshaled his consular corps forces and masterminded passage of the Rogers Act and had been an assistant secretary from 1924 to 1937. The first meeting of the Wives' Group, the first formal attempt by spouses to lower the implicit social barrier between "consular" and "diplomatic" wives, was held in the early 1930s, a luncheon at the Massachusetts Avenue home of one of the members. Fourteen women attended.[5]

Informal luncheon meetings had been held in the fall of 1928, prior to the founding of the Wives' Group. They also had been organized by Edith Carr and "a group of wives of consular officers stationed [for the first time] in Washington. The meetings gave the wives of the men who met officially at the department a welcome opportunity to chat and exchange experiences."[6]

The [American] *Foreign Service Journal reported in March 1929:* "*The women of the American Foreign Service met at luncheon on the first of February at the [American Association of] University Women's (AAUW) Club at 1634 I St., N.W. There were about 40 present. Mrs. Wilbur J. Carr spoke after the luncheon of the treaties of the different countries with the United States that are kept in the archives of the Department of State. She told of the beauty of the parchment on which many of them are inscribed, of the illuminated lettering, and of the almost barbaric splendor of the bindings and containers of many of them.*"

Mrs. Carr attended the luncheons for 25 years, throughout the existence of the Foreign Service Wives' Group.

As Caroline Simmons—whose husband, John Farr Simmons, went on to become chief of protocol in the 1950s—remembered in 1993, "It's true that we had a sort of social organization. I belonged to the wives' group when I came into the service in 1936. I remember our gathering for a large luncheon of Foreign Service wives in the ballroom at the Mayflower Hotel. At that time, it afforded a nice opportunity for Washington wives to meet the secretary [of state's] wife. I think it's very important to look at such an organization in light of the time in which it was formed. There weren't many women working in those days, so they had time to do things. There were very few women, actually, in the service, and the problems were different, people did things differently."

And the activities of Foreign Service women were reported differently. On Thursday, 19 November 1953, the Washington Times Herald *noted:*

Velvet hats took the spotlight in the receiving line . . . at [yesterday's] luncheon at the National Press Club, hosted by the wives of the members of the Foreign Service Association. . . . The two ranking ladies greeting the guests, Mrs. John Foster Dulles, wife of the secretary of state; and Mrs. Walter Bedell Smith, wife of the undersecretary of state, both chose small very effective chapeaus of this favorite material.

Mrs. Dulles' hat was a warm brown to match her wool crepe gown. Mrs. Smith's headpiece was black and topped off a black wool coat-dress which featured a black braid trim.[7]

"Sofa Can Prove a Hot Seat," warned Dorothy McCardle, reporting the same luncheon in the 19 November Washington Post.

"NO! NO!—Don't sit on that embassy sofa! Not if you don't want to get your protocol ears pinned back!". . . This was the wary word passed among newcomers yesterday at the luncheon given by the wives of members of the State Department's Foreign Service Association at the National Press Club Building.

You prefer sofas? And besides the guest of honor is seated there and you want to settle down for a nice little chat beside her? Well, don't! So far as you are concerned, my dear, that embassy sofa might just as well be a throne. Or a hot seat. It's not for you—not unless your hostess, the ambassador's wife, leads you to it. . . .

Anxious young wives crowded about Mrs. William E. Shepherd for the right answer at yesterday's luncheon-end. For two years, gracious and friendly Romaine [Alling] Shepherd was etiquette monitor to Foreign Service wives at the State Department.

"The right hand corner of the embassy sofa is reserved for the ranking guest of honor," she explained. "It's a pretty safe rule never to approach the sofa unless your hostess leads you to it and invites you to sit there."

And so to be safe, advised the more experienced wives, just regard every embassy sofa around the world as a social trouble spot. Avoid it, in favor of the stiffest, straightest chair in some distant corner. That way you're playing the social game the smart way![8]

But by 1959 the extensive change and growth that had completely revamped the Foreign Service had also changed spouses' expectations of their lives within it. The cancellation of spouse training at the Foreign Service Institute the following year was the final straw and fueled the women's resolve to organize—to represent their interests as spouses not only before the department but in other forums, including Congress. The Association of American Foreign Service Women was the result in early 1960.

June Byrne recalled:

Several of us had been talking about the need for a more formal organization. We felt that the problems being faced by Foreign Service wives were enormous. I'm referring to the wives of the young World War II veterans who were brought into the Foreign Service in 1946. It's now 1959, 14 years after the war, and these young couples were veterans of another sort. They were veterans of three or four posts and a couple of Washington tours. And we were all looking at the Foreign Service and at our life in the Foreign Service, trying to analyze it, and we just felt that there were problems there that needed to be addressed, problems that the State Department was unable, or unwilling, to address.

There was a suggestion box at one of the lunches, and I put in that suggestion box a strong statement that we should have a formal organization with elected officers. And this was read out at our next meeting. The jaws dropped, I mean, there was just hushed silence. It was heretical.

So I just stood up and said, yes, I had written that, and I felt that it was important for us to investigate the possibility of developing an organization.

The first board of directors of the Association of American Foreign Service Women (AAFSW), (from left) Hallijean Chalker, Marjorie Gallman, Ann Penfield (standing), June Byrne, and Nene Dorman, Washington, D.C., 1960. *Courtesy of AAFSW.*

We had a most perceptive, independent-minded wife of the director-general of the Foreign Service, Mrs. Waldemar Gallman. And she caught her breath, looked around, and said, "Well, all right, June. Why don't you . . . ," and then she named two other women who happened to be friends of mine, and she said, ". . . see what you can do to develop such an organization." And from then on AAFSW took off, not, however, without some resistance from a number of the more senior women, and from the department's administrative section as well.

June Byrne and her new group were very careful to continue the social side of the new organization. Coffee mornings and luncheons continued, but the group decided immediately to establish a more purposeful raison d'être. As its principal undertaking it would help raise funds for scholarships for Foreign Service children. A $1 membership fee was established (later raised to a scandalous $3), and a book fair, for which the department grudgingly provided a venue, was held

Mary Caroline (Mac) Herter, wife of former Secretary of State Christian A. Herter, conversing with her successor, Virginia (Mrs. Dean) Rusk, at an AAFSW tea, 21 February 1961. *John N. Richards, Sr., Department of State, courtesy of AAFSW.*

annually. Three decades later, the annual book fair had become a Washington institution and had raised over one million philanthropic dollars, but the venue at State now was threatened, for security reasons.

At the same time that the Foreign Service Institute eliminated its spouse training program in 1960, budget cuts stopped the housing information program in State's personnel office. To meet the department's housing needs, AAFSW was provided a desk in the Foreign Service lounge. Here, volunteers dispensed all important information on housing availability and on where, in those days of a rigidly segregated Washington (even though segregation had been outlawed by local ordinance), integrated neighborhoods, such as upper 16th Street, could be found. The desk proved so successful that it soon moved next door into a room of its own and became the Housing Office.

"In January 1962 we helped 228 people at the desk," June Byrne recalled. "We quickly realized there were needs other than housing, and we provided information on schools, jobs for wives, on posts abroad, local car and furniture rental, and other facilities, such as medical, and recreation. We really were very efficient [and] were getting to be very well known."

VIETNAM: THREE VIEWS

The American experience in Vietnam was one of the great traumas of the 1960s and 1970s. The effect of Vietnam assignments on Foreign Service families and careers, particularly in the attitudes of women toward this assignment for their husbands, generally reflected their state of health, their family commitments at the time, and in particular their husband's position in service—eager new officer, midlevel with career on hold, dedicated senior officer going for broke. Even though younger officers considered Vietnam a hardship post, their attitude was that Vietnam would provide excitement, an opportunity for promotion, and generous hardship allowances.

"Saigon [Ho Chi Minh City] was another world," remembered Virginia Bogardus. "I'm not sure I could ever go back there again. It is the only post I was glad to leave, definitely not our best hour in the Foreign Service. We arrived well before our American military buildup, when our troops began to arrive in great numbers."

My time was taken up with settling in and trying to get used to a strange land, to the tropical climate, which I thought was perfectly terrible. We arrived in January 1959, and the first attempted democratic revolt against the Vietnamese government occurred that same year. The second attempted revolt came in early 1961, and both were pretty scary. There was severe fighting right in front of our house, one of those lovely French villas which, I understand, has today been razed because it was falling down from termites. We loved the house. And we had a wonderful Vietnamese family who took care of us. All of this helped a great deal, but the life was so different. I think if I lived there a thousand years I would never adjust to the climate or the culture, even though a lot of French influence remained.

I could see the buildup of our troops. They weren't in uniform, but they marched down the street with their short hair and plaid shirts. I asked George, "Who are all these young American men? What are they doing here?" "They're with MACV [Military Advisory Corps, Vietnam]," he said. It was a buildup that seemed inexorable. Terrible things began to happen. Hand grenades thrown into restaurants and gardens. Life became very frightening. One morning there was fierce shooting back and forth on our street, then suddenly at noon there was a lull. I ventured cautiously onto the upstairs balcony, and saw, to my astonishment, white flags waving at both ends of the block. This was lunch break. After lunch and the usual siesta, the sniping began again.

The Vietcong began ambushing anyone who drove out beyond the airport, where the jungle began. So that put a stop to getting away from Saigon, except to fly out, which I tried to do as often as possible. I got off to Singapore twice to visit friends, and three times to Hong Kong. I just had to, because it was impossible to stay and deal with the situation in Saigon. For instance, much to my horror and quite by chance, I saw the first self-immolation by a Buddhist priest.

Throughout all of this, I had amoebic dysentery. I had no less than ten cures. When I look back on it, I don't know how I survived. This was the time also that I began to think the Foreign Service was asking a lot of the wives and children. In fact, both George and I were disillusioned at this point, I more than he. Like so many others, George had been unfairly treated in his career, and that, of course, reflected on me and I was very upset. So one day we sat down and talked about it.

My attitude was, let's go do something else. George, who had wanted to be a Foreign Service officer since he was 15, said, "To tell you the truth, in spite of everything, I do not want to change." "Well," I said, "if we choose to continue in the service we will not be bitter, we will not go around complaining as others do. We will accept the situation and live with it." So with that he volunteered for a second tour, and all together we had four and a half years in Vietnam! I can muster no desire to return.

The situation had changed dramatically five years later. "Vietnam. Alec's first post was Vietnam," said Catherine (Casey) Peltier, seven-times great-granddaughter of Abigail Adams, in 1987 about her husband's Vietnam service, which began in 1968. "He got a bottle of wine from his A-100 classmates [the junior officer indoctrination course] for getting the most rotten assignment. Of course, we were married about ten days later, but he had to say, 'No, I'm not married.' at the time.

[The separation] couldn't have happened at a better time. We had no kids, and there was a safe haven program. Alec left at Thanksgiving time, and the following April, right after Martin Luther King was assassinated, in 1968, I moved out to Manila, where I lived in more than Oriental splendor. We spouses used to say that we were the best-kept mistresses in Asia! Separate maintenance allowance, housing, medical care, all sorts of support. There was an officer [at the embassy] assigned to look after us.

But we were considered social pariahs. All of these unattached women! We had a terrible reputation, thanks to the activities of a few. But the thing that really chafed most of my friends, who were all under 25, was that they could not work. Our visa precluded working in the Philippines.

We had all been married for less than a year when we arrived in Manila. And there was only one other spouse like me who had never worked and knew what to do with herself. Naturally, there was an American women's association, and naturally, they had all kinds of worthy projects. So we dove into worthy little projects and had a fine time. Some of the others, who felt they had to work, were given jobs at the American school, even though they didn't necessarily have the degrees.

But it was a funny way to live, because if you were lucky and your husband had a decent boss, he was with you for a week every six weeks. At which time you dropped out of sight completely. When Alec and I were together, we were so young and shy, like a newly married couple, it was like a two-year honeymoon. I think I was 20 at the time.

But there were some weird consequences to living like that. One of our group was very social, and when her husband arrived, she wanted to have a little party and introduce him. The fact that every single one of her 14 friends was a woman didn't bother her. But at the party we all just sat there. We didn't know what to say or do. We were so conditioned to not even dare to smile at someone else's husband in case his wife would be jealous. Now that I look back on it, what a scream! But it was two very interesting years.

At the upper levels of the Foreign Service, a tour of duty in Vietnam could still be unsettling, especially at the height of the U.S. presence during and after the 1968 Tet offensive, which proved a decisive turning point in American involvement in the country.

"We had been in India for three years—a very exciting period in our lives— and then, lo and behold, Galen was posted to Vietnam," as the embassy political officer, recalled Anne Stone in a 1992 interview. "I was very angry. But if you knew Galen, you would know that he felt it was his duty. So many of his friends had had a Vietnam assignment: now it was his turn. And he would not refuse."

I knew his mind was made up, but I was angry. I really felt that, with five children, it was a lot to ask to have him go out there at that time when it was extremely dangerous. It was 1968, the time of the "Tet," and that was a very bad period in Vietnam.

But, being a dutiful Foreign Service wife, I bit my lip and carried on. Galen was in Saigon for fifteen months, and for me it was a long fifteen months with a boy and three girls in adolescence and a son of eight. It was a difficult time.

I went to visit Galen in Saigon after he'd been out there about eight months, I guess it was. They let me come at Easter, right to Vietnam, and it was very exciting. That was 1969. There's a funny story about that, because my visit happened to coincide with a visit of the new assistant secretary of state [for East Asian and Pacific affairs], Marshall Green, who was visiting all of the countries in his geographic area. His wife, Lisa, accompanied him to Vietnam, and since Galen was head of the political section at the embassy, I got in on all of the VIP things that were arranged for Lisa Green.

The first thing we did was take a ride over Saigon and all the surrounding area in an army helicopter, where you just had a seat strap. The doors were open on either side, so when the helicopter banked you were leaning over space. In the back was a soldier with a machine gun and in the front was another soldier with a machine gun.

The next thing I did with Lisa was ludicrous. We were taken down to the docks on the Saigon River, and we got onto an army launch, which was a good-sized craft. We were on the upper deck with a huge American flag flying from the stern, and there was a sort of awning over the top. We cruised the Saigon River and had a tea party on the top deck! There was Mrs. Creighton Abrams [wife of the U.S. Army chief of staff] and Mrs. Marshall Green, and I. It was wonderful.

We passed a small navy patrol vessel coming back from their patrol, and their eyes almost fell out of their heads when they saw us. Our only protection was a boat about the size of a bathtub, with two Vietnamese police officers between us and the Vietcong. The bank of the river opposite Saigon was just jungle, really wild. And that's where all the rockets were coming from every night, when the Vietcong aimed them at Saigon and just shot willy-nilly.

I stayed two weeks and felt like I was living in a Hemingway novel. It was very romantic, and very traumatic. Every night the rockets would come. It sounded like the Fourth of July.

The worst thing that happened to me was not in Saigon but when I was here in Dedham [Massachusetts]. Galen was going to come home on leave to be with us, and we were looking forward to his arrival in a week or two. Then one day the telephone rang, and it was a call from the State Department. A young man—I think he was young, he certainly was immature—asked, "Is this Mrs. Stone?" And I replied, "Yes, it is." And he said, "I'm afraid I've got bad news for you."

The children were right beside me, and they said I went absolutely white. It was a terrifying, silly thing for that young man to do. All he was going to tell me was that Galen would be delayed a day or two.

THE DUKE IN BAGHDAD

As in Africa and Vietnam, the Middle East experiences of Foreign Service spouses provided exhilarating, and often dangerous, options for service in a host country. The unrest caused by the mercurial shifts in Middle East politics, and the increasing importance of the region as the world's most important energy source, combined to create an atmosphere that at times proved surrealistic for these wives.

June Hamilton, spouse of the embassy's public affairs officer, was living in Baghdad in 1963. There had been three coup attempts between April and November, two unsuccessful. June Hamilton remembered a particularly gruesome episode during one of the earlier coups.

Because the fellaheen, the people, down in Basra were skeptical that this man they thought was so wonderful had been killed [Prime Minister Abdul Karem Kassim, who was overthrown by the Ba'ath Socialist Party], his dead body was pictured on Baghdad television and transmitted to Basra—and pretty much all over Iraq—to prove that he really was dead.

We had been told to tune in at six o'clock, and right after a cartoon of "Felix the Cat," Kassim appeared on the screen, sitting in a chair. He didn't look dead—he had a funny eye and always seemed to be staring anyway—but someone in uniform grabbed the body by the head and turned it so we could see for sure that it was Kassim.

In November, just before the Kennedy assassination, a fourth and ultimately successful bid, this time against the fledgling Ba'ath party dictatorship, was getting under way. At night fighting raged around the embassy, with tracer bullets arcing across the bridge that embassy personnel used to get to and from work. Embassy families were told to stay indoors and out of sight.

But the curfew was suspended for Americans and Iraqis alike when, as part of a months-long tour of Africa and Asia sponsored by the United States Information Service, Duke Ellington and his 15-piece band were in Baghdad for a series of free concerts of American jazz. "With the curfew lifted, we had to turn people away from the concerts every night," June Hamilton recalled in 1990. "We had listeners stacked against the walls of the 400-seat Al Khuld Hall."

June Hamilton wanted to give Ellington a special treat. "Most visitors to Baghdad wanted to see Babylon," she said, "but we took Duke Ellington to Ctesiphon, hoping to find the old sitar player." The traditional attraction at Ctesiphon is a ruined palace from the fourth century A.D. containing the largest unreinforced masonry arch in the world. June Hamilton took a chance on finding the "ancient blind man, who must have been 90 years old, who sat in the ruins playing on a single-string, bowed instrument," even though she had no assurance the aging musician would be there that particular day.

"Ellington fell in love with the little old man," she continued. "He was fascinated with the themes." Ellington himself told the same story in his memoirs.

Our manager, Al Celley, has a tape recorder on which he records the old man's performance. We have our pictures taken beside the arch, go over and have some coffee, smoke a water pipe. As we come back to the arch, Al Celley plays the tape of the blind musician's solo so he, the musician, can hear it, and scares [the old man] half to death. He knows that it is his playing, yet he realizes that he is not playing. We have the interpreter explain the magic to him.[9]

"Cultural visitors were supposed to be briefed in order to learn something about the country," June Hamilton recalled. And although Baghdad briefings traditionally were held in the USIS library, this time, because "these poor men [had] been on the road for months," she proposed, "Let's have a buffet brunch here at the house." But the Hamiltons had a piano, and the brunch briefing did not turn out as planned. Ellington and the band members attending learned little about Iraq, but the Hamiltons were treated to a private, impromptu concert; somebody was at the keyboard all morning and into the afternoon.

Although each of Ellington's Baghdad concerts was a standing-room-only success, the political situation in the capital caused some nerve-wracking moments. "We are told by the embassy that we should return to the hotel immediately after the concert, because there may be some trouble," Ellington wrote in his memoirs. "We rush back, and I bump my head as I scramble into the car. Late that night we hear a couple of planes flying around, approaching from different directions. We learn that they sent rockets or bombs into the front and back of some government official's house." Later, describing the Baghdad situation to the Beirut press, Ellington exclaimed, "Those cats were swinging, man!"[10]

THE SIX-DAY WAR

When the Six-Day War erupted on 5 June 1967—the result of prolonged skir-mishes and mounting tensions between Israel and the Arab nations—one Foreign Service spouse, Leila Wilson, literally had a foot in both camps. Her spouse, Evan M. Wilson, was consul general in Jerusalem, a city divided into Arab and Israeli sectors at the creation of Israel nearly 20 years before. Leila Wilson described those two camps and her involvement in the war in a 1987 interview.

Our principal consulate was housed above the official residence in the Israeli sector and was called the New City consulate. There was a branch office, the Old City consulate, in the Arab or Jordanian sector, where we had a small pied-à-terre. We would sleep there when we had an evening engagement in the Old City. As diplomats, we could cross freely between the two sectors, through the Mandelbaum Gate, which really wasn't a gate at all. It was a place where two roads crossed in the no-man's-land between Israel and Jordan, and it was closed to traffic at eight every evening.

Evan called our lives a tale of two cities. We had two of everything: two offices with two staffs, two residences, two cultures, and two sets of friends, who could never meet. We had only one cook, though. When we had a dinner in the Jordanian sector, I had to transport the meal from the Israeli sector. But the result was that we had good friends on both sides when the war began. The unfortunate result was that some in each group accused us of sympathizing with the enemy. And since Evan reported directly to Washing-ton and was independent of the embassies in Tel Aviv and Amman, each of them viewed us as suspect as well.

When the war broke out, there was heavy firing all around us. It seemed right outside our window, but the Marine guards said it wasn't that close. Nevertheless, shrapnel came in the windows of one room and damaged it, but no one was injured. I have never known why a group of "communicators"—perhaps six or eight of them, I don't really remember—suddenly arrived at the New City consulate at the onset of the war. They were in battle fatigues and boots and had brought equipment of some sort. Whether they were armed or not, I'm not prepared to say, but I suspect that they were there in case we needed to be rescued. They stayed at the residence until the war ended and left immediately afterward. During that time, we housed and fed

35 people. Evan says 30 in his book, but I was the one handling domestic arrangements.

When the UN failed to get a cease-fire, they moved their headquarters from Government House, in the demilitarized zone, into our bedroom, which fortunately was fairly large. We turned the UN people loose in there. They had a secretary with a typewriter, and Evan sent their communications to New York—to U Thant, who was then secretary-general of the UN—from the consulate command post upstairs. So, in addition to the communicators and the Marines, there was the UN crowd, plus a couple from the Hebrew School of Archaeology. She was a first-class typist and had been a secretary before her marriage. Evan swore her in at once, and she started to work. [At the height of the fighting, Evan Wilson reported in 1970 in *Jerusalem: Key to Peace*, the department "ordered the evacuation of the remaining three wives . . . but as I informed my superiors with some asperity, they were all working for me full time and, in any event, it would have been impossible to send them out with the heavy firing that was going on all around."][11]

Because there had been panic buying in the Israeli markets, I had bought extra food, and I suppose I was naive not to have bought potatoes and bread by the bushel. One day I got a couple of legs of lamb in the Arab sector, but at the time I didn't want to hoard or deprive the needy. It never occurred to me that we would be feeding 35 people. Normally, we were four, including the servants. When the Marine guard moved in, they did bring a great deal of their canned food, and that helped. No one, of course, had any idea how many days the fighting would last, and I feared that we were going to have to make what food we had last a long time.

We had turned our living room into a dormitory where people slept in shifts. There were people in every nook and cranny of the house. We were afraid the pipes might be damaged and leave us without water, so we filled two bathtubs. A third tub we left empty so it could be used by everyone. Some people were inclined to forget that there were 34 others waiting to bathe.

After the cease-fire, Evan didn't dare go to the Jordanian sector until he received absolute assurance that he would be allowed to return. He was in contact with the Old City office by intercom and knew that there had been heavy fighting. Some of the shells had exploded in the consulate, and there were gaping holes in the sides and roof. It was a miracle that everyone survived. There had been seven Americans and five of the local staff trapped there throughout the six days.

I was in the Old City for two days and visited as many friends and institutions as I could. After returning to the New City, I received a telephone call from one of my closest Israeli friends, who I had known for three years. I had not seen the current issue of *Newsweek*, which had arrived with unusual speed and reported that Evan was housing Arab snipers in the Old City consulate who had been shooting at the Israelis as they came through the Jordanian sector. An American reporter with the Israeli forces had wired the story to *Newsweek* without checking with Evan.

I returned my friend's call and was stunned by her reaction. "Just what do you think you're up to? What is Evan doing, keeping snipers in the Old City consulate? It's all in *Newsweek*." When I asked why she hadn't called Evan to verify the story as rumor, she snapped, "I don't think it needs verification."

This was the most shattering experience of my life. It was a terrible denouement to our time in Jerusalem. As Americans, we had tried to be evenhanded and trustworthy friends, to spread some truth about conditions on both sides, and in the end were considered nothing but liars.

IMAGES OF SURVIVAL

Marion Post Wolcott was known internationally for the photographs she took during the Great Depression. A member of a small group of photographers (including Dorothea Lange and Walker Evans) who worked for the federal Farm Security Administration from 1938 to 1942, she roamed the country, particularly the South, capturing on film startling images of the reality of American life in those years. One of her most famous photographs, of a stooped black man ascending an exterior stair (marked "Coloreds Only—Adm. 10 cents") to a movie house in Belzoni, Mississippi, is in the Museum of Modern Art in New York.

Largely unknown, but no less eventful, was her life after she left the government to marry Leon O. Wolcott, a widower with two children. After marriage, Marion confined her photography mainly to her family: she was busily bringing up Lee's children and having two of her own. However, when he accepted an AID appointment in 1959, Marion Post Wolcott had an opportunity for eight years to record on film her impressions of Iran, Pakistan, and Egypt. This record was virtually destroyed when the Six-Day War forced her evacuation from Cairo in the summer of 1967.

As her biographer, Paul Hendrickson, described it:

Anti-American feeling was rife in Egypt; once Marion got spat on as she walked to the embassy from her and Lee's apartment. They had been in Egypt about a year when the Six Day War broke out. On the night before their separate evacuations, husband and wife sat together on a sofa and destroyed slides and negatives. They knew the [Egyptian] government would confiscate them anyway and didn't wish to give them the pleasure. Marion and Lee got rid of about 200 images that night, which was not quite everything she had taken—or at least saved in [her] years overseas. It was not a lot, but it was an awful lot in another sense. She and Lee cut the pictures into little pieces, flared them brightly with matches. It was just something to do to ease the tensions. The next day she left the country ahead of her husband and flew to Athens. Lee was later evacuated to the Hotel Palestine in Alexandria.[12]

In a 1989 interview, Marion took up the story.

Marion Post Wolcott, probably 1939. *Trude Fleishman, Marion Post Wolcott Archive, Center for Creative Photography, Tucson, Arizona.*

I think I was too numb and too sad and too worried to really care about taking photographs once I got to the airport. I didn't have my camera with me anyhow, and the women and children who were being sent to Athens didn't have much time to wait there. I was so worried about Lee, not knowing really what was going to happen to him, because it was a very dangerous situation. We really didn't know whether we would see each other again. And we were still in love, so it was painful.

When we got to Athens, a lot of the women went to the Hilton, but I went to one of the smaller downtown hotels, partly because some of those women who had small children tried to take advantage of those of us without young ones. The mothers had been spoiled, I thought. They had had nannies, and they had almost forgotten how to cope with their own children, and they felt that the women who were alone should help them, in their trauma, take turns so the mothers could have more time off. They were envious of our freedom.

I thought that was presumptuous and said so, and wasn't particularly liked. Then several of the women who had been drinking too much in Cairo—and were perhaps on the verge of being alcoholic—did become alcoholics when they were separated from their husbands. I didn't like to have dinner with them, or even associate with them very much.

We could return immediately to the U.S. if we wanted to, or we could stay in Athens to wait for our husbands. Of course, I wanted to stay. I was interested in Athens—so much to see—but I tended to stay at the embassy just to find out what information they had. Mostly I just ate too much. But it was a learning experience. I felt that some of the women who were there alone were just glad to be free of their husbands and to be free of any responsibility to the embassy. Apparently, Cairo had been a nightmare for them: they seemed to resent having to tag along after their husbands, who had the interesting jobs.

A handful of Marion Post Wolcott's photographs from this overseas posting survived, among them, in Iran, a woman, completely cloaked in a black chador, buying a can of kerosene from a vendor with a tank truck bearing a "Standard Oil" insignia in Arabic.

8

THE WOMEN'S REVOLUTION

I had too many friends who were discombobulated, who felt they were nonpersons. They were neither flesh nor fish nor fowl within the framework of the embassies.

Lesley Dorman

Martha Caldwell, representing the Association of American Foreign Service Women, remembered that she felt a sense of history when she attended a lunchtime meeting of an ad hoc women's committee on 22 October 1970 in room 1207 of the State Department. The committee was a volunteer group of women officers, employees, and spouses concerned that the management reform studies of Deputy Undersecretary for Administration William B. Macomber, Jr.—detailed in the task force reports "Diplomacy for the '70s," released in July of that year—had virtually ignored women in drawing up a "management strategy for the '70s."[1]

Martha Caldwell was a volunteer spouse, the AAFSW representative at a meeting dominated by figures from the feminist movement in the foreign affairs agencies. Among them was Mary S. Olmsted, a high-ranking Foreign Service officer later appointed ambassador to New Guinea. Another attendee was Alison Palmer, who would initiate—and 14 years later win—a class action suit that charged the State Department with sex discrimination. Also present was Mildred Marcy from USIS, a friend of William Macomber who had facilitated the group's earlier meetings with the then-undersecretary. Although AAFSW was a decade old, Martha Caldwell was listed on the agenda as "representing AAFSW, formerly the Wives' Association."

"The group's recommendations," Martha recalled, "included abolition of any discrimination against women in a number of areas: recruitment, promotion, training, and career assignments, and an end to any discriminatory practice against married women or those who marry while in the service."[2] Martha Caldwell had resigned from the Foreign Service Auxiliary when she married Robert Caldwell in 1945. Four decades later, she remembered:

The group had also advocated greater training and employment opportunities for spouses and, among other issues, relaxing the regulation that a spouse had to have a power of attorney from her husband to cash a check with an embassy or consulate cashier! My report gave no indication of how acrimonious the meeting was. A number of the women were fiercely determined to take a stand for equality, others were considerably more moderate in their expectations.

The ad hoc committee was in the happy position of being wanted by all three organizations represented at the meeting: AAFSW, American Foreign Service Association [AFSA], and the American Federation of Government Employees [AFGE]. But the committee later voted to become the Women's Action Organization [WAO], with Mary Olmsted as president. Mary wrote AAFSW President Naomi Mathews that WAO would be more effective as an independent group yet suggested that the two organizations work together on mutual concerns. Any number of spouses felt—quite rightly, I believe—that their role was being diminished by WAO actions, and I believe there was no further formal communication between the two groups for several years.

Yet WAO and the Secretary's Open Forum panel were the principal advocates of the 1972 "Policy on Wives of Foreign Services Employees," which was drafted, after a series of debates by the 35 participants in the panel, by a committee of midlevel male Foreign Service officers and one spouse and went into effect without any official input from AAFSW, the organization that represented hundreds of women affected by it.

In spite of a reluctance on the part of "traditional" spouses, not to mention the Department of State, to move ahead with the times, women's issues dominated the decade for Foreign Service spouses. In addition to the 1972 "Policy on Wives," or the "1972 directive," as it is usually called, the decade witnessed the founding of the Family Liaison Office (FLO) in the State Department and the subsequent establishment of community liaison offices in missions abroad, development of a mental health program and educational counseling at State, and increased employment opportunities for spouses.

Yet how much really changed in the day-to-day lives of spouses at home and abroad when the "Policy on Wives" declared spouses to be independent individuals with no responsibility to the foreign affairs agencies? "Everything changed, yet nothing changed," declared the late Hope Meyers, who followed spouse issues at State for 17 years until her death in 1991.

Hope Meyers observed that the predictions of senior officials—that spouses, especially those of high-ranking officers, would continue to carry on the traditional work of diplomacy—were correct. None of the agencies, however, anticipated the change in spouse attitude once recognition was removed. Midlevel and senior spouses felt they had been "cast adrift"; some remained frustrated and bitter decades after their perceived rejection. The policy had a negative impact on younger spouses as well. In spite of a previous joint State/AID/USIA message on 11 August 1971 that mandated employment opportunities for dependents— the first significant policy change toward women in the Foreign Service—that mandate remained a "paper policy." [3] Young spouses often found themselves with nothing to do, a situation that created severe consequences for post morale.

Archaic as it may seem, recognition as part of the shadow cast by an officer during his Foreign Service career was a sufficient recompense for the majority of spouses in 1972. In his 1975 book The Angel's Game, William B. Macomber, Jr., who as deputy undersecretary for administration was responsible for implementing the "Policy on Wives," declared spouse recognition to be a casualty of the 1972 directive. Macomber "regretted" this lack of recognition but maintained that spouse participation was "a private matter between husband and wife, not an official matter between employer and wife." [4]

THE 1972 DIRECTIVE:
"THE DAY THEY FIRED THE WIVES"

Spouse issues, and women's issues as a whole, were not addressed in Deputy Undersecretary Macomber's early "Diplomacy in the '70s" reports. This omission was pointed out loudly to Macomber by the Women's Action Organization. As far as spouses were concerned, he responded in 1971 by instructing Dorothy Stansbury, director of the Family Workshop at the Foreign Service Institute, to convene a task force to address spouse issues. Stansbury, an ardent feminist, collected a sympathetic group to draw up guidelines and then, in a Machiavellian move, released them to the department, surely anticipating the furor that would follow.[5]

Under her direction, 27 women from the foreign affairs agencies and the Defense Department—senior, midlevel, and junior wives—met and drafted "Representational Responsibilities: Guidelines for Foreign Service Wives at Posts Abroad" (1971). None of the women selected was a recognized spokesperson for either traditional or feminist spouse groups.

The guidelines, also released as Management Reform Bulletin No. 20, made no proposal for reform but rather reiterated the status of the spouse; the bulletin circulated in the State Department without the consent of the drafters. The debate unleashed by the bulletin sparked the chain of events that led to the release of the "Policy on Wives," which came in an official announcement in January 1972 by Macomber, who declared, "We have . . . addressed the problem of a bill of rights for the spouses and dependents of Foreign Service employees."[6]

While giving token recognition to women's rights, the new policy spelled out not what a Foreign Service wife is, but what she is not: "The wife of a Foreign Service employee who has accompanied her husband to a foreign post is a private individual; she is not a government employee." It added that "the Foreign Service has no right to levy any duties upon her" and "the U.S. Government has no right to insist that a wife assume representational burdens." Few spouses of employees entering the service since 1972 have read the directive, which was circulated in the State Department and at posts abroad when it was issued but not officially since then.

What the directive did not do was recognize that the traditional duties of diplomacy continued and that spouses, now unrecognized and, as always, uncompensated, would continue to perform them. But in several ways the new policy was an improvement. It replaced the unofficial code of the "old" Foreign Service, in which "volunteerism" was officially enforced and wives were held in a rigid hierarchy based on the ranks of their mates.

The 1972 directive remained official policy in spite of the controversy sur-
rounding its origins and the lively debate it periodically provoked into the 1990s.
It resolved one set of problems for spouses, only to create another. Essentially, it
disenfranchised spouses, casting them into a netherworld of nonrecognition, while
making no provision for the representational responsibilities that remained the
sine qua non of diplomacy.

In retrospect, "the directive was probably 'trendy,'" recalled William Z. Slany,
State Department historian, in a 1992 interview. "There was an assumption that
the whole country had suddenly adopted a whole new lifestyle, which wasn't the
case."

In a 1974 interview for Radcliffe College, former Foreign Service Officer
Richard L. Williamson, chairman of the policy drafting committee, opined that,
given the opportunity, the majority of wives in 1972 would have vetoed the
policy.[7] "But," Williamson said, "[the committee members were] all grinning
like Cheshire cats. There were [previously] bizarre instances, where wives had to
do the shopping for an ambassador's wife, or where they were treated more as
servants than guests at social functions. But mostly what we were worried about
was the quasi-legal basis on which any [spouse] participation rested." The feminist
Carol Pardon, whose withering attack on Management Reform Bulletin No. 20
had appeared in the September 1971 Foreign Service Journal, was the only spouse
on the drafting committee.[8] Another principal architect of the directive was
William B. Milam, who went on to become American ambassador to Bangladesh
in the early 1990s. In private correspondence, Milam recalled that "the '72 Policy
is one of the things I have been connected with in the service of which I am most
proud."

What I wanted to do was to ensure that the system would permit—provide
the option for—a spouse to be an independent person when accompanying
her Foreign Service spouse abroad, without penalty to the employee. Frankly,
for some of us, if our spouses did not have the option, we did not have the
option of remaining in the Foreign Service.

Yet it did not occur to us in 1972 that the problem was much more societal
and universal, so that changing the mores of the U.S. Foreign Service was
only a small first step. Many parts of the world have yet to accept (and may
never accept) that spouses can be private and independent. We, the drafters
of that new policy, did not understand the different and complex pressures
on spouses at more senior levels. . . .

In any case, my spouse had found it impossible to totally avoid being a
public figure, though I believe that she maintains a lot of independence. She
receives no official recognition for any of [her public activities], and this is a

damned shame. I believe that the U.S. government should find a way to compensate spouses for public activities.[9]

Some aspects of the new policy were positive, most notably, the State Department's official acknowledgment of the presence of the spouse. And the department continued to recognize spouses in many other ways—diplomatic and official passports, travel fare, housing and other allowances predicated on spousal presence at post, language and other training, medical care, crisis evacuation, employment at post, pension rights for divorced spouses, and more. None of these benefits, however, resulted from the directive. And the Foreign Service continued to function most effectively when family members, particularly spouses, pitched in to help.[10]

But the absurdity of the new policy when measured against the real world demands of diplomatic life soon appeared. Kristie Miller, who had accompanied Alice Roosevelt Longworth to Japan and in 1973 had herself become a Foreign Service spouse, told an anecdote in a 1989 interview in which policy and reality met head to head.

In 1973 we were transferred to Caracas. Even though I had majored in Spanish, we had been in the Middle East, and I had studied and spoken Arabic. My Spanish just wouldn't come out when we first got to post.

I needed work papers right away to teach in the International School—I always found it incredibly stressful to get your job the minute you hit the post—but when I asked if one of the secretaries could go with me to the ministry of labor, I was told, "Well, you don't work for the embassy." So I said, "All right, I'll get the papers myself."

A few months later, when I was called to cook for the embassy Christmas party, I said, "Well, I don't work for the embassy. But my husband does, and he makes a dynamite meatball. Ask him." The cook was going to make them in any event, but I was just making a point. I must say, my [former] husband was very supportive. He got on the telephone to talk to his boss's wife about meatballs!

The next day at school, every kid in my high school class knew that I had refused to make meatballs. It was obvious that not everybody had absorbed the '72 directive.

The generational difference in spouse attitudes toward the 1972 directive is clearly demonstrated in the views of Stephanie Kinney, who entered the service

Bill and Kristie Miller Twaddell on vacation in Ecuador, February 1975. *Lynn Magruder, courtesy of Kristie Miller.*

as a spouse in 1971 and later became a Foreign Service officer, and Marlen Neumann, whose service experience was as wife of the ambassador to Afghanistan and Morocco.

Stephanie Kinney's experiences in the early 1970s summed up the problem for newly unrecognized spouses. "Either he chooses between his career and me, or I have to choose between something for me in my life and him, or we have to change the Foreign Service," she said in a 1992 interview. "Of the three options, the last one seemed preferable!"

I took the Foreign Service exam in October. I was elated some months later to be told that I had passed. I took the oral exam and was thrilled to death to learn that I would be the second married woman to be admitted into the service. So I was thrilled, but I had to wait on the list the same as everybody else. Being "a water lily floating on the sea of culture," I had been interested in USIA and thought it would be a natural métier for me. But President Nixon at that time, having little faith in the younger generation, put a freeze on hiring for junior officers. This was the period of Vietnam, and Nixon must have figured he didn't need any more rabble-rousers in the government than he already had. So I accompanied Douglas to Mexico, which was his first assignment, and kept myself busy down there.

I won't go into all the details, but I had to leave Mexico and reenter as a ordinary citizen to take the job I was offered. All the rigmarole and frustration and, to my mind, foolishness, that I had to go through to teach in a local school and to earn $5,000 a year—as opposed to the $13–15,000 that I would have been earning for the equivalent work in the United States—was hardly worth the effort. I came back thinking, "This is really crazy." So I took my frustration and fury at the system and marched myself off to Dorothy Stansbury's wives' seminar at FSI. And I figured I'd just go hang out there and see if I could meet people who might be interested in the same thing I was.

This would have been in the summer of 1973. The directive had come out in 1972. The fact that it had come out was what made it possible for the embassy to support my efforts to work in Mexico. And so the '72 directive was very important for me in an indirect kind of way.

LOGICAL IN WASHINGTON, UNWORKABLE ABROAD

When her husband, Robert G. Neumann, was appointed as noncareer ambassador to Afghanistan in the autumn of 1966, Marlen Neumann brought a wealth of experience to her role: world traveler, teacher, editor, linguist, and poet. As president of the League of Women Voters in Los Angeles, California, and a member of Governor Pat Brown's commission to investigate the 1965 Watts riots in Los Angeles—the only woman among the eight members—Marlen Neumann had had wide experience as a volunteer civic leader.

On her arrival in Kabul, Marlen transferred that expertise to her new diplomatic life. "I felt an ambassador's wife was a good two-way communications point," she remembered.

She should know what is happening in the host country so she can help others find their place. She can also help by knowing what the American community can contribute to the host country. With that in mind, I organized a Women's Advisory Council, which was made up of the wife of the head of each section at the embassy (political, economic, administrative, etc.), plus the USIS, AID, Peace Corps, and CARE women. Counting a few mothers and aunts and the children [of officials assigned to Kabul], there were about a thousand Americans in Afghanistan. I tried to reach all of the women.

Now this worked beautifully as long as we had the old system of senior and junior wives. But when the '72 directive came out, all of a sudden there weren't any more senior wives. Each group of women had to get together to decide who would represent them on the Women's Advisory Council. Later I discovered that it had become a plum among the American women to be on my advisory council. I didn't think of it that way, felt the council was no longer as useful, and I really didn't use it the last year I was there.

That's when my civic experience came in very handy. I never had any hierarchical authority as a leader in civic affairs. I had always had to network and compromise with people, get along with them, and find out what each was interested in and willing to contribute. So when the directive, the new system, descended on us, it wasn't too difficult for me. I just had to shift gears.

When younger, postdirective wives arrived in Kabul, some of them were apparently resentful of the organization. But after being there for a while, most of them joined in. We were so remote, so isolated, there wasn't much else for them to do. When Robert was assigned as ambassador to Morocco, my reputation had preceded me back to Washington, and I was very kindly and gently informed in the department that Rabat was different from Kabul. "Don't organize the women when you get to Morocco."

I had not been in Rabat very long when some embassy wives came to me. They lacked intellectual stimulation and wanted something to do. I suggested that we try something from my League of Women Voters days, when we had "Know Your Town" studies. We organized a "Know Your Embassy" study with, for example, an AID wife finding out what the Peace Corps did, and the Peace Corps finding out what the political section did, and, as a result, finding out about our husbands' various jobs.

There has to be a leader at a mission abroad, and what the leader or what his wife does is like dropping a pebble into a pool. The ripples go out. And if there is an ambassador's wife who doesn't drop any pebbles in any pool and there aren't any ripples, then everybody is at loose ends. It then devolves on the deputy chief of mission's wife to fill in, but she never has quite the authority. And sometimes the deputy chief of mission isn't married, or his wife isn't there, or the deputy chief of mission is a woman who cannot be expected to fill two roles, and it becomes very difficult for the wives of less senior officials at post. Policies made in Washington do not always work at posts abroad.

In spite of the efforts of women like Marlen Neumann, morale in American communities abroad continued to ebb, and nowhere more than in Kabul. Three years after her departure, the embassy in Kabul sent an unclassified cable to the department on 8 June 1976 stating that "dependent spouses' morale and overall productivity and happiness of Foreign Service couples can be adversely affected when the spouse 'has nothing useful to do.'" The cable noted that the embassy was employing spouses on an hourly basis in part-time jobs and requested information on spouse employment programs at other posts where "the occupation of spouses has been dealt with." Suicide, nervous breakdowns, rampant alcoholism at post, and resort to the drugs readily available in the streets of Kabul showed that post morale had bottomed out. In 1979 Ambassador Adolph (Spike) Dubs was assassinated in a violent coup d'état that installed a pro-left regime.

The steady erosion of morale in Afghanistan, and in many other posts abroad, pointed to a need that was well recognized among spouses in Washington, if not by the higher echelons of State Department management. In March 1977 the Forum Committee of the Association of American Foreign Service Women issued a report, "The Concerns of Foreign Service Spouses and Families," that summa-

rized the results of a survey of 9,000 spouses and correctly identified as its most important recommendation the reestablishment of "a new relationship between the Department of State and the spouses of Foreign Service employees, based on a recognition of mutual responsibilities." [11] *The Forum Committee's research indicated an urgent need for psychological counseling for families both at home and abroad, whether precipitated by political crises resulting in evacuation or just the normal rotation of assignments.*

One spouse, in a late 1980s interview, revealed a personal example of why an organized program by the State Department to address the mental health of spouses and dependents was desperately needed.

We came back to the United States in 1966 and bought our first house, which was very thrilling to me. It was in McLean, very nice, and it had three bathrooms. The children went to public schools. And then the drug years started, the hippie years, the long-haired years—I think maybe our sons were the first longhairs in Virginia. They insisted on having long hair, which caused all sorts of trouble in the schools because people were against it. But the boys wanted to be different—what they thought was "different" in those days.

So we had sort of hard years with the teenagers—they were all teenagers by then, except the youngest, who was in grade school and got along fine. In 1968 we had another child while we were in McLean, so then we had five children. We all lived a suburban life, affected by frequent deaths in our neighborhood from overdoses and things like that, several suicides. It was really a sick time in the U.S. Our sons running off to concerts in Baltimore, hitchhiking in rain in the wintertime, and at night doing dangerous things. Everybody was a little out of control. They were good years for my husband's career, but not so good in other ways. We had Vietnam, and the assassinations of Martin Luther King and Robert Kennedy. The first time the baby left the house was to protest at the National Rifle Association. I just put him in his carriage and took him along.

Then we went to Istanbul, where the two older boys were in school in Ankara—boarding school, because the local school didn't have grades above elementary. Our daughter was a freshman in college. It was a considerable change to suddenly have the family fragmented. The boys were very wild, running back and forth on ferries and on buses, just having a good time. It was a year of drugs and people being caught with drugs. All these kids were running around in what we called "the bowl" at Robert College, smoking hashish, and they didn't care if they were caught or not. We were just lucky they got away with it—that was their attitude, they weren't afraid or worried about anything. I considered it rather unthoughtful.

Then the school in Ankara was disbanded, and for the next six months the boys had to go to Karamursel, a Turkish naval base across the Sea of Marmara where some Americans were stationed. They could come back and forth on weekends by ferry. Everybody was smoking hashish. They didn't seem to realize, or care, that their father would probably lose his job if they were caught. They were just thinking about themselves. . . . They could see that people were getting thrown in jail for a long time for very minor offenses—what they considered very minor offenses. The situation ultimately resolved itself because they just never got caught. We were lucky.

THE CIRCLE WIDENS

Foreign service cohesiveness continued to erode during the 1970s, both in Washington, D.C., and at posts abroad. The 1972 directive was only a part of the cause. At home, demographics were another factor, as they had been since World War II. Earlier Foreign Service families had tended to know one another socially, and personally, and had lived in exclusive neighborhoods in the District of Columbia: around fashionable Sheridan Circle, in mansions on Woodland Drive and on Meridian Hill's Crescent Place, and later in restored Georgetown and in nearby suburban Chevy Chase, Maryland, and McLean, Virginia.

As the service became more reflective of America's democratic society, the once easy problem of communication among spouses became more difficult. By the 1970s Foreign Service families were spread out in the suburbs; in the 1990s they were scattered still further afield in exurban Washington. Foreign Service salaries had not kept pace with the cost of housing, and in a society in which the majority of women worked, one-income Foreign Service couples were searching for housing in a real estate market dominated by two-income families.

Spouse employment also affected Foreign Service cohesiveness. Women's rising expectations—and economic needs—created demands for increased spouse employment opportunities and for expanded communication between the now disenfranchised spouse and the State Department. The department continued to regard spouses as a faceless monolith. But nowhere were their diverse talents—both inherent and acquired—more evident than in the groups that lobbied for jobs, a spouse representative at the State Department, and solutions to a host of spouse concerns that surfaced at this time. The three principal groups involved in these negotiations were the Women's Action Organization; the Research Committee on Spouses, which incorporated a detailed proposal for a spouse skills bank and was later taken over by a third group, the Forum Committee of the Association of American Foreign Service Women.

THE BROADER CONTEXT: AAFSW FORUM

The broad impetus for changing the relationship between Foreign Service spouses and the State Department drew its inspiration from within the ranks of the Forum Committee of the Association of American Foreign Service Women. The organization's 1977 report set the agenda for a discussion that has continued into the 1990s. The report addressed compensation and recognition of spouses for both representational responsibilities and contributions to mission effectiveness; the lack of such support had been a source of much rancor to many spouses in the years since adoption of the 1972 directive. The report's longest recommendation called for establishment of the Family Liaison Office.

Jean Vance remembered this gestation period in interviews conducted during the winter of 1990–91.

Fifteen years ago, being chairman of the Forum Committee was considered a revolutionary role. I was the second vice president of AAFSW, and I was really brought along by the young women who wanted changes. They were the ones who persuaded me to fight for what they wanted. I knew they were right, because of my experience in the service, and I felt the same way they did about many of their concerns. In 1976, when we formed the Forum Committee, it was quite an upheaval for AAFSW. The board was very traditional and was reluctant to finance our idea, but we prevailed. I chose my committee from the young women who were very desirous of having changes made. And I listened to them very carefully, and then we went on from there.

We had five committees: family life, modern Foreign Service wife, orientation, reentry to Washington, and women in transition. The transitional woman's husband was about to retire, or she was getting a divorce, or she had recently become a widow.

We had a big meeting with tremendous attendance. And the women were very bitter. They stood up and spoke out, many for the first time, about the injustices which had occurred during their husbands' careers. One woman after another popped up to share her ideas. There were women who had been very happy in the Foreign Service and had nothing to complain about and they also spoke. One universal complaint was that the department gave information to the husbands which wasn't necessarily passed on to the wives. Women were especially interested in the available medical facilities, which was very important because they were responsible for family health.

They wanted better language training, and child care facilities so they could attend classes at the Foreign Service Institute. They wanted to attend the area studies courses, which were available only to employees and not to family members. They wanted greater allowances for children to travel to post from schools in the United States. They felt they went to too many parties and neglected their children as a result. The career women wanted jobs and bilateral work agreements with many different countries. They felt they would be more effective if they were working—preferably in their own fields—where they would meet host country nationals in the business or academic world instead of just traveling the social circuit.

We sent 9,000 questionnaires based on these concerns to women all over the world, and we got an overwhelming response. Then we drafted the Forum report. First we stated the problems, and then we made recommendations, based on the five committees' findings. First, we recommended that a new relationship be established between the Department of State and the spouses of Foreign Service employees, based on recognition of mutual responsibilities. The second recommendation was to create a family liaison office. There were 11 [recommendations] in all. The most difficult to cope with—one that has not been done today—was to review and clarify representational responsibilities and explore ways to compensate spouses for their work and expenses.

We presented the Forum report to Secretary Vance in March 1977. It took us exactly six months.

Lesley Dorman, the longtime president of AAFSW, deserved enormous credit for marshaling her forces, as well as keeping lines of communication open between these women and the State Department. In a 1987 interview, she remembered:

The first person we went to see was the director-general, Ambassador Carol [C.] Laise. She was extremely nice, but we exercised caution at every turn. We did everything most professionally. We always had a member of the particular "labor union" along—in Laise's case, someone from AFSA, which represents State. We did the same thing for USIA and AID. We covered our tracks from stem to stern.

AAFSW is a nonprofit, autonomous organization, separate from State, and in my opinion, therein lies its strength. Eventually, we became lobbyists—indeed, we did pay our dues to do that—and as a result we have a very sound reputation on the Hill, partly because of the work we did lobbying for FLO [Family Liaison Office].

I always took members of the Forum steering committee, called "the

Lesley Dorman, president of AAFSW, and Carol C. Laise, director-general of the Foreign Service, meet to discuss AAFSW projects, 1977. *Courtesy of AAFSW.*

group," with me to meetings. The group did change along the road, as people were posted overseas, but Jean Vance and I remained in place. Before we met with Ambassador Laise, we had presented the Forum report to Henry Kissinger, then secretary of state, and to Lawrence Eagleburger, who was in the department at that time, and to the directors of USIS and AID.

As a nonprofit, we have to watch our budget. Therefore, I asked Ambassador Laise if she would be willing to have the department send copies of the Forum report to posts, with a mandatory telegram requesting that meetings be held at post to discuss the report, which hopefully everyone would have

Secretary of State Cyrus R. Vance cuts the ribbon to open the Family Liaison Office, with Janet Lloyd, first director of FLO, March 1978. *Robert E. Kaiser, U.S. Department of State, courtesy of Family Liaison Office.*

been given an opportunity to read. The group felt that it was necessary to substantiate the findings of the report, and Laise did agree to have it sent abroad with a covering cable signed, of course, by the secretary of state, who by that time was Cyrus Vance. Then we went to see the undersecretary for management, Ben[jamin H.] Read, and then Secretary Vance. Meanwhile, I had talked to Gay Vance and apprised her of what we were doing, because she had agreed to be AAFSW's honorary president, which was customary for the wife of the secretary of state. She attended our lengthy meeting with the secretary, as did Carol Laise and, of course, the members of the group. The secretary agreed that we had a very wise plan.

Then I briefed the secretary again, which was a terrifying experience because the room was packed with his full team. I recall at the briefing that Warren Christopher [deputy secretary of state] said, "Lesley, go to the Hill." I responded, "I've been to the Hill." He replied, "Lesley, go back to the Hill."

From there, we chose the office space for the FLO, and then Jean Vance and I sat on a panel to choose the director of FLO. We went through a great number of résumés, and from those we initially interviewed ten candidates.

They were then winnowed to five, and then USIS and AID members were brought onto the panel. I had pointed out to Ben Read, "They are, after all, part of the foreign affairs community." It was all very fair, and Janet Lloyd was chosen as first director of FLO.

As editor of the AAFSW News from 1977 to 1978, Margaret Sullivan gave a voice to the spouse revolution. She gathered and disseminated news by monitoring committee meetings and by reporting the Forum Committee's progress.

THE SKILLS BANK SAGA

Another of the players in this drama was Cynthia Chard, a determined young woman—she had just turned 30—who was ahead of her time and willing to take the risk of going public to promote an idea. In November 1976, with Women's Action Organization support, Chard went solo to Congress to seek authorization for a spouse skills bank in the department.[12] *She was the first to grasp the potential of lobbying Capitol Hill for legislation that addressed spouse problems.*

Chard worked with Senators George McGovern (D-S. Dak.) and Joseph R. Biden, Jr. (D-Del.) of the Senate Foreign Relations Committee for passage of Public Law 95–105, which was congressional authorization for the department to use appropriated—public—funds on nonemployee spouses, without which the Family Liaison Office could not have been established. President Jimmy Carter signed the bill on 17 August 1977. For their efforts, Senators McGovern and Biden and Cynthia Chard received WAO's Marilla Marks Young Ricker Honor Award for contributing the most to the advancement of women in the foreign affairs community.[13]

Working from the dining room of her renovated Capitol Hill town house, Chard devised and, with the help of volunteer supporters, mailed 4,672 questionnaires to spouses of State Department employees, 2,040 to AID spouses, and 1,589 to USIS spouses. The response was enthusiastic and, in fact, statistically exceptional. Chard took the results to the press. On 1 October 1976, an op-ed piece in the Washington Star editorialized, "It is a crucial first step towards utilization of human resources at all U.S. missions and possibly in Washington."[14] *Chard earlier had written a proposal asking the State Department to establish and fund a spouse skills inventory. An article in the October 1977 State Department Newsletter (now State magazine) reported: "The Senators noting the resistance of State to the legislation added a clause requiring the Secretary of State to report to Congress on his implementation. Secretary Vance tasked 'the director general, the information systems office, and the deputy undersecretary for management to meet with Cynthia Chard as soon as possible to develop a proposal for the institutionalization and implementation of the Skills/Talent Bank.'"*

Cynthia Chard recalled, "We began lengthy negotiations for updating and computerizing the skills bank in September 1977. The department even reported to Congress that they were going to offer me a contract."

But after unproductive negotiations with State, I offered to donate my files to the Family Liaison Office. In March 1978 I received a letter from Janet Lloyd, director of the newly established Family Liaison Office, dictating the conditions for acceptance of my files, stating that FLO would develop its own skills bank and noting that mine was by then out of date. Rather than permitting me to donate my files [there is a State Department regulation that prohibits donation of one's time to the U.S. government], State insisted I receive $3,000, to which I responded in writing that this sum would be used to defray some of the costs of operating the bank and was in no way to be equated with the value of the spouses' skills or the work involved in designing and operating the skills/talent bank.

As I look back on it all, the highlights were working with the Senate Foreign Relations Committee and succeeding in "spearheading the quiet revolution that shook the State Department to its core." [15] Negotiations with the department were difficult. Many lacked vision, and most were distrustful of my access to Congress.

After success in the private sector and coordinating the secretary of commerce's trade investment mission to Algeria, Cynthia Chard was offered a Commerce Department Foreign Service reserve officer appointment, for which she earned a Sustained Superior Performance Award in 1985.

GOING UPSTAIRS: A TACTICAL VIEW

While Jean Vance and Lesley Dorman at AAFSW were producing the report that led to the creation of the FLO, and Cynthia Chard was building the first spouse skills bank, Stephanie Kinney finally achieved her goal of joining the Foreign Service and, as a representative both of dependent spouses and of the State Department, succeeded in bringing the Forum report to the secretary of state's attention.

When Douglas was assigned to the department in 1976, I went to Dorothy Stansbury at the Family Workshop at the Foreign Service Institute, and that was the beginning of all the events that led to creating the Family Liaison Office. I cried on Dorothy's shoulder, said how awful I thought the spouse situation was. And she directed me to Hope Meyers, who was, I think, touched by my fervor and energy and the younger generation coming on.

I began meeting in what became known as the Research Committee on Spouses. We would meet every Tuesday in the department, initially to talk about all the things that we didn't like, and then to start identifying things that we could do to make a change. We got information from the director-general, we learned as much about management as we could. We talked about the problems that resulted from taking away the old structure without putting anything in its place.

Our frustration derived largely from the fact that, although we had been declared "private persons" by the 1972 directive, there was nothing private about our lives at all. Our lives were totally circumscribed by our husbands' professions and their vagabond existence, dragging us from pillar to post with no chance of career continuity, pay, or anything else. We decided that there was one thing worse than being an adjunct to your husband: it was being a nonperson; we didn't officially exist. At least before, you existed. You were recognized in officer evaluation reports. There was a certain responsibility owed to you because, although you weren't paid, it was recognized that you did certain work and therefore the department dealt with you.

I felt at the time that it was the six of us in the research committee against the world. There was a growing sense of empowerment by gathering information and being together. Also, [as I was pregnant], a wonderful irony about being an impending mother starting this little nascent revolution.

A questionnaire that Cynthia Chard and I did was one of the most seminal acts of the Research Committee on Spouses. It was a very unscientific questionnaire, about two pages long, with considerable space after each question. It was distributed to as many male officers as we could find in the department. We got a tremendous response back, about 33 percent, which is very high for a questionnaire like this. Twenty-five percent of the respondents indicated that the working status of their wife would influence their next assignment. And at that point, I said, "Aha, this is our handle. This is not a women's issue. This is not a malcontent's problem. This is a management concern." And from that point on, we started attacking the issue as a management issue.

We collated the information and sent it in a small report to Carol Laise, who was director-general at that time. Periodically, I was disappointed because Carol didn't seem to give us the support that we thought we deserved. But we kept at it. In that same time frame, Cynthia Chard also put together a spouse skills/talent bank. I spent many afternoons at Cynthia's house addressing thousands of those forms to send out.

The ironic thing was that, in the midst of all of this, I had taken the Foreign Service exam again in 1975, passed, took the orals, passed, and became an FSO [Foreign Service officer] in my own right in September of 1976. The first year I was in the service, I spent more time promoting and helping direct the "revolution" than I did working as a Foreign Service officer.

I started working from inside the service; now I was able to provide the link between the outsiders and the insiders. Sometime later I was "interviewed" at a luncheon at the Foreign Service Club and later told that the director-general wanted me to come up and "solve the spouse problem," on which I was known to have just a few opinions.

This meant working with Carol Laise, who initially had not been receptive to the spouse issues. But my relationship with her was very respectful because, one, she was dealing with the issue, and two, she had given me an opportunity to help address it. Politics mattered, and politics had made addressing the issue unavoidable. What Carol really wanted to do was some larger, serious managerial and organizational reform within the Department of State. She couldn't make much progress in that, but what she could do was address the spouse problem.

There were problems because the position I was supposed to have was an FSO-2, and I was an FSO-7. But I became part of a small unit called "policy coordination." The four of us were Carol's policy people for the management reforms that she was trying to undertake.

We were able to make the most progress in the spouse area, my field. I was asked to write Secretary Cyrus Vance's response to the Forum report, since I had had a large hand in developing the recommendations for it. There was no question as to what the secretary's response was going to be! He would establish the Family Liaison Office. The question then became, "How are we going to get the memo cleared and onto the secretary's desk?" And therein lies an interesting story about the importance of networking and the power of women.

Once I was assigned to the director-general's office. I spent most of my time acting as liaison between the external spouse organizations and militants and internal management, trying to keep confrontation to a minimum and incremental progress forward maximized. Meeting, networking, conversations, cocktail parties, talking to the right person, planting the idea, seeing it come back to you, were all part of the process.

I would often see something "management" was going to need two or three weeks hence and have a conversation with the right spouse leader so that she would come up with the idea about the time we needed it. I spent a lot of time suggesting or planting ideas about what was needed next.

When President Jimmy Carter was elected, Jean Newsom called me. She was the wife of the former undersecretary for political affairs, David Newsom. She was a friend of my husband's parents and had been interested in what I was doing and supportive of the spouse movement. And she invited me to lunch with some of her friends, Gay Vance—Mrs. Cyrus Vance—among them.

The basic idea was that the wives of senior officials needed a good project, and the Forum report filled the bill. And so we would meet every Thursday in the secretary's conference room upstairs. We would bring a bag lunch, and we would invite speakers from both sides of the issue. All was very decorous, but very purposeful. I was the youngest one in the group and the only one who was an official of the department. Once again, I was serving as a link between the official and the unofficial.

When the secretary's response to the Forum report was ready—the memo which I had drafted recommending the establishment of the Family Liaison Office and a number of other things—I announced with great glee that the memo was ready to go upstairs [to the secretary's office on the seventh floor of the State Department], but we were expecting problems because it was well known that the administrative and executive officers in the department did not welcome the prospect of the FLO. They had opposed us all the way. There were one or two enlightened ones, but as a group, the administrative officers of the Foreign Service were not enthusiastic about what we were proposing: a Family Liaison Office to be run by spouses with a direct link to senior management. They correctly foresaw that this would eventually result in similar offices in embassies overseas.

I was worried about the memo getting through because I knew it had to have all sorts of clearances from the executive directors. I expected them to hold it up, which had begun to happen. Mrs. Vance wanted to know, "When is Cy going to get it?" And I said, "Well, I don't know. We're having some trouble with clearances from the executive directors, but it'll get there eventually." And she said, "Stephanie, you do have an extra copy of it, don't you?" And I said, "I suppose that could be arranged." And she said, "I think Cy would be very interested in reading this tonight." So she took it home and tucked it under his pillow. And within 24 hours, we had the secretary's blessing.

9

HELD HOSTAGE

Our society has changed, and if we want to continue to have the best and the brightest as part of the Foreign Service, then it has to reflect the changes that exist in society as a whole. . . . All of the issues that face the United States also face the Foreign Service people. What we put up with 20 years ago wouldn't be understood today.

Marlene Eagleburger

For spouses overseas in the Foreign Service, three concerns overshadowed the 1980s: the threat of terrorism, of being held hostage; the nagging sense that Washington assignments were the fast track to promotion; and the narrowed window to career advancement imposed by the Foreign Service Act of 1980. Certainly, the 444-day captivity of American hostages in Tehran, beginning 4 November 1979, did nothing to ease the fears of spouses scattered at posts throughout an increasingly volatile world.

Whether these beliefs were true or not was, and still is, debated. But the perception was growing in the 1980s Foreign Service that careers were made in Washington, D.C., not abroad. Instead of seeking assignment overseas, officers jockeyed for good jobs in the foreign affairs agencies at home. Some of this must be attributed to the women's movement and the reluctance of spouses to disrupt their career paths, to go abroad without a job, or to move their families abroad in an uncertain world. During this period, officers extended their stays in the United States to the limits, often requesting exceptions that enabled them to remain in the capital despite department regulations.

UNCOMPENSATED SPOUSES

The Foreign Service Act of 1980, while benefiting spouses in some areas, made it more difficult for them in others. The new process of opening "windows" for promotion meant that upper-mid-level officers, many with children bound for college, were suddenly out of a job if not promoted within a certain time frame. Spouses without careers, and without incomes, could not provide adequate financial support during such a transition. By placing new strictures on the "up or out" rule, the Foreign Service greatly limited the options available to a member family. While the spouse's perception of herself was changing from housewife to disadvantaged partner, the service continued to resist her ability to build her own financial safety net in the mobile Foreign Service life.

Marlene Eagleburger, the spouse of then-Undersecretary Lawrence Eagleburger, was the first high-profile spouse to propose a paycheck for Foreign Service spouses who were representing the United States overseas. In 1992 her husband became the first career Foreign Service officer to serve as secretary of state. In a March 1984 op-ed article in the Washington Post headlined, "'Mrs. Foreign Service' Deserves to Be Paid Too," Marlene Eagleburger took the substantial risk of going public with her views.[1] "Americans love a bargain," she wrote. "The U.S. government gets the biggest bargain in town when the Department of State hires a married person for the Foreign Service. Since the days of Ben Franklin, wives have been expected (read required) to carry out representational duties while serving abroad at an embassy or consulate.

"The time has come to pay spouses in the Foreign Service for their representational work abroad," she continued. "It is one thing to give a party for friends every few weeks. But in the Foreign Service, dinners, luncheons, etc., are weekly business—the business of the U.S. government."

The Associates Proposal:
A Framework for Employing Spouse Skills

"You would be able to say, 'I have functioned as a Foreign Service associate,'" explained Sue Low, the principal force behind the Foreign Service associates proposal, in 1987 and 1993 interviews. The idea was to create a program for utilizing spouse skills—in mission-related and host country jobs that would

further U.S. interests and offer spouses mobile career continuity. With the chang-
ing times, spouses, especially the younger ones, were reluctant to forgo careers.
They were concerned about jobs that would provide them with social security and
health benefits. The formal proposal grew out of the 1985 Association of American
Foreign Service Women study, "The Role of the Spouse in the Foreign Service." [2]
Sue Low continued:

[The committee] was galvanized by Penne Laingen's matter-of-fact observation that we needed a questionnaire to find out how Foreign Service spouses
really did assess their lives. To everyone's surprise, about two-fifths of the
spouses answered, candidly critiquing the Foreign Service context of their
lives. The responses clearly called for action.

First, we underlined the need for the department to support the traditional
role of the volunteer, support that was sadly lacking. Second—which proved
the most recalcitrant—was recognition of the key role of spouses in representational functions and the related question of spouse compensation. While
aware from our own experience of the central importance of this issue, we
concluded that the time was not ripe to pursue it—the department had
responded flatly that funds were not available. Attitudes on the Hill were
epitomized by Senator [Claiborne] Pell's (D-R.I.), that until the wife of the
president was salaried, wives of ambassadors should not expect to be paid.
Thus, the third aspect, the employment issue, became the focus of our effort.

The breakthrough came when Senator [Charles] Matthias [R-Md.] introduced an amendment to the State Department authorization bill, mandating
a pilot program to test the feasibility of the Foreign Service associate proposal.
[But] in October 1986, at the moment when the pilot program was scheduled
to begin, Gramm-Rudman budget stringencies knocked out its funding.

Patricia Barbis, who had returned from overseas assignment in Greece in 1979,
recalled in a 1992 interview why spouses grew increasingly resentful of their
'officially unofficial' relationship with America's foreign affairs agencies:

When I first came back from Greece, I said, "I'm never ever going to
volunteer or work for a women's group again. I've done it. I've contributed
much more than anyone should be expected to give." But with the Foreign
Service Act of 1980 under consideration on the Hill, I began working on
that legislation with Marlene Eagleburger, whose husband was at the time

undersecretary for political affairs. We lobbied in the area of taxes, employment, and spouse compensation, to try to make life better for family members in the Foreign Service. I was motivated because I felt that the Foreign Service had let me down. We had just come back from our most difficult assignment in Athens, where the CIA station chief had been assassinated, my husband had been under a death threat, and while I was there alone with the children and packing to leave, our household effects had been burned. I didn't think the department had been helpful to me.

I had begun working in public relations in 1979, and I was able to put that experience to work. Marlene and I were interviewed by Cable News Network. I was in Washington, she was interviewed in New York, and the anchor was in Atlanta. He asked me, "How did you get the job you have now, and what are you doing?" and I said, "I am working now for a very major international public affairs agency, Hill & Knowlton Public Affairs World Wide, and I am doing many of the same things that I did in Foreign Service as a spouse, only now I am being paid." Then we were asked, "What does an ambassador do if he does not have a wife?" And we responded, "He hires a social secretary or a residence manager to handle all the things that his wife, if he has a wife, does for free. And the government will pay for that social secretary or manager, if there is not a spouse. But they will not pay a spouse." That is still true today, and it's blatant discrimination.

The following year I worked with Patty Ryan, who was president of the Association of American Foreign Service Women while I was vice president. Along with Marlene and me, she was very interested in legislative issues that could benefit family members. The three of us started having meetings in an anteroom of Marlene's husband's office.

Our first consideration was to find some way to compensate senior Foreign Service wives—we weren't saying "spouses" so much at that time because there were very few male spouses. We also began looking at the possibility of pensions for divorced wives. It was really our group—Pat Ryan, Marlene Eagleburger, and I—which germinated the idea that Foreign Service spouses had to look out for themselves. Spouses are not eligible for social security if they have spent their time volunteering for the government. So if you've spent a great deal of time out of the U.S., if you don't have any work history, if you don't have social security, and if your husband divorces you, you are as poor as anything. And if you were the spouse of a senior officer, you had had considerable responsibility, because certainly an ambassador's wife or senior counselor's wife, deputy chief of mission's wife, for the most part are very responsible, well-educated people who, if they had been in any other endeavor, would in some way have been recognized or paid.

Gradually society was changing in the United States so that a two-income family was becoming almost essential. If a Foreign Service family was going to have a mortgage and educate their children, it was inevitable that they needed a second income.

We made many arguments like that. Then we did a grass-roots campaign. We called on every member of the Senate Foreign Relations Committee and every member of the House Foreign Affairs Committee. Marlene had no trouble getting the appointments and the entrée. Some of our ideas later evolved into the Foreign Service associates proposal.

In the early 1980s, under Reagan, we were in a recession, and so the idea that senior wives would be reimbursed in any way just simply could not fly. Although we did manage to get Senator Charles Matthias to introduce a bill providing for the secretary of state to establish a pilot project to allow spouses to work. And a former ambassador was hired within the department to start working out the details. But in the end, it wasn't fully appropriated. We had meanwhile become aware that compensation had to be across-the-board for everyone, not just senior wives. A great deal of intelligence and ingenuity was shown through the 1980s in looking for different approaches to compensating spouses.

Marlene Eagleburger remembered the same period with a different, but comple-mentary, perspective in a 1993 interview.

Having been overseas as an ambassador's wife gave me a different perspec-tive than I had before. The focus that we eventually reached was influenced by the fact that when I arrived in Belgrade, that embassy was divided in two camps: those women who decided that the only way their self-esteem could be enhanced would be to do no representational activity at the post (and they were absolutely gung ho to be employed in some manner); the other group was women staying home with children, doing representational work—that was the way they wanted to go.

But the trouble was, they were making life very difficult for one another: the hurtful comments, the nastiness. There was no empathy, no understanding— certainly at least [not] from those who were talking in rather strong terms— on both sides.

I was floored to see this going on. One of the first things I did was to call everybody together and say that I thought this had to be resolved, that there had to be understanding and empathy for everybody's position and beyond anything else, tolerance. That led me to begin thinking about the role of women in the Foreign Service both from the point of view of employment and from that of somebody who really felt that they wanted to do the representational work.

I started to think, to recognize that there was a problem which I had not recognized before.

When we went to Belgrade, there were at least three officers who were there without their wives. These officers did not do a poor job, but I thought it was abnormal. To me, married people belong together.

They all were married and had children. It wasn't just the spouse they left behind. I am not saying this is good or bad, I'm only saying that this alerted my mind to something going on that the Foreign Service, not being terribly adventuresome, had not really focused on.

Gay Vance, wife of the secretary, had started a brownbag lunch once a month for wives of senior officers, to which I went. We began to touch on these issues. Some women were uncomfortable, others were angry that things were changing and they didn't know how to cope with it. I was somewhat amused when one senior wife suggested that a pin might be nice to hand out to wives in recognition of their contribution, and maybe if we were lucky we could get a tea with the wife of the secretary.

I thought, "These aren't answers, these are little gifts that are supposed to soothe." I felt that we had to make some serious recommendations and proposals. We wanted to help the women who wanted to do representational work but who, perhaps for financial reasons, took a PIT [part-time, intermittent, temporary] position, or the women who felt that in this day and age their work should be compensated and therefore felt they would only do the minimum. There was a case in Belgrade where, when the husband gave a dinner at home, the wife hired a cook and she sat upstairs, she would not participate.

In a lot of embassies—the Canadians come to mind—the wife receives an allowance for getting her hair done, buying dresses, things you wouldn't do [as frequently in private life]. The Canadian government felt that since these were expenses incurred on behalf of the government, they would pay for them. Normally, we don't go dancing in long dresses and black tie to the local pub: these clothes are examples of expenses strictly related to the business we are in.

So we decided to try the Internal Revenue Service. The first step, we learned, was getting an okay from the Treasury Department. The IRS granted us the right to deduct these expenses—babysitting, for instance, which many of us in Washington in those early years could ill afford to pay for four nights a week, or [buying] long dresses. So at least there was some relief on the tax return. I think that sort of gave us a 'high' to take on bigger and better problems.

We were at a dinner party one night at the home of Kay Graham, publisher of the *Washington Post*, and sitting at my table was [editorial page editor]

Meg Greenfield. We were talking about wives in the Foreign Service and how they worked and got nothing for their work—[no] recognition, money, zilch. And Meg looked at me and said, "Why don't you write an article?"

So, there was my challenge. I ran home, got out the yellow pad and the ballpoint pen, and started. I must tell you, it was a labor of love, but it was labor. Meg ran it as it was—and it was pretty long.

That started the public reaction to the whole idea of the role of the wife in the Foreign Service. I say "wife" because for the most part we are talking about wives.

The next developments were about money. When you go up to the Hill, you not only have to talk to the people and get them all lined up on your side but you have to get the money people on your side. So one of the very first persons I called on was Congressman Henry Hyde, Republican from Illinois. I approached him with great trepidation—not that I don't like him personally, I do, but he's a very conservative man, and I thought I would have a very hard sell and perhaps end up with a no.

I walked in ready for battle, trying to be charming, to get this man on my side, because he was the House member who held the pursestrings. He graciously escorted me to his sofa, sat down, and before I could say a word he looked at me and said, "Marlene, I know why you're here. You don't have to go through it all." And I thought, "Oh Lord, I'm dead, it's going to be a big fat no." He looked at me with his eyes twinkling, and he said, "The women in the Foreign Service do the most wonderful job. Anything you want." I couldn't believe it! I just sort of sputtered, "Thank you," and he said, "Be in touch, you've got my support. If you need a cosponsor of the bill, I will be happy to do so."

While my husband was in government, our goal was . . . compensation for spouses—not just jobs but compensation for those who decided to do representation rather than do a particular job already existing in a U.S. embassy. Representation would be viewed as a job worthy of pay.

This was adulterated, if you will, when we left. I shouldn't be surprised. I know this town very well. But when you leave office, be it State Department or any other agency, you leave your power behind. And it became evident to me very quickly that the direction I had hoped we would continue to move in was being diluted and changed. This is not to point any fingers, it's merely to state the obvious.

Frankly, had I known what was going to happen, I would have pushed much harder for a resolution before we left government. Unfortunately, you live and learn. I'm not going to say that I think the Foreign Service associates proposal that was finally submitted is bad; I don't. But to me, there was an intellectual arrogance in the proposal. In other words, there was an underlying premise, in my view, that only a "job that existed in a U.S. Embassy that was recognized as a job" would be good enough for the spouse. In fact, this implied that anybody who wanted to do the crummy work of representation wasn't good enough; it was a stepchild rather than a legitimate child.

For me the whole thrust of the pilot program was entirely in the wrong direction, because it did not address the underlying fact that, however you slice it, representation is here to stay, and whatever other pilot projects you put in—as far as jobs are concerned—have nothing to do with the issue I was talking about. So I, frankly, was not disappointed when the pilot project was not funded.

DIVORCED FROM THE FOREIGN SERVICE

They had taken part in diplomatic life because of the kinds of people they were and because of what was expected of women in those days. "We viewed it very much as patriotism," Miryam Hirsch said. "We were working for our country and took pride in doing it." But then, in some cases after as many as 30 years, their marriages fell apart. Alcoholism, homosexuality, male midlife crisis, and spouse and child abuse reached into their lives, often with devastating consequences. Almost all of them believed that service-related stress, or war-caused separations, led to their divorces.

In the late 1970s, when they first organized as a combination support group and political action committee, they called themselves Women in Transition but soon changed their name, when divorce was no longer a transient phase in their lives, to Displaced Foreign Service Partners.

The experiences of Jane Dubs following the assassination of her former husband, Ambassador Adolph (Spike) Dubs, in Afghanistan in February 1979 illustrated the catch-22 in which these women found themselves. On 28 May 1979, after Spike Dubs was killed, People magazine featured a photograph of President Jimmy Carter comforting his widow—his second wife, of three years' standing. At the far reaches of the audience, Jane Dubs, who had been his wife for 30 years, stood watching, not yet realizing that the assassination had cut off her only means of support, $650 per month in alimony. She was literally one step from welfare, ineligible for social security or any government-sponsored health benefits, and physically disabled. As a volunteer and as a widely traveled Foreign Service spouse, she had had no opportunity to create a financial safety net of her own.

In a 1993 interview, Jane Dubs told a story that, at the time, had strengthened the resolve of Displaced Foreign Service Partners.

His name was Adolph, but everyone called him Spike. His fraternity brothers changed his name. They were thinking of Hitler and said they could not have an Adolph in the house. He was a naval officer during World War II, and we were married in January 1945. Then he went to graduate school, and I worked for four years to help put him through. In December 1949 he went into a training course at the Foreign Service Institute to get ready to go to Germany the following year. So I was married to him when we started out in the Foreign Service.

During the next 25 years, Spike Dubs had been steadily promoted and had received a superior honor award. Jane Dubs firmly believed that she had contributed to his success.

Spike was 52 when he was assigned to Moscow in 1972 as deputy chief of mission and minister counselor. He was chargé d'affaires for 13 months, so I had the duties of the wife of both the deputy chief of mission and the ambassador. I especially remember sitting for hours during the Soviet May Day parade in Red Square while all of their military might rolled by.

While he was on the Soviet desk, before going to Moscow that second time, I started feeling that something wasn't right. . . .

I wouldn't accept the fact that there was any problem. In those days, you didn't share that type of thing with your friends, and I couldn't bring myself to confront Spike. Today, with all the media exposure—like on "Donahue" and "Oprah Winfrey"—it would be much easier to bring my feelings out in the open. . . . Our divorce was final in January 1976, after a 30-year marriage; a year and a half later, he was appointed ambassador to Afghanistan.

After Spike's kidnapping and murder, I went to the State Department and asked what part of the pension I would get, and the woman I talked to said, "You don't get anything." My jaw dropped, and I said, "But I was the Foreign Service wife for 26 of my 30 years of marriage. She was the second wife for less than three years and didn't even go to his ambassadorial post with him except to visit at Christmas." The woman said, "That doesn't matter. She's the wife." So I got absolutely nothing, and the alimony stopped.

I then went to two employment agencies, and later to a government employment office, but I became totally discouraged. I just went home and curled up and went into deep depression. My very, very closest Foreign Service friends were still abroad, and I didn't have my church nearby. Didn't have any money for counseling. There was also no money for health insurance or for treatment, so for the little things that were bothering me, I didn't go to the doctor. My support at that time came mainly from members of AAFSW.

Right after the divorce, I had $650 per month alimony, but when Spike was assassinated that stopped, and when the second wife died it didn't make any difference at all. Not at all. She got the entire annuity until she died, and when she died nobody got that annuity. I called the State Department, but they said no. All I received was a small percentage of Spike's share of their joint will.

Since Spike Dubs had anticipated retiring after his service in Afghanistan, his wife Mary Ann had remained at her job as an editor of the "Daily Digest" for the Congressional Record, *in Washington. After her husband's death, she served as a director of the Afghan Relief Committee, raising funds to aid more than one million Afghan refugees in Pakistan. In 1980 she joined the Foreign Service herself and was stationed in Mexico when she was diagnosed with leukemia. She died in 1985. Jane Dubs died in 1993.*

PENSION RIGHTS WON

While the question of compensation for active spouses remained unresolved into the 1990s, the experiences of divorced, long-service wives like Jane Dubs fueled a campaign that finally resulted in congressional action to grant retirement and health benefits to women who had voluntarily served the U.S. government abroad. But even this battle had its own bitter irony. The problem was that the Foreign Service Act of 1980, which went into effect on 15 February 1981, granted pension and health benefits to those spouses divorced after its effective date, thus neglecting many of those who had worked for reform. Displaced Foreign Service Partners had to continue its efforts for another seven years before the government recognized the value of what often was a full career of service. Even with this victory, as one spouse—a staunch feminist who divorced after the 1980 act but remarried before age 55, thus losing her pension rights—pointed out, "The department did not view the pension as having been rightfully earned by me. In their male chauvinist minds, it was just something to tide me over until I found another man to support me. If I had earned the pension, why didn't it continue to be mine whether I remarried or not?"

Patricia (Patty) Ryan, chair of legislative liaison for the Association of American Foreign Service Women, helped gain passage of the 1980 legislation and served later as president of the organization. Even in 1993, she said, "I am still embroiled in the campaign for protection from penury for divorced or widowed women from the Foreign Service and from CIA." She recalled the attitudes of the time in a 1992 interview.

Until the middle 1970s, any family issues in the Foreign Service had been dealt with by getting the ear of the wife of someone important and getting her to persuade her husband that something should be changed. Frequently, it was changed. This system had its imperfections, but it worked to a degree. It was becoming increasingly clear, however, that women had legitimate needs which required official solutions, and we could address those needs without being considered self-centered, unpatriotic, backsliding, whatever. A younger generation was emerging which had not been trained to be self-abnegating, and this group had to convince the AAFSW board that they were going to lobby Congress for their rights. They made some hair stand on end but did ease the board into accepting the fact that we had to lobby Congress for some of the benefits we felt Foreign Service women were entitled to.

One of the events of the 1970s which affected spouses—in an unanticipated way—was the institution of no-fault divorce. No-fault had the effect of creating a situation in which American women married for many years no longer had any leverage to protect themselves financially during a divorce. In the old days, if a husband of 25 or 30 years wanted to marry his secretary, at least he had to provide a comfortable living for his former spouse, if he was able. He had to buy her out with an adequate income. Now with no-fault divorce, that no longer existed.

This was the story the Association of American Foreign Service Women Forum was hearing over and over again by women who felt that they had spent many years not only in a marriage but in a career. They had really bought into "two for the price of one," and nobody was prepared for the fact that suddenly at 50 or 55 these women would find themselves with half a house, if they were lucky, as their sole lifetime economic equity.

Unfortunately in our court system, the winner is the person with the best knight, and if you can't afford to buy yourself a good knight to represent you in the tournament, you're going to lose. And it was typically the women who did not have the resources to hire the right knight, and they would be left with almost nothing.

Yet they expected the courts to rule in their favor. Their view was that they had worked hard to be good Foreign Service wives, to be good mothers, they had spent years supporting the service all over the world, and they therefore expected the outcome of the divorce to be good for them, too. They discovered too late that it wasn't going to work that way. Motherhood and good deeds were not counted as having much weight in a law court.

It soon became apparent that our best strategy was to argue that the mobile Foreign Service life absolutely precluded any opportunity for a woman to create a pension or benefits for herself on her own. If she could work, it was part-time: perhaps at this post, perhaps not at that post. And she earned pesos or krona; she was paid poorly. She was working because she simply wanted to do something. The only certain thing was that spouses could not have gotten pensions for themselves.

After the passage of the Foreign Service Act of 1980, Displaced Foreign Service Partners continued to lobby until it achieved success in 1987, with much assistance from Representative Patricia Schroeder (D-Colo.) and Senator Nancy Kassebaum (R-Kan.). In the department, the group found that it was dealing not with Foreign but with Civil Service officials, who did not comprehend the role mobility played in the women's inability to develop a safety net of their own. On Capitol Hill, because they were former wives of diplomats, the "partners" were presumed to be independently wealthy.

"The Story of the Struggle" by Miryam Hirsch, which appeared in the February 1989 AAFSW News, *celebrated the victory.*[3] *In it, she paid tribute to all who were involved in gaining enactment of the legislation: the women affected, who testified, lobbied, wrote, and walked the halls of Congress by the hundred; the AAFSW, particularly Lesley Dorman and Pamela Moffat; and the State Department. The Displaced Foreign Service Partners' cause had been further aided when the Central Intelligence Agency granted precedent-setting survivor and health benefits to CIA wives in the "displaced partner" category. The bill was signed into law on 24 December 1987 and was, according to Miriam Chrisler, "the best Christmas present any of these women, who gave so much to their country, ever received."*

FOLLOW THE FLAG

As spouses moved into the 1980s, terrorism was changing the face of the Foreign Service and contributed to a growing reluctance to serve overseas. In 1980 there were 278 terrorist attacks against Americans, resulting in 10 deaths and 94 injuries.⁴ Embassy and consulate buildings increasingly became fortresses. With the Iran hostage situation, foreign affairs agency wives were thrust into the blinding glare of a national spotlight. In her study of 14 hostage wives, the Foreign Service spouse Leila Dane documented the differences in the women's reactions to prolonged stress. They had affirmative, unanimous agreement on only one question: "Did you feel your behavior might be reported in the media?"⁵

The State Department bureaucracy, during the Iran hostage crisis and its aftermath, perhaps inevitably in such an unprecedented situation produced mixed results and got mixed reviews. Moorehead Kennedy, in his memoirs, reflected on his encounter with the department's personnel rules and on his wife Louisa's involvement in the rescue effort, after being freed.

"I had my own reason for irritation with personnel. In order to flesh out my performance file, for I had accomplished nothing in fourteen months of captivity, I submitted letters of thanks and commendations which I had received for my media work immediately after our return: from Barbara Walters, from Ambassador Shlaudeman in Buenos Aires for a broadcast in Spanish, from Ambassador Hartman in Paris for one in French. And many others. A much-embarrassed personnel officer informed me that none of these was acceptable, because they mentioned Louisa. To protect Foreign Service wives who chose to lead their own lives, and not be pressured on a two-for-the-price-of-one basis to serve as unpaid adjuncts to their husbands' careers, no personnel record could ever mention a spouse. It was a good rule, to which, however, an exception might have been made in these unusual circumstances. But none was."⁶

Regardless of personnel rules, spouses were deeply involved in both official and unofficial responses to the taking of the hostages in Tehran. With ten years' experience in the Middle East, a wealth of contacts, and an informal channel to information that most spouses lacked, Louisa Kennedy was different from most

Foreign Service wives. She became a spokesperson for the wives of hostages and worked telephones at the State Department to keep families scattered around the country current on the situation in Tehran.

Louisa Kennedy remembered meetings of the family members with President Jimmy Carter and Secretary of State Cyrus R. Vance, early in the hostage crisis, in which it was stressed—and the families agreed—that while everything would be done to free the hostages, the interests of the United States came first. This was the message she took to the American public when she was interviewed by Barbara Walters on ABC News and when she appeared on NBC's "Today" show.

In March 1980 morale was at a low point. Iran's head of state, the Ayatollah Ruhollah Khomeini, announced that the fate of the hostages would be decided by a then-nascent Iranian parliament. It was becoming increasingly clear that the situation of the American hostages in Iran was not going to be resolved quickly and, in fact, could go on indefinitely. For the spouses, the prospect of a continuing emotional roller-coaster ride was daunting. Louisa Kennedy and her fellow hostage spouse Penelope (Penne) Laingen organized the Family Liaison Action Group (FLAG).

FLAG settled in for the long haul. Its president was Katherine Keough, wife of the former superintendent of the American School of Tehran, who had just happened to be in the embassy on business when the hostages were taken. They used donated office space in downtown Washington. The State Department, Louisa Kennedy remembered, found the hostage spouses much easier to deal with as an organization outside of the department and kept them informed of initiatives and developments, with the notable exception of the rescue attempt by U.S. troops.

TIE A YELLOW RIBBON. . .

Penne Laingen, whose husband was chargé d'affaires in the Tehran embassy, had a very personal view of spousal reaction to the hostage taking, as she recalled in 1986 and 1990 interviews.

The hostage crisis was a terribly public, international crisis, and when I was on television, I think I was, in the minds of the American people, the wife of the chargé d'affaires being held in Tehran. And how I behaved reflected not only on Bruce but perhaps on the whole Foreign Service and other Americans abroad. If I had gone on television and cried nightly, if I'd flown off to Iran, or criticized President Carter or U.S. government policy, I think I would have heard in two minutes just how private a person I was. How can you be private when you are on the public stage, as those of us caught up in the Iran hostage crisis were? I got no support from the department in that role. The hypocrisy of State's official policy toward wives has gnawed at me for years.

In March of 1980, about five months after the takeover, I went to lunch in Annapolis with some former POW wives, who said that the hostage families needed to get organized. We had a lot of questions which were not being answered by State—legal, financial, administrative, medical, whatever. For instance, should we pay income tax, an issue about to be raised that time of year. As an ambassador's wife, I had learned the importance of teamwork in a crisis situation and knew that we would be more effective speaking as one voice. So on 22 March I called the hostage families in Washington together, and we founded FLAG, the Family Liaison Action Group. I began editing the FLAG newsletter, which was distributed to the hostage families all across the country.

After the aborted rescue attempt, I was called in the middle of the night by the department, with assurance that Bruce was all right. And at about 5 A.M., my son and I woke to find the media people banging on the door. We hid out, didn't turn on any lights, and they eventually left. A few hours later I went to church, feeling very sad about the families of the eight men who had died in the rescue attempt, and feeling sorry for Jimmy Carter and the terrible decision he had had to make.

Later on Sunday I called the White House—I had a contact there—to say that I wanted President Carter to know that I supported his actions, and if he could do it again, to "hit 'em again harder," that sort of thing. The next day the *New York Times* printed a "telegram" to that effect that "I had sent to the President." I was really angry. I had prayed over that private message of grief, and it had been released to the *Times* without my permission. I guess it showed President Carter that one hostage family supported him, but I was never as happy with him after that. The other wives were upset with me as a result of the *Times* article, wanting to know how I could support such a foolish thing.

Almost immediately after Bruce was taken hostage, I had "tied a yellow ribbon 'round the old oak tree" in our garden. Then one day a *Washington Post* reporter called to ask how I managed to keep my composure. We discussed religion, family support, and the support of the POW wives, and how extremely important they all were. Then I mentioned the public demonstration of outrage—by then the term "Irage" had been coined—which I didn't think was helping our situation. I said we needed a lot of patience to deal with the hostage crisis and suggested that people tie a yellow ribbon to express their feelings.

"Have you tied a ribbon?" she asked. And when I answered yes, she thought it was a wonderful idea and wrote about it in the *Post*.[7]

She also began hanging yellow ribbons in Reston, Virginia, where she lived. Soon afterward, I answered the doorbell one snowy night to find an AID wife standing there—with a station wagon overflowing with children and dogs at the curb—to tell me that she had just appointed herself chairperson of the Yellow Ribbon Committee. She and her sister began hanging yellow ribbons around the White House and along Massachusetts Avenue.

Well, the idea just snowballed. I think the whole country was ready to be united behind something, and the yellow ribbon was an easily grasped symbol. I was invited to attend President Carter's State of the Union address in January 1980, and that night, with Senator [Thomas] Harkin [Democrat] of Iowa, I put a yellow ribbon on the Sam Rayburn oak on Capitol Hill. In May I went to the White House to festoon a Georgia maple with a yellow ribbon, compliments of Mrs. Carter. That summer I tied a ribbon around the Wye Oak in eastern Maryland, the largest oak in the country, with Governor Harry Hughes. The tree was so large that instead of a ribbon we had a bolt of yellow cloth, and he went around one side of the tree and I went around the other, and we swathed that giant tree in yellow. FLAG had also started a campaign to hang yellow ribbons at every governor's mansion in the country. The most exciting moment, however, was when Bruce and his colleagues finally came home in January 1981. Bruce removed the yellow ribbon in our front yard as all the neighbors and friends looked on and cheered.

Penne Laingen's yellow ribbon became an American folklore symbol.[8] *In 1991 she presented the original plastic ribbon that had hung on the oak in her garden to the Library of Congress.*

TEHRAN BEFORE THE FALL

Long before the hostage crisis erupted, Tehran was an increasingly uncomfortable post for American diplomats and their spouses. Pearl Richardson, whose husband Cecil was consul in Tehran during the period when Shah Reza Pahlavi's government fell to Muslim fundamentalists, and who nearly became a hostage herself, recalled in a 1987 interview that the political and social situation steadily deteriorated during the late 1970s.

We were having to evacuate thousands . . . 60,000 people, something like that. The military had just built a multimillion-dollar commissary. It was open like three days, and Cy [Cecil Richardson] thought that the parking lot would be a good staging point to process evacuees. So he took our car and drove to the commissary grounds. As he got out of the car, a teenager put a gun to his head and told him not to come back. The Hilton Hotel and the embassy eventually became the staging points for evacuees.

My attitude was that I was going to stay there with him. If he's going to die there, it's going to be perfectly fine for me, too. We'll go together.

But Cy called me February 2d and said, "Pearl, you will tell me on the telephone right now where do you want to go, Rome, Athens, Frankfurt, or home?" I said, "Wait a second! I'm not going anyplace. You get me a job." He said, "Pearl, we're not hiring you, everyone is going." I said, "You never told me this." He said, "I know I didn't, but that's it. And you're leaving the day after tomorrow."

I must admit, I really thought my evacuation was temporary. I thought I was going to be back in three months, and that's why I didn't go home. That's why I went to Rome. Eventually, Cy was evacuated from Damascus (where we were on vacation) to Rome, and then right on to the United States. But they're not evacuating me, because they said, "You've already been evacuated." And I said, "Don't worry, I will make my own way back to Washington," which of course I did.

WORKING THE HOSTAGE HOTLINE

Pearl Richardson continued her story:

We got to Washington officially in January [1980], and the first thing I did was go into the State Department and ask if there was any group working on the Iran problem that I could volunteer for. And from that day until the day I left, 8 August, I worked every single day, except weekends, from eight in the morning until six at night.

I felt that this was my way of saying "thank you" that my husband wasn't a hostage. I also felt it was very, very important for the State Department to have this volunteer group, because what we ended up doing was not only counseling families and talking to families every day, but we were taking calls from congressmen, senators, the press, and giving them advice.

We had, in one case, I can only call her a child bride, a second wife of one of the hostages, and she wasn't living anywhere near the Washington area. She couldn't open a checking account. She didn't have a power of attorney from [her] husband. We managed to call the bank, explain the situation, and get her a checking account. We got her a job.

There was a family of one hostage that heard absolutely nothing for 444 days, except when the Red Cross went in, he was allowed to write 50 words on a message paper. Other families heard all the time. Some people, if they used their real names, the letters never got to their husbands. If they used an alias that the husband was aware of, that letter got there.

One woman called, very excited, to say, "I just got a letter from my son." And she started reading, "Dear Mom, I'm well and I'm playing a lot of scrabble, hearts, and . . ." I said, "Wait a second. Repeat that." And I had everyone pick up the phone, and I said, "That means he's with two other people, because you cannot play hearts with fewer than three people."

Richardson remained with the volunteer spouses on the hostage hotline until she accompanied her husband to a new assignment in Lima, Peru. But she kept a promise to the many she had counseled over the months—when the hostages were released in January 1981, Richardson flew to Washington from Lima for the occasion.

221

It was primarily through the efforts of one woman that the Department of State's former disregard for the welfare of evacuees, once they were removed from danger, was transformed into one of ongoing concern. Betty Atherton, perhaps more than any other spouse of her generation, employed the privilege of rank in "getting things done," especially in her efforts to improve the status of the family within the Foreign Service. She was interviewed in the late 1980s, when she was chairman of the Mental Health Committee at State.

When the families were evacuated from Iran in December 1978, it was assumed, as it had been apparently in most previous evacuations, that eventually they would return to post. By January it was obvious, as it apparently had been in most previous evacuations, they would not return to post. On the contrary, by then and definitively so by February, it was clear that not only would there be no return to post for families, but most of the official staff would be evacuated.

While it was true that, as one of the officers on the Iran desk in the department put it, the families were out and safe so why be concerned, I was. With verbal permission from Henry Precht, who was on the Iran desk, a group of us set up the Iran Evacuee Support Network Program (IESNP).

For the next several months, we contacted the families who had been evacuated to determine what we might do for them and soon discovered the immediate need was helping them get in touch with each other. They felt disoriented, lost. They had been so abruptly uprooted, so cut off from husbands and fathers who had remained in Iran, so totally out of contact with all that had been a part of their lives.

Some were still full of anger and resentment. Some had tried to get their household things out of storage so they could settle back in their homes or rent an apartment, only to learn that without power of attorney from the employee, they could not have access to their own things. The separation allowance proved inadequate, particularly for those women who, without power of attorney, could not even collect their husband's paychecks. We were overwhelmed with the myriad of problems the evacuees were facing.

Our program volunteers became an advocacy group for the evacuee families. We visited the appropriate offices in the State Department to determine what could be done to cut the red tape and provide access to household goods, money allotments, etc. Our early efforts went into trying to meet crucial needs. Just alerting the department to where the system was proving cumbersome and unresponsive brought results.

All the top management was cooperative. Perhaps one of the most painful yet productive steps we took was arranging an afternoon meeting of the evacuees in the Washington vicinity with the top management people. It provided a forum for venting concerns and for everyone to become aware of the others' problems—both the problems facing the evacuees and those facing management. It was, I believe, the first time evacuees and management had ever met together. While obviously all the problems were not solved, there was, at least, the beginning of a building of trust and understanding between them.

In 1977 the Association of American Foreign Service Women had recommended improving the evacuation procedures by sending a specially trained temporary duty officer to safe haven posts to help evacuees with information, counseling, and financial assistance. The department had not responded to the request.

This event [the Iranian crisis] resulted in a lengthy paper with recommendations for changes in the evacuation system. As a result, the department made a thorough study of the evacuation procedures and revised them, making them more relevant and effective. Other benefits derived from the IESNP included the establishment of another position in FLO with responsibility for working with the department on evacuations; the helpful "What Do I Do Now?" booklet; and, what I find amusing as well as satisfying, FLO now has permanent offices in all the space we had acquired for a supposedly brief time.

As far as getting the rooms in the department for our evacuation office was concerned, let me start with the fact that I knew the rooms were there, and I knew they were empty, and they were very near FLO [just inside the C Street, N.W., or diplomatic entrance, to the department]. We were not an adjunct of FLO, and that was interesting. We were just nearby, but they supported us absolutely.

I had tried several times on the telephone to reach the person who was responsible for the assignment of the rooms. After three days of total failure, I took a big thick book with me one morning, and I went down to the complex of offices where he was located. I announced to the receptionist that I knew he was a very busy man but I needed just a few moments of his time, and that I had brought along a book to read and I would just be sitting there, and whenever he had a minute I'd appreciate having a chance to talk with him.

The offices were like a suite with a corridor, and I could see him dart from office to office. I watched him dart back and forth several times and debated whether I would interrupt. I decided, no, I had a big book to read. It was about noon—or one o'clock—when he decided that he had time for me. He was very nice. I told him that Mrs. [Cyrus R.] Vance, wife of the secretary of state, had sent her regards and appreciated all he would be doing to help us out in this time of need. We got the rooms on the promise that we would be out of them by May, that this was purely a temporary assignment.

On 21 March 1979 Betty Atherton sent a memorandum to Undersecretary of State David Newsom, outlining the accomplishments of the semiformal group of women who led the evacuee-support efforts. In typical government shorthand, the memorandum outlined a tremendous amount of work to help the displaced, and often distraught, dependents of officers who at that time were besieged in a hazardous duty post and who would, in six months, become hostages until January 1981. The support group made five recommendations for future evacuation situations: the United States should be the safe haven for all evacuees; the Overseas Briefing Center, a part of the Foreign Service Institute, should train family members going to the field on evacuation procedures; the department should assume responsibility for keeping family members informed; there should be a realistic separate maintenance allowance; and a network of affected individuals should be established for each evacuation situation.

"These were all approved by Secretary Vance," Betty Atherton continued. "They were actually instituted and were in place for several evacuations, especially the one from Sudan in 1986 after Cleo [A.] Noel and [G. Curtis] Kurt Moore were assassinated. It seemed to have been the most successful, because the crisis management people and the support network were in place in the department. There was time for the planning to take effect, and apparently the evacuation went as smoothly as an evacuation could go."

TERRORISM, FOOD SHORTAGES, TEACHING
ENGLISH AS A SECOND LANGUAGE

In 1980 Kristie Miller found herself in Maputo, Mozambique, as spouse of Deputy Chief of Mission (and later Chargé d'Affaires) William Twaddell. It was the time of "the emergency," the war waged against the government by the rebellious Resistencia Nacional Mozambicana, or Renamo. The war had started in 1976 and was to expand dramatically in 1981. But by the time Kristie Miller arrived, it had ruined the national economy and much of the transportation and communication infrastructure, not to mention the prevailing rural society, where six million Mozambicans confronted food shortages. Soon afterward, the mantle of American first lady in Mozambique fell squarely on her shoulders. She recalled in a 1989 interview:

When the border between Mozambique and South Africa was open, we went to Nelspruit for food. It was an eight-hour round-trip drive. One time I went with the wife of a political officer. He wanted her home by nightfall because he had heard rumors that the South Africans were going to attack that night. Our car was overloaded with food, and we had a flat tire, but we made it back before dark. The attack didn't come that night, but later.

The ANC [African National Congress], the black African group from South Africa, was living on the outskirts of Maputo, in Matola. Maputo is practically on the frontier of South Africa. One night the South African army just strolled across the border, walked into Matola, and killed all the ANC, cut off their ears. The Mozambicans were shocked. This would have been in late January or February of 1981. Some people blamed the Americans for the raid, and we received a bomb threat one night when we were having a dinner party at the house. Bill wanted to keep it quiet, but I made him tell our guests. I thought they should decide whether they wanted to stay or leave. They left!

Under any circumstances, the trip to Nelspruit was an arduous one to have to make every six weeks. It was like driving round trip from Washington to New York for groceries. I thoroughly resented it when a member of a visiting congressional delegation said to me at one of our dinner parties, "Well, I hope this food isn't from South Africa." Our alternative for shopping was to go to Swaziland, but of course that food came for the most part from South Africa; certainly all of the shelf foods did. They tacked 10 percent on for importing it, so since the goods were South African anyway, I didn't see any high moral ground in going to Swaziland.

When the worst of the drought hit, we had to import food not only for ourselves and our dinner parties but I imported tons of maize for the workers. Finally the embassy truck was commandeered and used to bring it in by the truckload because the Mozambicans were on such short rations.

With the unsettled political situation and food problems, Kristie Miller found comfort in pursuing her ten-year career as an English teacher. This also helped her husband gain access to Mozambican officials and foreign diplomats.

Frankly, I found the endless round of diplomatic parties excruciatingly boring, and I just set myself up as the American Language Institute. In fact, the political section wanted to put me on the payroll because I was working at the Chinese embassy as an English teacher. I just started recruiting students at these dull parties, which were so boring and where I had nothing else to do. Everybody wanted to learn English because it really is the diplomatic language. In the Chinese embassy I had 35 students, including the ambassador there. I had several Hungarians, a Pole, a Swede, a Dutch woman, and other Europeans. Eventually, the Mozambicans unbent to the point where they allowed me to teach the women who were the ranking Communist party members.

THE ONLY DECISIVE VOICE DEMANDING
AN INVESTIGATION

Meanwhile, half a world away in El Salvador, Mary Anne White, spouse of U.S. Ambassador Robert E. White, was witness to and a potential target of the terrorist acts being carried out by Salvadoran right-wing death squads. White remembered in a 1987 interview:

While we were still in Paraguay, Bob was told of the possibility of being assigned to El Salvador. I was not happy at that news. But I didn't think there was much point in my objecting, as things always happened the way the State Department determined. So after Bob's confirmation hearings in Washington, we were sent to San Salvador in March 1980. That was, of course, probably the most difficult year of our lives, because Bob was not only hated by the Salvadoran military, he was hated by the Salvadoran oligarchy. The evident danger in the country was palpable. Bob and I couldn't even go to the movies without a motorcade, a large security entourage.

Bob would allow no embassy official or functionary to be photographed at any time. And if anyone were accidentally photographed, he or she was immediately sent out of the country, as that person would become an immediate target. Bob was constantly being photographed. As a result, of course, there were plans to kill him, which fortunately never happened. He did things that I found extremely dangerous. He went to mass at the cathedral when Archbishop Oscar Romero was speaking and exhorting the military to put down their arms, at least not to shoot innocent people and to remember their responsibilities to their own people, to their Christian principles.

Bishop Romero was an astonishing man. He had been chosen originally because he was a very conservative pastor, and Rome felt he was quite safe and would be quite in keeping with the conservative nature of the Catholic oligarchy in El Salvador. But when his mentor and confessor, Father Rutillio Grande, was gunned down on his way to market along with an old man and a young boy—Rutillio Grande having complained about the government's torturing, killing, abuse of the citizenry—it transformed Archbishop Romero. And he, in turn, following the sermon in which he exhorted the military to change, was assassinated, and I remember that evening vividly.

I never went to mass at the cathedral because Bob felt that if there were an attack on him, we couldn't afford to be concerned about me; I was really a handicap.

Following Archbishop Romero's assassination, Bob called Washington, and the department agreed to his suggestion that all families and women be evacuated. We were evacuated to Guatemala, where kind embassy people took us in. Ten days later, after most of the evacuees had been sent on to the United States, I went back to El Salvador. I had previously been given a job as emergency evacuation coordinator for the entire American community, but I had not yet begun working when we were evacuated to Guatemala.

After my return, I began developing a warden system throughout the country, buying CB radios so I could contact people, talking with Southcom, the southern command, about planes that would be available, about how they would be outfitted and how they would come in. But since I had not begun my job before I was evacuated to Guatemala, the department said that I was being given special privilege to stay in a war-torn country with my husband. So I was sent off to Vermont, which turned out to be fortunate, because our second daughter had broken her leg. I stayed with her for eight weeks and also saw our other four children.

Then I went back to El Salvador at U.S. government request as the emergency evacuation coordinator. It was a minor position but salaried, and I got to meet a lot of people who were in the American business community. Also, they found out that Bob and I weren't really such ogres after all. We did manage—security motorcade and all—to relax and take people along with us from the embassy.

The house was on the street, with nothing but a 14-foot wall in front and a cliff on the other side, which any attackers could have easily scaled. A serious assault would have very been difficult to counter, so a safe haven had been built into the house before our arrival. It had double steel doors, a bathroom, water, emergency rations, bullet-proof vests, guns, and a shortwave radio. We always were aware that marines were patrolling the grounds and just trusted that all possible avenues of approach had been guarded. Even our windows, which were supposedly bullet-proof, weren't considered bullet-proof by State security, and heavy metal shields had been installed on some of them, between the drapes and the panes. We couldn't see them, so they didn't disturb. It was amazing how, if you accepted the fact that machine guns went off every night, bombs were very close, [and] your electricity went off, you learned to live with it.

Of course, after Archbishop Romero's death, there was a 7:00 P.M. curfew, and if you put your foot on the streets after seven, you were liable to be shot. There was just no equivocation, no allowing for an error. Anyone without a Salvadoran government pass had to be inside.

It all blends together after a while. Tortured bodies, and the deliberate mutilations, and the killings. The pulling of doctors out of emergency rooms, and not only killing the patients but the doctors disappearing, obviously murdered as well. It really came to a head for us personally in the brutal murder of the four American churchwomen, two of whom, Jean Donovan and Dorothy Kazel, we knew well. We had invited Jean and Dorothy for dinner and overnight, and so they drove up to San Salvador in their white Toyota van. We had invited two or three others from the embassy and had a great time.

The next day, we were having breakfast upstairs, because Bob as usual was having an official breakfast downstairs. The time got away from us, and at 11:30 one said, "Oh my heavens. We've got errands to do before we pick up two Maryknoll nuns who are arriving at the airport." Off they went, and we promised we'd get together soon. The next day, the priest who was in charge of the Cleveland, Ohio, missionary contingent in El Salvador, which included Jean and Dorothy, called to ask if by chance they had stayed over. I said, no, that they had left at 11:30 the previous morning. Well, of course, we started the search. Bob had gone to the international airport, accompanying some Canadian visitors who had come for the funeral of the FDR (Democratic Revolutionary Front) opposition leaders. The FDR men had been murdered the week before when the military, in plain clothes, had surrounded the building in which they had been meeting and took the top five leaders away. Later they were found murdered brutally. The Canadians who had come to attend this funeral were potential targets, and with no resident Canadian ambassador, Bob accompanied them to the airport.

On the way, he heard that the women were still missing, and that a burned Toyota van had been found. Bob and his entourage headed toward the vehicle, where they found a farmer who said that bodies were being buried at that moment right up the hill. So the motorcade took off, up through the fields, and found the graves into which the women's bodies had been placed. Bob immediately ordered that they be exhumed. The men who had buried them did not want to do this, of course, because soldiers had ordered that the bodies be covered. Bob insisted, and so they were dug up. He was unable to talk about it when he came home. The women had been raped and brutally murdered. Bob said that it was something that the Salvadoran government was not going to get away with this time. And so he began the first steps to require an investigative team from Washington. The bodies were taken to a local funeral home, where we had a memorial service for them the following day. The Salvadoran government did not cooperate in investigating this terrible situation. The United States government was having difficulty also in deciding how to handle it. The only decisive voice demanding an investigation was that of my husband.

The murder of the churchwomen was followed only a few weeks later by the murder of the Salvadoran head of the agrarian reform and our two labor advisers, Mike Hammer and Frank Pearlman. They were having a sandwich at the Sheraton Hotel when a group of armed men came in, began shooting, and killed all three. They were good friends of ours. The military was upping the ante, because between Reagan's election in November 1980 and the inauguration in January, an unofficial liaison team was sent down to Central America, and to El Salvador in particular, to pass the word to the Salvadoran military that, really, with the new U.S. administration they needn't be terribly concerned about the human rights policy. The emphasis was going to be on counterterrorism, not human rights. In effect, these unofficial transition teams sent signals to the military that such action could be taken during Carter's lame-duck interval. As a result, the situation worsened considerably after the 1980 election—the killings were up, the tortures were increasing, the disappearances were increasing tremendously in number.

Bob was called to Washington early in 1981 and relieved of his post. In spite of his protests about the ineffectual U.S.-Salvadoran investigative efforts, Bob was given an office in the basement of the State Department, next to Senator Edmund Muskie who, after a brief appointment as secretary of state, was cleaning up his office. After this two- or three-month period, under a rarely used provision, Bob was forced to retire from the Foreign Service.

10

A FUTURE FOR THE
FOREIGN SERVICE SPOUSE?

*1992 marked the 20th anniversary of two important events: the 1972
directive on wives, and the opening of Disney World. Both created
fantasy worlds, but only one of them has been successful.*

Christine Shurtleff, President, AAFSW

*A vast generational gulf separates the affluent American Foreign Service wife
of 1914 and the declining number of spouses willing to accompany their officer
mates abroad in the 1990s. The former lived in a cocoon, in a stratified society,
and mingled with like spouses at home and abroad. She saw the Foreign Service
as an extension of her domestic support role. The latter, in many cases, had little
interest in a mate's career and found the mobile life that accompanied it a profound
deterrence to her or his own aspirations and accomplishments. Nonetheless,
each of these spouses was linked solidly to her times and to the continuing
representational needs of diplomacy.*

*The lifestyle of the early diplomatic wife, who served primarily in European
and Latin American capitals, was not necessarily dramatically changed by the
Foreign Service: she already was comfortable with travel, servants, and VIPs,
and like the British in the days of the Raj, she took her lifestyle with her. She and
her husband dressed for dinner even when there were no guests. These women
rarely, if ever, strayed outside their circle, and they created an impression of the
service that is not completely lost in the 1990s.*

*Contemporary Foreign Service spouses continue to enact that role. Why?
Because State Department policy throughout the twentieth century, changes in
regulations notwithstanding, has placed the burden of spousal participation in
representing the United States abroad squarely on the shoulders of the couple
and, consequently, on their relationship. After the 1972 directive, a wife was
officially entertaining for her spouse, not for the U.S. government.*

The changes in the relationship between spouses and the department had begun in the 1960s, when the back-channel influence of spouses of senior officials resulted in the founding of AAFSW and the resumption of spouse training at the Foreign Service Institute. It accelerated in the 1970s, when spouses discovered the efficacy of direct lobbying in Congress. The Family Liaison Office at the State Department and community liaison coordinators (CLOs) at nearly 200 posts abroad began to provide counsel and advocacy for spouse and family concerns. So-called tandem couples—two-income Foreign Service families—were accommodated, to a degree, in assignments. Spousal skills were inventoried and increasingly utilized during assignment abroad. State stepped up employment initiatives for spouses.

Foreign-born spouses were recognized with support groups and counseling. The threat of the AIDS virus, particularly in African posts, was met and, after a fashion, responded to. But in the 1980s, despite the efforts of influential spouses, like Marlene Eagleburger, who lobbied Congress, the spouse's inherent role in diplomatic representation went unrecognized. There would be no paychecks for spouses.

More recently, a handful of spouses of senior officers skirted the compensation issue. Arriving at post with their high-ranking mates, they found a housekeeper position on the residence employee roster. Prohibited from taking the job themselves (and assuming they personally were not entitled to a housekeeper), these spouses did not object to the removal of the position from the residence employee roster. Nor did they challenge the right to take the job themselves. (An enormous tangle of bureaucratic process surrounds the creation of a housekeeper job.) No spouse has filed a discrimination suit against the department for being denied equal access to the job. Why? Because no spouse was willing to jeopardize her officer mate's career.

Those spouses did, and still do, manage a domestic staff; function in a foreign language; feed and house a parade of American VIPs; orchestrate entertainment for thousands of host country contacts; and perhaps most demanding, play a public role that meets the expectations of the host country culture. Yet their only outlet for carrying out the traditional work of diplomacy has been as a volunteer.

Patricia Ryan reflected on such issues in a 1992 interview, a decade after she served as president of the Association of American Foreign Service Women.

Spouses of my generation were not subject to the same difficulties that younger people are experiencing in the service. When my generation went into the Foreign Service, it was a very good option, because I was more involved with my husband's work than I had been, for example, in suburban Chicago. His work overseas was a chance to live abroad, and I found the issues interesting. Of course, my options at that time were more limited than the young woman's today.

A young woman today, who has been trained to be a lawyer, has spent many years working on a career. She expects to use these dearly bought skills in the workplace. She expects to perhaps take a few years out for childbearing and early child-rearing, but she expects to spend most of her life working. In earlier times, for the middle class—and perhaps the Foreign Service was then typically slightly above middle class—the women did not really work.

Things were beginning to change by the time I was out of college in 1952: usually you worked for a couple of years until you had children, and then maybe later on you might go back and do some kind of job, something small. Women were educated in all respects like men, except when they got out of college there were few avenues. Pearl Buck said that in China women are educated for the role that they're going to have in their life, and that in America women are educated for a role they're not going to have in life.

There was no sense of a career other than to be supportive of your family and raise children and give your husband the support that he needed to make it possible for him to go out and earn the living that would keep the family afloat financially. You would keep the family afloat emotionally.

Some of the older women have seen the efforts to change things as somehow a repudiation of their lives. They suspect that the younger women feel that the older women were patsies to do the things that they did, whereas the older generation saw those activities as very worthwhile and important contributions. And in fact, they're both right. The older women did make important contributions, but they were patsies because they didn't say, "This is a worthwhile contribution I'm making, and the government doesn't get worthwhile contributions unless it pays for it, just like every other business."

I have known women who have been estranged from their husbands and would not necessarily have done the Foreign Service things they did simply to advance their husband's career. They did them rather because they felt they were overseas and had responsibilities to do things in the local country that reflect well on America.

It has given the Association of American Foreign Service Women a certain Janus face, looking back and looking forward. I think in the 1970s, when the Forum report was being written and older women were being confronted by the rebellion of younger women against things that they had long accepted— maybe not liked, but certainly taken as the way the world was—they found it very threatening.

To a certain extent, the older Foreign Service looks at the new Foreign Service and says, "Well, they're not tough. They want too many comforts." But what I see more is the inability of older people to understand why a young woman wouldn't want to entertain in foreign countries, would want to have her own career, and wouldn't be willing to subordinate her own career to her husband's.

There was a lot of cramping of personalities. By the time women were older, they were embittered because of the lack of scope in their own lives. I've seen lots of women in the Foreign Service who could have done marvelous things but they were just in the wrong generation, the wrong place at the wrong time.

FROM OFFICER TO SPOUSE

Some spouses of earlier decades, through a combination of talent, hard work, and luck, carved out careers that foreshadowed the 1990s. In the 1920s there were five women Foreign Service officers. Three resigned to marry. In the 1930s, in part because of the Depression, which removed women from the workplace, there were only two: Frances E. Willis, who became the first career woman ambassador (appointed by President Eisenhower to Switzerland in 1953), and Constance R. Harvey, who was appointed consul general to Strasbourg, France, in 1959.

In the 1940s, with the expansion of the Department of State as a result of the rapid emergence of the United States as a world power, women in increasing numbers entered the Foreign Service as special staff officers. Later they moved laterally to officer positions in the Wriston program. Most were placed in the two career branches considered least desirable, administrative and consular. A knowledgeable, ambitious, and motivated handful used these assignments to master the bureaucracy and to rise to senior positions. Among them were Carol C. Laise and Joan M. Clark. Laise was appointed ambassador to Nepal in 1966 and director-general of the Foreign Service in 1975. Clark was appointed ambassador to Malta in 1979 and director-general in 1981. Both women also had assignments as assistant secretary of state. Most women officers of that era, however, married and left the service. As of late 1993, 81 career Foreign Service officers at the State Department were women, out of 772 senior officers.[1]

According to Ann Morin, an authority on U.S. women ambassadors, three additional women—Mary S. Olmsted, Margaret Joy Tibbets, and Mary Vance Trent—joined Willis and Harvey as career officers in the 1940s. Of the women mentioned above, only Carol Laise married and remained in the service. She wed as an ambassador and, consequently, was not subject to the social pressures that forced other women officers to resign upon marriage.

This group paved the way for the 1950s, when women officers were no longer that rare and Phyllis Oakley, Alice Pickering, and others entered the service as career officers. Alice Pickering resigned to be married during her first assignment and never returned to officer status throughout her husband's extraordinary career. In a 1992 interview she recalled:

I had been a USIS officer in the department and in The Hague, and when I was married in the Netherlands, I thought I had to resign. I think this is why I have been so aware of spouse problems, especially the legal problems of women who are not officers in the Foreign Service. I have suffered, as far as employment is concerned, all through my years as a spouse.

I must say that when the resignations were challenged, the department did come around—at some point I learned that I could be reinstated, in the early 1970s, if I had resigned on the basis that it was mandatory upon marriage. However, I was to be reinstated exactly as I left. I had been in only one year as a junior officer. My possible reinstatement came 17 years after I had resigned, the same year my husband was getting his first ambassadorship. I thought that it would be very difficult to find in a small mission a job that wouldn't conflict. I would also have been the most junior member of the team. So I chose not to reinstate myself.

It was fair. I could have done so. And I knew some other women who did reinstate. I want to observe, though, that the ambassador's wife, the deputy chief of mission's wife, the consul general's wife, or any spouse whose husband is in a senior position, still has a difficult, if not impossible, problem of being able to work in an embassy, or even a related agency such as USIS or AID. It has been done, I know, but the department still actively discourages it.

OMAN OR BUST

Alice Pickering had a secondary reason for not rejoining USIS: she and her husband had found that getaway trips—as opposed to post-to-post travel—were "something we needed for our own personal morale. To keep your mental health, I think everyone needs to find either an avocation or an interest outside the specific work they're doing. In our case, and for many Foreign Service couples overseas, that interest is travel and experiencing other cultures." Pickering continued:

My husband particularly enjoys traveling by land. He feels he doesn't really know the country unless he's on wheels . . . he can stop and go where he wishes rather than being confined to public or air transportation.

Although we made a round-trip across the Sahara, 26 driving days from Nigeria to Algeria and back in 1983, I think our greatest travel saga was in the Middle East. When we were in Jordan, we began by exploring the desert areas, and during our first year there, 1974, we made a major trip to "the Gulf," as everybody now knows the Persian Gulf. The purpose of that trip was to go to Oman. We took two and a half weeks, did a lot of camping. We organized ourselves with a group from the embassy, including our son, who came out from college. We had two four-wheel drive vehicles, and we learned a great deal about desert driving, resources that we could use later on our Sahara trip. For instance, we learned how to use sand ladders in case we got stuck. And we learned the importance of having reliable compasses, good navigational equipment, and spare parts for vehicles, as well as lots of food and water. But still, there were times when we felt that camels were a safer means of travel!

For two years we had lived in Zanzibar, where everyone had talked about Muscat and Oman. The sultan of Zanzibar had been from Oman, in fact Zanzibar was always very closely linked with Oman. Our goal was to get to the sultanate of Oman, which meant driving through Saudi Arabia, on to Qatar, and then across the vast wastes of the Empty Quarter [Rub el Khali] of the great Arabian desert. When we finally reached Muscat and were driving through the city to stay with our ambassador, who lived in one of the wonderful old traditional houses, we were so thrilled. We kept saying, "It looks just like Zanzibar!" We saw dhows, the Arabian vessels that go on the monsoon back and forth from the Gulf countries to East Africa, or on to India.

We returned from Oman driving back through some of the same route, but on the return trip we went to Kuwait, flew to Bahrain, and back to Kuwait. Then we drove along the famous pipeline road back to Jordan.

I mention the "famous pipeline road" because that's the road that we saw on television during the Persian Gulf War. It was used extensively by the UN's military forces and, of course, by many people fleeing to Jordan. In New York everyone at the UN was amazed because my husband knew every area, knew the routes, and knew the roads. You never know when these travels are also going to become politically important! [Thomas Pickering was ambassador to the United Nations mission during the Gulf War.]

TANDEM COUPLES

In the foreign affairs agencies, the most significant recognition of the necessity for two-income families has been the rise of the tandem couple: both spouses work in the Foreign Service, and the service itself cooperates in assigning them abroad so that family life is at least possible, if not ideal. At the time of her January 1989 interview, Phyllis Oakley had been a Foreign Service officer and part of a tandem couple since 1974. She had just completed a tour as deputy spokesperson for the Department of State, a high-profile position that made her a familiar figure on television screens nationwide during evening newscasts. Her husband, Robert Oakley, had just been appointed ambassador to Pakistan, when Oakley reflected.

I would not put it that I'm going out to Pakistan to be the ambassador's lady. I would put it that we are being assigned to Pakistan. Bob was named ambassador immediately following Arnie Raphel's death. [Ambassador Arnold L. Raphel died in a mysterious plane crash in northern Pakistan on 17 August 1988.] We didn't know what we would do after the new administration took over, and we had decided that, having been in Washington for four and six years, respectively, we really wanted to go overseas again, and Pakistan is the kind of post that we were both looking at. And so it's a fulfillment of something that we've thought about rather than a complete change of pace.

Let me say that when I went to Zaire in 1979, and Bob was posted there as ambassador, which was his first ambassadorial position, it was done with the understanding that I could work. And I was the first ambassador's wife who was permitted to work in her spouse's embassy. Harry Barnes [then director-general of the Foreign Service] did it almost as a test case to see what would happen. There I was on loan to USIA, as the cultural affairs officer. So, in other words, I always felt that we were posted to Zaire, and Bob was the ambassador, and I worked.

Now we're going to Pakistan. Bob is posted as ambassador once again. It is always with the understanding that I will work. And I am in the process of negotiating now with AID to work with their Afghanistan mission on cross-border assistance and the repatriation of the refugees. I was the Afghanistan desk officer for three years from 1982 to 1985, so this just suits me to a tee.

It is not the same kind of job that I've just left in the department, which was certainly visible and important as far as the enunciation of American

Phyllis Oakley, deputy spokesman, Department of State, Washington, D.C., 1986. *Courtesy of Phyllis Oakley.*

foreign policy. But I look forward to a change of pace, which the Foreign Service does provide with various assignments. I look forward to leaving Washington after six very hectic years in which I've worked hard. And so I look upon this as a great opportunity, and something that we both feel is right for us to do at this time.

I will be the ambassador's wife. But being the ambassador's wife has changed so much, as we all know. When we went to Zaire, it was a post where almost all the wives worked. They needed people to work in the school, the recreation association, English teaching. There were a lot of projects, and so almost every wife who wanted to could work. Some of the jobs were not at the level at which these women would have worked here in Washington. But it provided most women with some sort of outlet in Kinshasha.

The same is true of Pakistan: the deputy chief of mission is a wife, part of a tandem couple; the head of the political section is married to an economic officer; the new economic officer going out is married to the budget and fiscal officer, and I could go on. And I think the embassy residence runs very well. There's been a good professional staff established over the years.

The one aspect that is always difficult is how much time you have to devote to meeting women from Pakistan and participating in their activities. I'm just going to have to see how I can juggle it all. But it doesn't faze me. When we went to Kinshasha, everybody kept saying, "You're doing two jobs. You're running the residence as well as working as a cultural affairs officer. I said it was a piece of cake in comparison to Washington, where the hours are longer, where you run a house and raise children and don't have as much help. I had a lot more time in Kinshasha in those two jobs than I had in one job in Washington. Now Pakistan's going to be busier. There are more delegations coming through, there's more activity. The women are more emancipated. There are more cultural activities and things like that. So in that sense, I'll be busier. But I think it's doable.

The Foreign Service is always a career, not a job. And you get paid for being what you are in a career, and not for a job that stops at five or six in the evening. Somebody said to me the other day, "What an interesting life you have. Here you were Afghanistan desk officer for three years. Then you became the deputy spokesperson for the State Department. Now you're going back to Pakistan, where your husband's the ambassador. You're going to work on repatriation of Afghanistan refugees. Gee, what a life!" I hadn't thought about it in these terms, but I guess that's true.

If Bob had never gone to Vietnam, however, I probably would never have gone back to the State Department. Let's back up to Khartoum, Sudan, for a minute. I didn't have enough to do there, but I played bridge and tennis and swam. I had a lot of Sudanese friends, young wives, and I spent a lot of time with them. I studied a little bit of Arabic, not as much as I should have. And then I did some volunteer teaching at a high school. There were a lot of temporary things, very much in the traditional mold of what a diplomat's wife does. It was pretty much the same in Abidjan, Ivory Coast, in West Africa.

In 1965 Bob volunteered to go to Vietnam, and then after he was assigned, families were no longer permitted. So that was a very difficult period because it meant, what should I do? Should I go to Bangkok or Hong Kong, where the wives were waiting with the children? I think I would have stayed on if we had been at one of those posts, but I didn't particularly want to move there with the children and be part of that community of women waiting for their husbands.

So our families decided that I would be better off in Shreveport, Louisiana, where Bob's mother and grandmother lived. It was a smaller community than where my parents were living in southern California, the living expenses would be less, and I could rent a little house. It had two main results. One is that I think our children really felt at home in the United States and part of a community, going to a school where their father had gone and everybody was related and concerned and small-town. The other result was that I went back to work.

I went by the local college in Shreveport and said, "I don't have a Ph.D., but I have done some teaching and if you ever need anybody to substitute or to fill in, I'm here and I'd love to do it, and I will have some time." The head of the history department said, "Thank you very much, we're fully staffed, I can't possibly see how we could ever use you." I had this kind of down feeling that nobody wants you, you can't do anything. Then a professor had a heart attack, and they needed somebody to fill in on short notice in summer school to lecture ten hours a week—two hours every morning in American history. And he said, "I think you can do it."

So I really scrambled and got ready and found that teaching was very difficult to do with two young children, four and six, without a husband, even though I had help. I mean I didn't have somebody to take them to the swimming pool or off to the park while I was trying to grade exam papers. I taught in the evening division the following year, which was much more manageable because it was just one three-hour lecture a week. And all of a sudden, my brain worked! Once again, I was doing something that was intellectually stimulating, it was fun. It took seven years after Bob's Vietnam assignment, but I became a Foreign Service officer again.

After almost three years in Pakistan, Phyllis Oakley returned in July 1991 to the State Department, where she served as a deputy assistant secretary in the Bureau of Intelligence and Research.

Marguerite (Margo) Squire and her husband Ross Wilson were another tandem couple; Squire herself combined an active career at the USIA with being a Foreign Service spouse and mother of two sons. She had the further distinction of being a third-generation Foreign Service officer. When interviewed in 1993, she was on maternity leave.

I should be going back to work in six months. I'm still debating whether or not to extend my leave for another year and really work for an assignment two years from now, when we'll be going overseas. It's tough, because Ross was promoted a year ago and I, ironically enough, was just promoted while I was on leave. You know, I laugh that if I stay out long enough, I can become an ambassador! I just won't get paid!

It clearly gets tougher as you go up, and Ross is now debating whether to try for the Senior Foreign Service, which will make it even that much harder trying to get jobs together. So we're sort of at a turning point really. Does my career take precedence? Does his career?

Most tandems who have found jobs together have found they have to alternate taking the lead job. We went to Moscow because of my job there. Ross ideally would not have gone back to Moscow so soon directly from Prague. But it certainly didn't hurt his career, and it was a wonderful time to be there. We came back here now very definitely because of his job. That's fine. We'd been out for five years. It's sooner than we wanted to come to Washington, but fine.

But now he's wondering, "Should I take the lead and then try to get the job?" And I'm not sure I want that. Again, as a woman I have concerns about family. Again, I wonder, "How driven am I? How driven do I want to be?" Yes, I really enjoy the Foreign Service life, and it's very hard for me to imagine not working as an officer overseas.

Many people think that it's an ideal situation to be a tandem. But I think you really have to want to be a Foreign Service officer, as I do, to do a good job and enjoy it. I really don't recommend that people take the Foreign Service exam unless they're committed to being an officer. You're not a free agent, you have to support your government, no matter what. Fifty percent or 90 percent of what you do is junked or it never goes anywhere, and you have to live with that. You have to live with all the dignitaries who come through, the senators and their wives, and everything like that. Spouses who are teachers or have a portable profession I envy to some extent, because they are in some ways much more flexible.

I am constantly being asked, "What do you think about being a tandem and joining the Foreign Service?" And I always respond, "Think before you do it. The Foreign Service can be tough for everyone. For a single officer, it's tough. It can be very lonely. For an officer with a family, it can be doubly tough. First of all, safety is always a concern. When we were growing up, there wasn't as great a fear of terrorism as there is today.

It's a hard life for families, because when you are overseas as a tandem you're both working all the time. And particularly with U.S. Information Agency, since your job is outside of the office and so you're doing that much more entertaining and receptions and traveling around to all the various

Tandem couple Ross Wilson and Margo Squire, Prague, Czechoslovakia, 1986. *Courtesy of Patricia Squire.*

centers, and you're involved with the academics and the cultural types who are leading the after-hours lives. It's much harder when you have children, and Ross and I really worry about how we will manage when we go abroad again.

We were working all the time when we were assigned to Moscow. Without children, the work was exciting and rewarding because the two of us could do it together. With kids, you don't want to work as hard as that.

I really had two role models for the Foreign Service: my father, as the officer with the strong, traditional Foreign Service sense of service, and my mother, as the mother of a movable family. That has very definitely come across, and I feel that I have an obligation to serve, but I also have an obligation to my children. It may seem corny, but a love of one's country and a need to really represent the country is there. I can remember feeling as a child that I had to act a certain way or I would bring dishonor to my country. When my father was in Vietnam for two years and we were back in my mother's hometown in Massachusetts, I can remember in junior high they had a little softbound yearbook and eighth-graders got different awards. I had the best manners because of what I had learned overseas. You curtsied, you shook hands, you did all the things that goodwill diplomats did, and you certainly never did anything wrong.

My father was in Vietnam for almost two years, and having no father for that time was really hard. If you ask any Foreign Service dependent what the hardest adjustment is, it's coming back in preteen or teen years, or even university years, when you've been overseas for a long time. I was coming from Moscow, and of course that was sort of exotic, and we went to my mother's hometown, Gardner, Massachusetts. The furthest most of my classmates had been was Boston, maybe Maine. One girl had been to California. But I was coming from the moon. And when you're that age, you don't want to be different. That's really at the point where you just want to meld in with everyone else.

I was 13. And so to be hauled up in front of assemblies and in classes and, "Talk about the Soviet Union!" Well, Russia. "Tell us about Russia!" And of course, when we were in Moscow, we were constantly bombarded by anti-American propaganda. There were posters everywhere comparing the Americans to Nazis, and there was a lot of anti-Vietnam sentiment, obviously. You'd see American soldiers bayoneting Vietnamese. There was a lot of propaganda in general about what life was like in the United States.

I had thought, "Oh, it's going to be such a relief to go back to the U.S., because it's home and you don't have that." And so to come back and find anti-Russian propaganda was very interesting to me. There was the sense that Russia was a big concentration camp.

The question I kept getting was, "How did I escape?" Because there was this idea, somehow twisted in people's minds with, again, Nazi Germany, of this huge barbed wire fence that I had somehow climbed over. It was a shock to me to find out that, no, the United States wasn't totally open and totally objective. That was the hardest move I ever made because, here it was my country, and why did I feel so uncomfortable coming back?

My mother basically had to give up her career for the service, and all my life I heard, "You have to be your own person, you have to have your own career." My husband and I were engaged, and we were visiting his family in Minnesota when we decided to get married. I called my parents—this was while I was still in graduate school in Washington and I hadn't gotten an offer from USIA yet—and my mother's reaction was not, "Congratulations," although they loved Ross, but, "Are you sure you want to marry him when you're not in the Foreign Service yet?"

And my father, who was on the line, said, "Listen to your mother." Because obviously he knew what effect his career had had on her. And there I was, educated, college and master's and everything, and I guess they saw it in terms of the old Foreign Service when the wife was an appendage—I would be following Ross around the world. My mother would argue that since 1972 it's become worse because before that at least to some extent wives were credited. She, unlike most women, liked the old [service], where wives were included in their husbands' evaluation.

But I would just hate that. Ross being rated by whether I entertain or how well is just crazy. But for my mother, that was very important because that was her contribution. But it's not expected of me, and it really isn't even of the spouses who aren't Foreign Service officers nowadays.

BUSINESS—BUT NOT AS USUAL

Karen McCluskey was of the right generation and was in the right place on three occasions—New York City in 1987, Vienna in 1989, and Washington in 1992— to establish three cross-cultural consulting businesses. She left the first two behind when her spouse was transferred. In 1992—considering her husband's inevitable transfer from Washington—she realized she could not overcome the mobility inherent in Foreign Service life. Karen McCluskey felt there would never be a right time in service life for her personal ambitions, but she retained a loyalty to her husband's profession. Her successes, nonetheless, paved the way for professional achievement by later spouses. She exemplified how determination and hard work could overcome both host country barriers and hidebound State Department rules. In a 1992 interview, she remembered:

I always wanted to get into international business. That was a goal of mine long before I went to the Sorbonne. It's why I chose my two majors, business and French. When I was at school in Paris, I met Tom, now my husband, and we both wanted to get overseas again as fast as we could, and we both worked toward that. He got there first by being accepted into the Foreign Service, so I went with him. He said he would have gone with me if I had gotten a job first. I'm not so sure, I think it would have been hard for him.

I actually arrived in Turkey thinking naively that I would be able to work in the local economy. I couldn't imagine why I wouldn't be able to do that. I had a business degree and was darned if I'd be stopped by anyone. Well, I was stopped by myself because I had no Turkish language skills. We found out very shortly before moving that we were going to Turkey, there was no time for language training. I barely had time to sell the car.

After we arrived in Istanbul, I interviewed with Citibank and a couple of other American businesses, which politely told me, "Sorry—if you have no Turkish language skills, we can't use you, we have no place for you." So I went to the consulate, and I got two jobs actually—one lasted the entire tour, an administrative writer-researcher job, which I loved. I did take language classes, and by the end I was translating Turkish newspaper articles into English to support the reports we were sending back to Washington. During the last of our three years there, I held the community liaison officer job concurrently with the writer-researcher job. But I learned that there's no such

247

thing as two part-time jobs, you have two full-time jobs. I also went to evening school for Turkish language, so I was pretty stressed out. But I enjoyed it.

When we went to Nairobi, I worked at the embassy for the commercial attaché. Then there was Gramm-Rudman-Hollings [budget cuts], and my job was one of the ones that had to go. Luckily, the community liaison officer job opened up at about the same time, and I applied. Having been a CLO before was a big help, and I got the job, which was very different from the job in Istanbul, a small post where we had about 50 families. Nairobi, in contrast, had 300 families, with a large AID contingent. We did a series of workshops on cross-cultural adjustment, families overseas, job searching in Kenya, job search skills, volunteer opportunities, and reentry to Washington, all those kinds of things. I feel good about what I did in Nairobi. It's what got me my next job in New York City. Nairobi was a rough posting, I have to say, but I miss the game parks, and I miss the open expanses of land and the Massai, and I miss the Kikuyus, the exotica of Kenya.

But I also felt I had gone as far as I could in the system as a Foreign Service spouse—I didn't think I could get much more meaningful work in view of my goals for my life, my background, and my education. I wanted career progression, and I couldn't see it happening going to another foreign posting.

Then we went to New York. I managed to parlay my experiences into a training manager job at one of the largest banks in New York, Manufacturers Hanover Corporation, and was promoted in less than a year to a management slot in the corporate training department. We lived right in Manhattan, so I could walk to work. I'm a city person, I love the pulse of the city. I, of course, hoped all along that I could pull Tom out of the Foreign Service in New York so that we could live there forever, but that didn't work out either.

Then Tom got Vienna. That was a really hard decision, for both of us—harder for me, I think, than for Tom—because I really was on my way and had focused my very haphazard experiences overseas into a very organized career. At this same time, we also got pregnant. We decided—with the pregnancy and the fact that I could legally work as an independent contractor-consultant in Vienna—perhaps this would be a good move. After consulting with a lawyer, the family liaison office, and a few others, I decided to start my own business in Vienna, an exciting new opportunity. But in a way the move came at a bad time for me, because I was really taking off. I now know if I'd stayed I'd have made it into an assistant vice president slot.

Anyway, I was giving up a lot, but you know, you make your decisions. When I got to Vienna, I started German classes right away. I'd taken a short evening course at New York University, and I continued with two intensive courses as soon as I arrived. Then I called an Austrian lawyer and said, "Please work out the details and let me know how I can set up a business on the local economy."

To make a long story short, I got some wonderful contracts right away.

My business just took off, in part, I think, because I was a mystery, the Austrians just couldn't believe that a pregnant American would want to do training programs and write for them. I remember the interview I had on the day I was due; it was my best contract the whole time I was there. When I waddled in, which, of course, I was doing at nine or nine and a half months, the interviewer looked at my stomach and just smiled slightly. I thought, "I've got to say something about this, I can't just ignore it." I said, "Well, you can see I'm pregnant." He said, "I see that, when are you due?" I said, "Today," and his eyes just got really big, and I said, "Don't worry, I think she's going to take her time. I don't think she'll be here for a while." He just laughed, and it set a wonderful tone for that meeting, and I got great contracts from that organization. Meghan was born a week and a half later. I hired an Indian woman to take care of her, and my business just took off. I also taught at two universities there, Webster University, based in St. Louis, and the Austrian School of Tourism in Vienna. I taught human resource management.

I have to say, I got a lot of resistance from the people around me because setting up a business was something that had not been done by an embassy wife before. There were a lot of naysayers who said, "You're making waves, don't do this." I said, "I want my business to be internationally successful some day." So I went for it. I hired an accountant, I kept in touch with the lawyer, and I was very comfortable knowing that I was working legally and paying taxes and that no one could ever complain about my right to work in Austria. I wanted to start a good reputation that would continue year after year. The cost to me was giving up my diplomatic immunity, which was a big cost and something to be concerned about. But the immunity was only given up during the hours I was working. So when I was at home, or if there were an evacuation, I still had that protection.

I have to say, it felt really good to be successful, legally successful in a country where I was told I'd never be able to establish a business. And the best part about it was, I know of a couple of women who came after me who were then able to do the same thing. I'd done some of the groundwork. I turned a lot of my contracts over to one of those women, I know she's doing a great job with all of them. But it was really hard for me to give it all up because to market my services and build the client base took six months out of a two-year tour.

And then it was time to leave. I wanted to stay longer, but after a lot of family discussion, we decided to return to the U.S. It was a hard decision, but it has paid off for me to come back to Washington. I registered my business as Global Training Associates soon after I got here, did all the necessary licensing, and converted part of my basement into an office. I've built a client base once again, and this time I don't want to say goodbye. Obviously at some point Tom has to go abroad again, but we're hoping it can wait. We want any move to be years away. There are some posts I would consider messing up my business for, which is how I see a move—destroying my client base again. I think that's a realistic way to look at it. I have a deep commitment to the importance of the training programs I conduct in management, communication, and cross-cultural issues. So the bottom line is, am I better off as a result of my Foreign Service years? I have a good marriage and a beautiful daughter, I have some wonderful experiences overseas to draw from that have nothing to do with work and some that do. Would I have had those things? No, and that would be a big loss. So in some ways I am better off having spent those years abroad. I've tried to make the most—professionally and personally—of my overseas experiences, but from a career perspective there was definitely a cost.

FOREIGN-BORN IN THE FOREIGN SERVICE

"I had been in the Foreign Service for 23 years before I had any support from a foreign-born spouse group," recalled Magda Cooper, a native of Lima, Peru, in a 1992 interview. But the State Department did slowly respond to growing numbers of foreign-born spouses, to whom service in Washington was doubly difficult, as was posting to yet a third country and culture. There were many reasons why Foreign Service officers increasingly married foreign nationals while at post. One certainly was the growing reluctance of potential American partners to live the uprooted Foreign Service lifestyle. Cooper's experiences were hardly unique among foreign-born spouses.

More and more American women want to stay in the United States and pursue a career. They are very frustrated by the fact that they cannot pursue their own career if they move every few years, while foreign-born spouses more or less conform to the mobility, the Foreign Service situations.

I had short-term jobs, like I worked teaching Spanish when we were in Helsinki, Finland. When I came back to the States, I either worked as an interpreter or taught Spanish at the Foreign Service Institute. Again when I went overseas, I did voluntary work. And when I came back to Washington the last time, I had a job in the director-general's office. I was the manager for Foreign Service Day for four years. In 1988, when we were transferred to Grenada, the deputy director-general told me he was happy to assign my husband as chargé but was sorry to lose me as manager. My reply was, "You do not have to lose me if the government needs me." The following year a contract to do Foreign Service Day—a four-month project—reached me in Grenada. Every year while we were in St. George's I returned to Washington to do Foreign Service Day.

So it's not that we foreign-born spouses sit idle. We do a lot of things, but we are very realistic. We know that our life is such that every few years we have to change our life patterns. We do that in order to stay with the family, stay with our husbands. Our families are a very high priority in our life. I would never consider not providing an orderly home for my children. For me, I would be uncomfortable. But once I get them settled, I go and look for a job.

As a result of [a 1986 Overseas Briefing Center] workshop, I think there was an awareness of the differences between foreign-born spouses and American-born spouses, because for the first time some of us had an opportunity to speak out, to express our feelings. I must say, most of us were real achievers, and we just wanted to make OBC realize that, because our cultural backgrounds are different, we look at life differently. But it doesn't have to be better or worse. Just different. Unfortunately, there was no follow-up to the workshop, but we in the group continued to have monthly meetings.

A lot more has been done in recent years to make our lives more comfortable. Still, we have tremendous hurdles to pass in order to be effective and to be happy at the same time.

We have to make new foreign-born spouses, especially those who just come into the United States for the first time after they got married overseas, aware of what is available for them. Take advantage of language training. Plan. Try to get a job when you are overseas with the government so when you come back you have the president's executive order [which increases civil service job options for returning spouses] and you are able to be reintegrated in your job in Washington. If you don't tell the spouses what is available, there is no way they're going to find out, and the foreign-born spouse group is a fantastic way to keep everybody informed. Sometimes coming back to Washington can be the most difficult posting. When I came back to Washington in 1966, there were not any of the support systems that we have today. The State Department then was not well organized for spouses. They didn't have the Family Liaison Office.

I lost a child in Washington. But I didn't speak about it because in those days I thought, "Well, who is going to listen to me?" A tragedy's a tragedy, but if you have your immediate family with you, it's a support system. And now we have support systems within the State Department. We have workshops. We have networking. If a woman gets breast cancer, there is a group.

There's also a problem in coming back to the States, which is your spouse's home country. You realize how culturally different you are from each other. This is something the husband never really understands, because you are trying so hard to adapt that you ignore your inner feelings and you don't talk about it.

I met Ford, my husband, when he was assigned to Lima, Peru. I had been in the United States, at Chatham College in Pittsburgh, and I had come home to my family in Lima after that. Ford had to submit his resignation when he told the department that we were going to get married. It took over six months to hear back from the State Department whether they had approved his marrying me or not. That was a true love test! Then, immediately after, we were transferred to Glasgow, Scotland. But the department would not allow a foreign-born spouse to go overseas before getting her naturalization papers. So we came to the States, and in three weeks I got my U.S. citizenship. We didn't have a choice. Nowadays foreign-born spouses can choose. In my personal experience, it has been to my advantage, because I have been able to get federal jobs here in Washington in the department. After all, your children are American, so they want the mother to have the same citizenship. At least, my kids feel that way.

I can understand why some foreign-born spouses want to keep their passports. First of all, dual nationalities are now recognized in many countries. If the marriage doesn't work and they want to return to their country and they don't have access, for instance, to the legal rights that they had before, because they gave up their citizenship, where do they go? It has pros and cons.

We also provide information on the selection-out process, which, unfortunately, is going to affect a lot of our future middle-career officers because of the "windows" promotion process. The bottom line is this: we have to be prepared for it. Should our husbands have to leave the service in their, let's say, early forties, we should both as a couple be contemplating a second career. Also, providing funds, savings, for us and our children. What happens if the husband is selected out when you are paying college education? Or you're having parents who need care? That could perfectly well happen when you are in your forties and fifties. So we are warning the families, "This can happen to you. Let's be ready."

I feel very comfortable as a spouse, thanks to some fantastic role models that I have had through the years, both American-born and foreign—foreign spouses that became ambassadors' wives. They gave me the guidelines to be myself, not to try to impress anybody by being somebody else. Yet serve with dignity, because it is a responsibility. It's not a game. I think our image overseas is very important. We represent one of the biggest countries in the world. It is important for a foreign-born spouse to speak English well. Any extra bit of education that she has adds to her as an asset, to this organization and to her husband. So I never stop learning. I have tried to join all the Overseas Briefing Center workshops that there are whenever I'm in Washington.

When we go overseas as a couple, the local people view us as the two for the price of one, unfortunately. No matter how many new laws exist in the department, that's what they expect from you. So the more dignity and the more importance that you give to your job, the better projection you make. The host country feels that they deserve the best. Even though State's policy may say that a spouse is not judged, the reality is that we are judged, by local people especially—the way you entertain, the way you conduct yourself, the contribution you make. The diplomatic career will always involve the spouse. The foreign-born spouse is another dimension of the American culture, since we have many, many foreigners in the United States.

AIDS IN AFRICA

The epidemic spread of the human immunodeficiency virus (HIV) and acquired immunodeficiency syndrome (AIDS) in Africa, while initially met with a panicked reaction by Foreign Service officers and spouses, eventually became just another challenge of serving in an overseas post, recalled Linda Bell in a 1991 interview.

AIDS was absolutely rampant throughout Zambia. Yet the embassy personnel did a flip-flop, from being almost paranoid, hypersensitive, about it to accepting the situation. Prior to our arrival, there had been such hysteria that Lusaka was the first mission in Africa, I believe, to start universal AIDS testing of all local employees. They refused to hire anybody who was HIV positive. Remember, it wasn't so long ago that we still weren't sure whether the mosquito might transmit AIDS.

I think everyone was more educated when we arrived in 1988, because the concern had diminished considerably. We were aware that this was an AIDS-infected area, and we still chose to go there, and you just assumed that everybody in your household was exposed to AIDS. If mothers were worried about young children and their contact with baby handlers—there really wasn't much likelihood of the children getting it, except perhaps in the case of a wet nurse—I think the mothers just took more upon themselves. A servant washing dishes or preparing food or brushing up against you or even hugging the children is not going to infect you or the children with AIDS. It was probably better not to test them because it really wouldn't make much difference one way or another. They could be HIV positive this week; perhaps two months ago they were negative.

Near the end of our tour, the embassy needed four new local employees. The policy was to medically AIDS-test anybody short-listed for these jobs. Embassy personnel knew it would be difficult to fill these slots, because the former hysteria had more or less written that into the rules. There were 20 candidates tested for the four positions, and out of the 20, 18 were HIV positive. That's when it was decided that the time had come to be more flexible, because the embassy couldn't operate efficiently under those circumstances. After all, a person who has tested HIV positive still has five, perhaps more, very active working years. Also, somebody might be hired who is HIV negative and yet walk across the street and be hit by a car. We lost just as many employees through automobile and other accidents.

So I think the whole feeling was, just assume they're HIV positive and give them a job, they need a job. They're still productive elements of the community, you can't put this stigma on them. You just have to make sure that your behavior is such that you don't expose yourself.

The embassy had a policy of providing coffins for family members of local Agency for International Development, U.S. Information Service, and embassy employees. (We had a fairly large employee network because all the carpentry, plumbing, electrical, and other work of that kind was done by embassy contract employees.) By the time I left, they were making a coffin a week. A couple of years earlier, it had averaged about one every three months. The carpenters used every scrap of lumber, even the used boxes from the commissary, which I was managing. A lot of those coffins were for infants under the age of two. I don't know what the percentage might have been, but certainly the majority were AIDS victims.

It was very sad. You had to harden yourself a bit to survive. I can't recall statistics of the number of deaths in Lusaka every day, but it was absolutely phenomenal. The city's main cemetery was just down the street from us, and there was a constant stream of trucks full of people coming or going to an African funeral. Sometimes there were four or five funerals at the same time. One day you'd pass an open field, the next day there would be all these little crosses. Where there had been funerals, now little headstones.

NO FREE LUNCH

The Report on the Role of the Spouse in the Foreign Service—a research study conducted in 1985, but still the most comprehensive account of spouse attitudes— found that the women most content in the Foreign Service were those with time for their families and occasional representational entertaining, and with a chance to work at post.[2] With a little belt-tightening, and with part-time or entry-level jobs for spouses during Washington assignments, couples could manage a mortgage with children in college. But since that report, the steady ratcheting up of housing and education costs, and the general cost of living, have made a second income a necessity for Foreign Service families. Mary Bowen explained in a 1990 interview.

Before I had children, I remember being frustrated looking for work in Bogota, Colombia, trying to find some sort of career path. That was in 1974, before the service encouraged spouses to work in embassies. I had secretarial skills, and I went to the personnel officer in the embassy to apply for a job. I was willing to do anything. I was "fresh" out of school and had worked before, but I was not encouraged. Later, when I told one of the secretaries I had applied, she said what a shame: they'd flown someone down [from the U.S. on] temporary duty, for a job that I was capable of doing. So the department was not yet aware of the resources it had in spouses at post.

I did teach English as a second language in a Colombian school for one semester. I did some substitute teaching at the American School there. On my own, I did a little freelance translating for a neighbor-translator who had extra work. And I did some tutoring with individual students, Americans and others. But it was really in Bogota that I realized I had to do something about a career path. I was frustrated then, and I realized that I would have to be adaptable. There could always be blocks to what I wanted to do. But once I started having children, I put a career to one side.

After Bogota, we went to Bukavu, Zaire, and were there during very difficult times. The country was broke, the economy was very bad.

Our son, Andrew, was born while we were there. I arrived in Zaire with Joanna, my daughter, as a one-year-old, and then had Andrew in Kenya. I flew to Nairobi on a missionary plane when I was seven months pregnant and stayed in a family hotel. I took Joanna with me, and my mother met me there.

My husband had to stay behind in Bukavu, so I took a taxi alone to the hospital when it was time and had my son.

My mother had contacted the embassy in Nairobi and asked them to radio to Bukavu because there was no telephone contact; the whole country of Zaire didn't pay their long-distance phone bills, so they had no such phone capability. The embassy said it would send a cable. Cables only went to Kinshasa and then by pouch to Bukavu, which would have taken a very long time. Finally radio contact was established—Andrew was born on a Friday and John was able to get a Saturday plane and arrive that day. We waited about a week before going back to Zaire, the time interval the doctor thought right before the baby should travel.

I was fortunate in having two babies in Bukavu because they gave me something to do. I didn't work for nine years and only began again when we went to Brasilia, where I started working right away in the embassy. Even though my youngest was in preschool, I was leaving the children for a time with a caretaker who spoke a language they didn't speak, and it wasn't easy for them to adjust to that.

But there would always be someone at home, and we had the advantage of being in a family environment. We were in a compound, and there was a sense of security. Brasilia, of course, is so isolated there was a great interdependence. The friends we made in Brasilia are closer than those we've made since then, even though they're more removed in time. There were enough people at the embassy to really find someone we had things in common with.

We bought a house in Falls Church [suburban Virginia] when we came back from Africa 12 years ago. It was a very small house, and it was a serious disappointment. We chose a tiny house inside the Beltway [shorter commute to the Department of State] rather than moving way out to live more comfortably. It was a very, very small house. We kept it while we were overseas, and a year ago we moved into it. We knew that it was too small, and so we sold it recently and moved to a slightly larger house. It was only because our first house was inside the Beltway, and because I'm working part-time, that we could buy the second house.

If we were living on John's salary alone we would not be in this larger house, where we are quite comfortable. We have a part-time salary and a full-time salary, and that's okay because we don't have the children in college yet. I don't know what that's going to be like. My part-time salary is entry-level. I have a graduate degree and have been out of school for many years, and I'm still working at an entry-level salary. Part of that is because of moving around for the Foreign Service, but it's also because of my children. In fact, I feel it's more because I was fortunate and I could stay home with my children when they were little, or at least stay home most of the time.

Now we have contingency plans. We're here for three more years. My oldest is a sophomore in high school. When she starts college, we'll probably go overseas again, and my husband says he wants a post with the biggest hardship allowance possible. I'm also working on a library degree, knowing that when we go overseas there's a very good chance that I'll not be able to use it. I can always go overseas and work again as a secretary or as a substitute teacher, but I think I'll have to work full-time with the oldest in college. We have two more children, and at one point we'll have all three in college. That's when we do have to find a differential post, that's not a joke.

I think if I were bringing in a respectable salary with my library degree we might be less inclined to go overseas. Right now I earn so little that it doesn't matter; I would probably earn more overseas. I think my husband would consider retiring early if I had a career—a job which I really liked and where I had a good salary. I think all along he's always been open to leaving the service; I don't mean that he's not dedicated but, for instance, when we first bought our house—before the Foreign Service Act of 1980—his salary was very, very low, and considering the size of our family, we were practically eligible to receive free lunches at school!

The schools always sent around a little letter about the free lunch program, and I remember looking at it one year and thinking, "Oh, last year we fit!" We laugh now, but it wasn't funny then. And he was seriously looking for another job at that time, just because if he didn't earn enough to support his family in Washington, why stay in the service? But then they did pass the 1980 act, and he received a significant salary increase. We're kind of planning that when my husband does retire, he'll retire fairly young and that will be my chance to work, using my library degree. These days I don't see anyone pressured to have children and stay at home. All I see are financial pressures for women to work.

THE ENDANGERED SPOUSE

As the responsibilities of the Foreign Service continued to increase during the 1990s, and the increasingly qualified spouses' reluctance to leave careers and relocate abroad grew, the presence of spouses at post abroad continued to decline. But when there, they found enhanced employment opportunities in more substantive positions.

Joan Pryce offered positive views of her experiences working as the employment program coordinator in the Family Liaison Office in a 1992 interview.

We have doctors and lawyers and farmers and pilots and chemists and all kinds of people in the Foreign Service spouse pool. We're working to establish more bilateral work agreements so that people have access to employment on the local economy. This should broaden the range of employment. But we also have to look at expanding other opportunities. More creative use of contract employment, maybe through AID or through other organizations. Being able to hire spouses as consultants or as temporary contractors.

I think networking is very important. If you have a spouse coming into the Foreign Service who is a lawyer, woman or man, they feel like they're starting from ground zero. They have to find out where lawyers have worked. "How do I go about getting a legal job in the Middle East or the Far East?" If we had an established network, they could take advantage of [the experience of] other lawyers who have already done that groundwork in those regions. So I think networking is an area where we have to really expand.

And then internally, there are two areas where I think we need to expand. One concerns the people who are interested in continuity between mission employment overseas and U.S. government employment in the Washington area. When they come back to Washington and they would like to work in the State Department and make use of their experience gained in temporary positions in a mission abroad. We need to develop better continuity for them, to get credit for their overseas service. And we need to develop a system so that spouses—say working in a secretarial job in one post—can be assured of at least getting the highest previous rate at the next post, or perhaps have some kind of a promotion pattern, or way to move up in particular kinds of jobs that are at a number of missions.

We want to look for more substantive jobs for spouses in the mission, and as we face budget cuts within the Foreign Service, I think there's a real opportunity to do that. There may be shortages or gaps when Foreign Service officers are not at post, and we may have spouses who are skilled in certain areas, have had the appropriate training, and can fill in.

And the last thing I would say is that we need to work for a more flexible attitude toward senior spouses working. This is another trend. We have more and more spouses of ambassadors and deputy chiefs of mission spouses working in our missions, and this often creates what is considered to be a conflict of interest or a perceived conflict of interest. And yet somehow it isn't fair to a professional spouse who has the appropriate skills not to be able to put them to use if she or he can manage to work without a conflict of interest.

Another, more pessimistic view on the status of spouses was expressed in 1992 by U.S. Ambassador to Bangladesh William B. Milam, one of the original architects of the 1972 directive.

Even with [spouse] compensation, which I think is a long time away in any case, I believe the structure of the Foreign Service and of our work overseas will change dramatically in the next two decades. Not only will spouses probably not be so involved in public activities, frankly they will not need to be. And as for representation officers will have to learn to do it by themselves.

The role of spouses is changing—and right under our own eyes—yet I think we fail to notice it. This is the trend of the times, and I believe it is inevitable.[3]

"1992 marked the 20th anniversary of two important events: the 1972 directive on wives and the opening of Disney World. Both created fantasy worlds, but only one of them has been successful," wrote AAFSW President Christine Shurtleff in 1992.

The 1972 directive established a policy that, in effect, describes spouses as non-persons, and does not allow for any recognition for the positive endeavors of spouses who choose to pursue the traditional spousal role. . . . Spouses of senior officers may no longer be judged in the sponsoring employee's efficiency reports, but they are still judged by the foreign society in which they live. . . .

The present climate is one that fosters the image that the only way to fulfilled life overseas is to work within the cocoon of the embassy. When the expectation of a meaningful job does not materialize, demoralization sets in. There is a growing trend among officers at all levels to bid on assignments according to the availability at post of jobs for their spouses. Among senior officers, particularly, there is a growing trend to not accept certain assignments or to go to post without a spouse who has found meaningful work in the U.S. The result of all these factors is that the image we are portraying in host countries overseas is not much different from recent images the world had of the Communist Bloc countries: all nationals working behind the walls of secured fortresses. It is ironic that as family members from former bloc countries are seen moving more freely in marketplaces overseas, savoring the daily contact with citizens at all levels in the host countries, our American family members no longer have the time to do so because they are holding jobs in the embassy.[4]

The 1985 research study The Role of the Spouse in the Foreign Service *drew two dramatic conclusions: the spouses of senior officers had the most negative attitudes, primarily because they received no recognition for performing the role expected of them, yet 61 percent of respondents felt that the ambassador's spouse should provide a leadership role. These conflicting tensions facing the traditional spouse in the Foreign Service remained unaddressed in the early 1990s. Meanwhile, these spouses, a dwindling part of diplomatic communities abroad, continued without compensation or recognition in a volunteer support role, some more comfortably than others.*

The State Department, ever resistant to change, has been consistently reluctant to recognize spouses' talents, skills, and potential. It has, when pushed, responded to the need for increased spouse employment—in tandem arrangements, with more in-house jobs, more bilateral agreements with foreign governments, and greater assistance to spouses seeking employment abroad. But spouses have provided the primary impetus for this progress.

And the department has been slow to recognize that there are many different solutions to the spouse dilemma, including recognition—other than the usual Foggy Bottom rhetoric—that the traditional, supportive spouse provided valuable services to U.S. government policy aims abroad, services deserving of compensation. There are precedents for this solution in any number of countries.

In 1993 the disadvantages caused by the lack of official status for spouses gained a glimmer of recognition on Capitol Hill. As Senator Joseph Biden told the Senate Foreign Relations Committee: "One of the things we vastly underestimate in this government is the sacrifices that spouses, male or female, make, allowing career diplomats to pursue their careers. I am of the view, and I am in a distinct minority, that . . . an ambassador's spouse should be paid, because they are required, as a matter of course, to provide certain duties and functions on behalf of the United States government. In short, their entire life is consumed by the job." [5]

Also in 1993, a federal appeals court declared First Lady Hillary Rodham Clinton a "de facto officer or employee" of the government, the first time the judiciary extended official recognition to the role of the spouse. [6] *Both were further evidence that women in the United States, and in the Foreign Service, "are establishing themselves in the mainstream of public life."* [7]

Mary Bowen receiving a transcript of her interview at the Foreign Service Spouse Oral History Program annual meeting, DACOR Bacon House, the retired Foreign Service officers club, Washington, D.C., 1992. *Courtesy of Carl L. Nelson.*

Appendix:
The Foreign Service Spouse Oral History Program

Interviewees

The following women and men were interviewed for the Foreign Service Spouse Oral History Program through August 1993. The asterisks following or within names signify: (*)—post–Foreign Service married name; (**)—divorced, Foreign Service name no longer used; (***)—Foreign Service officer husband's name; and (****)—maiden name, not used in the Foreign Service. As a rule, the maiden names listed below (e.g., Soell, Quinn, Glassford, White) signify association with U.S. government foreign affairs agencies or Washington, D.C. prior to marriage. Transcripts of interviews and supplemental interview materials quoted in the text are available from: Association of American Foreign Service Women Oral History Collection, 5125 MacArthur Blvd., N.W., Suite 36, Washington, D.C. 20016-3300.

Adams, Frances

Atherton, Betty

Austin, Lillian (Lee) Soell

Barbis, Patricia Quinn

Bartlett, Joan

Bartz, Patricia

Beam, Margaret (Peggy) Glassford

Bell, Linda

Bennett, Janet

Bennett, Margaret White

Berle, Beatrice

Blake, Regina (Gene)

Blane, Dianne (Deedee)

Bloch, Stuart Marshall

Bogardus, Virginia (Ginnie)

Bond, Ruth

Bourne, Lucie

Bowen, Mary

Briggs, Lucy

Brown, Peggy Ann

Buckley, Richard

Byington, Jane

Cabot, Elizabeth

Caldwell, Martha Painter

Chard, Cynthia

Child, Julia McWilliams

Chipman, Théophania (Fanny) Bunand-
  Sevastos
(Chrisler****), Miriam
Clubb, Mariann
(Cluett*), Catharine Johnson
Cooper, Magda
Cooper (King**), Marguerite
Daly, Anne
Dane, Leila
Davis, Mary Kay
Day, Susan
(Deane****), Sara
Deason, Joan
Dillon, Caroline (Sue)
Dinsmore, Amelia (Perk)
Dixon, Frances
Dorman, Lesley
Dorsey, Carolyn
Dubs, Jane
Eagleburger, Marlene Heinemann
Elbrick, Elvira (Elfie)
Emmerson, Dorothy
English, Anita Grew
Ensley (Kotula**), Ruth
Fenzi, Jewell
Forbord, Nancy
Frechette, Barbara
Freeman, Phyllis
Glazer, Mildred
Grady, Joanne
Green, Lispenard (Lisa) Crocker
Hamilton, June
Handley (Milam***), Faith
Hanson, Muriel
Harper, Lisa Manfull
Hart, Jane

Hartman, Donna
Hirsch, Miryam
Holmes, Marilyn Strauss
Ingraham, Susan
Irving, R. Allen
Jassie, Lois
Johnson, Jane
Jordan, Yvonne
Kahn, Ruth
Kaiser, Hannah
Kane, Dagmar
Keeley, Louise
Keogh-Fisher, Sue
Kerr, Margaret
Kidd, Mary Horak
Kidder, Dorothy
Kinney, Stephanie
Kolarek, Frances
Kormann, Elsa
Laingen, Penelope (Penne)
Lane, Betsy
Lane, Cornelia
LaPorta, Ann
Lee, Eleanore
(Lévitt*), Lilla Grew Moffat
Lewis, Hilda
Lewis, Sallie
Lion, Elizabeth (Liz)
(Little*), Ruth Smith
Long, Anne Alling
Low, Helen (Sue)
Lyon, Elizabeth (Elsie) Grew
Macomber, Jr., William B.
Marcy, Mildred
Martin, Elizabeth (Betty)
Massey, Suska

Mathews, Naomi

Matlock, Rebecca

Matthews, Nancy

McCarthy, Marija

McCluskey, Karen

McGeehon, Dale

McIlvaine, Alice

Metcalf, Doris Magnusson

Meyers, Hope

Miller (Twaddell**), Kristie

Mills, Francesca

Minutillo, Maryann

Moffat, Pamela

Morgan, Margaret (Peggy)

Morin, Ann

Motley, Judy

Murphy (Tymeson***), Patricia

(Nanny*), Matilda (Tillie) Cowles

Neumann, Marlen

Newberry, Susanne Davis

Oakley, Phyllis Eliot

Palmer, Margaret Jones

Patterson, Janet

Patterson, Marvin Breckinridge

Peltier, Catherine (Casey)

Perez, Kristine

Peterson, Esther

Pickering, Alice Stover

Prince, Dorothy

Pryce, Joan

Razi, Joana (Eggie)

Rice, Mary

Richardson, Pearl

Richmond, Pamela

Rowell, Lenora (Le)

Ryan, Patricia (Patty)

Sandin, Donna Hersey

Schoenfeld, Aida

Schweitzer (Derham***), Joleen

Service, Caroline Schulz

Silberstein, Fanchon

Simmons, Caroline

Slany, William Z.

Smith, Judith (Judy)

Smith, Laura

Sokolove, Hazel

(Spencer*), June Beakes Byrne

Spiers, Patience

Squire (Wilson***), Marguerite (Margo)

Squire, Patricia

Stearns, Antonia

Stibravy, Roma

Stillman, Chris

Stone, Anne

Sullivan, Margaret

Swanson (Salisbury***), Suzanne

Switzer, Sheila

Teare, Jeanie

Trent, Mary Vance

Tymeson, Craig

Vance, Jean

Weiss, Mary Louise Barker

Weisz, Yetta

White, Elizabeth (Betty) Moffat

White, Mary Anne

Whitman, Sue

Wilson, Joan

Wilson, Leila

Wolcott, Marion Post

Wyatt, Susan (McClintock**)

Memoirs and Correspondence

AID collective memoir, 1947–53 (Priscilla DeAngelis, Florence Keppel Dennis, Margaret (Marge) Luikart, Rickel Marvin, Anita Paige, Peggy Pope, Ruth Redstrom, Evelyn Strachan, Lois Hermanson [Young*]). Unpublished typescript, Harry S. Truman Library, Independence, Mo.

Suzanne Anderson, 700-page correspondence, c. 1930–60. Unpublished typescript, Suzanne Anderson collection.

Clemence Jandrey (Boyd*), Foreign Service correspondence to her mother, 1938–59, 7 vols. Unpublished typescript, AAFSW Oral History Collection, Washington, D.C.

Loretta Jones, "Offspring" (1956–81), the memoir of her husband, Harold Jones. Unpublished typescript, Harold Jones collection.

Anna Durkee Smith Kemp and Bernette (Nettie) Chase Kemp, correspondence, 1915–25.

Louisa Kennedy, afterword to Moorehead Kennedy, *The Ayatollah in the Cathedral: Reflections of a Hostage* (New York: Hill and Wang, 1986).

Mildred Ringwalt, "Memoirs of a Foreign Service Wife: 1938–58."

Edith Sebald, "Burma Interlude: Reminiscences of an Ambassador's Wife: 1952–54." Unpublished typescript, Hoover Institution on War, Revolution, and Peace, Stanford University, 1967.

Notes and References

Introduction

1. John L. Brown, "Abigail Adams' First Post," *Foreign Service Journal* (January 1962): 26.

2. L. H. Butterfield, Marc Friedlaender, and Mary-Jo Kline, eds., *The Book of Abigail and John: Selected Letters of the Adams Family 1762–1784* (Cambridge, Mass.: Harvard University Press, 1975), 354.

3. Ibid., 355.

4. Isabella Key Reeves, *A Diplomatic Tea* (Casper, Wyo.: Oil City Press, 1938).

5. Joan Ridder Challinor, "Louisa Catherine Johnson Adams: The Price of Ambition" (Ph.D. thesis, American University, 1982).

6. Suzanne Anderson, letter to her mother, 1951.

7. William B. Macomber, Jr., *The Angel's Game* (New York: Stein and Day, 1975), 127–29.

8. Joseph C. Grew, *Turbulent Era: A Diplomatic Record of Forty Years, 1904–1945*, vol. 1, ed. Walter Johnson (Boston: Houghton Mifflin, 1952), vii.

Chapter 1

1. Butterfield, *Book of Abigail and John*, 378.

2. U.S. Department of State, *Register of the Department of State* (Washington, D.C.: Government Printing Office, 1922).

3. Edith O'Shaughnessy, *A Diplomat's Wife in Mexico* (New York: Harper and Brothers, 1916), 232–34.

4. Ibid., 298–309.

5. Excerpted from Catharine Johnson to Mr. and Mrs. Charles H. Requa (her parents) of Harbor Springs, Michigan, 6 July to 8 August 1919.

6. Bernette Chase Kemp to Anna Smith, 5 December 1916.

7. Anna Smith Kemp to Mary (Mae) Smith Jackson, November 1919.

8. Hope Ridings Miller, *Embassy Row* (New York: Holt, Rinehart and Winston, 1969), 12.

9. [Anonymous], "A Consul's Wife: An Efficiency Report by One Who Knows," *American Consular Bulletin* (January 1923): 8.

10. Rose H. Fales, "The Making of Diplomacy," *Foreign Service Journal* (October 1974): 42.

11. U.S. Department of State, *Register of the Department of State* (Washington, D.C.: Government Printing Office, 1925), 234–38.

12. Homer L. Calkin, *Women in American Foreign Affairs* (Washington, D.C.: U.S. Department of State, 1977), 66.

13. Ibid., 74, 91.

14. Miles M. Shand (Bureau of Appointments), note to Chief Clerk Ben Davis; cited in Calkin, *Women in American Foreign Affairs*, 38.

15. Thomas DiBacco, "An Outsider's Historical Perspective," in *Foreign Service Associates: Concept and Controversy, A Forum* (Washington, D.C.: Center for the Study of Foreign Affairs, Foreign Service Institute, U.S. Department of State, 1986), 37–39.

Chapter 2

1. Judith Grummon Nelson, "Personal Prologues to Pearl Harbor: Diaries and Letters of a U.S. Diplomatic Family in China and Japan" (unpublished). The Boardman-Grew meeting characterized the personal ties that connect families over time and distance in the Foreign Service. In 1932, a year and a half after his historic flight, Russell Boardman's sister, Sandra, married Foreign Service Officer Stuart Edgar Grummon, who on the eve of World War II was assigned as first secretary to the embassy in Tokyo under Ambassador Joseph C. Grew. In her diaries, Sandra Grummon noted that Grew's admiration for her brother also extended to her. (Grew was impressed by Boardman's courage and felt the historic flight had bolstered Turkish-American relations.) In 1954 the Grews' granddaughter, Lilla Lyon, and the Grummons' daughter, Judith (Nelson)—both delivered by a Nazi doctor in Peking—found themselves classmates at Radcliffe College.

2. Grew, *Turbulent Era*, 900–903.

3. Diplomatic and Consular Officers Retired (DACOR), "The History of DACOR Bacon House" (Washington, D.C.: DACOR Bacon House Foundation, 1992), 3.

4. Christine Sadler, "Thursday's Child: Cornelia Bassel of Clarksburg, West Virginia," *National Historical Magazine* (Daughters of the American Revolution) (April 1938): 63–64.

5. Avis Bohlen—whose husband, Charles E. (Chip) Bohlen, served as ambassador to the Soviet Union, the Philippines, and France, and as deputy undersecretary and acting secretary of state—epitomized the ideal Foreign Service spouse. When she died in April 1981, the *Washington Post* reprinted President John F. Kennedy's graceful

tribute to her written at the time of his appointment of Charles Bohlen as ambassador to France in 1962: "She was ideal, first of all, because she was American through and through, but never shrill, or narrow, or self-congratulatory. Then she quite wonderfully combined gaiety with natural dignity, warm friendliness to everyone wishing to be a friend, with thorough understanding that those representing the United States must never imitate spaniels." In 1982 Pamela C. (Mrs. W. Averell) Harriman, who herself became ambassador to France in 1993, established the Avis Bohlen Award as "an ideal way to recognize [the volunteer contributions of] Foreign Service wives." The $2,500 award, presented annually at the Department of State, remains the only officially sanctioned payment to spouses for their support of U.S. foreign affairs.

6. Rosemary Levenson, "Caroline Service: State Department Duty in China, the McCarthy Era, and After, 1933–1977," vol. 2 (Regional Oral History Office, Bancroft Library, University of California at Berkeley, 1978), 31–33.

7. Sara M. Evans, *Born for Liberty: A History of Women in America* (New York: Free Press, 1989), 164–72.

Chapter 3

1. "Foreign Service Jobs Are Open for 300 Women," *Minneapolis Tribune*, 26 September 1943.

2. William L. Shirer, *Berlin Diary: The Journal of a Foreign Correspondent 1934–1941* (New York: Alfred A. Knopf, 1941), 286.

3. Milton Lomask, "Lively Memories: The Life of Mary Marvin Breckinridge Patterson" (unpublished manuscript, Washington, D.C., 1992), 99.

4. Marvin Breckinridge Patterson, talk delivered to the Society of Women geographers, Washington, D.C., 6 December 1986.

5. Lomask, "Lively Memories," 112.

6. Jefferson Patterson, *Capitals and Captives* (privately published, 1966).

7. Ann Denton Behlen, "Mary Marvin Breckinridge Patterson: From Career Broadcaster to Career Diplomatic Wife" (bachelor's thesis, Harvard University, 1982).

Chapter 4

1. Cornelia Lane, letter, 3 August 1945.

2. Levenson, "Caroline Service," 94–97.

3. Paul R. Porter, ed., "Greece at the Turning Point," Group IV Papers (unpublished, Harry S. Truman Library, Independence, Mo., 1981–82).

4. Ibid., 7.

5. Ibid., 11.

6. Suitable housing for American families was extremely scarce. They rented the

summer homes of wealthy Greeks, who then demanded them back during the summer months, regardless of the contract.

7. Loretta Jones, excerpted from Harold Jones's unpublished memoir, "Offspring."

8. Edith Sebald, unpublished memoirs, 1952–54 (Hoover Institution on War, Revolution and Peace, Stanford, Calif.).

9. Morris Weisz, "Labor's Role in World Affairs: A Memoir from a Socialist in the State Department," *Horizons* (Summer 1990): 8–11.

10. Clemence DeGraw Jandrey Boyd, Foreign Service correspondence, 1938–1959 (7 vols.), AAFSW Oral History Collection, Washington, D.C., vol. 4, 640–45.

11. U.S. Department of State, "Statement by Secretary Dulles on Personnel Integration Programs, 8 September 1954," *Department of State Bulletin* 115 (27 September 1954): 444–46.

Chapter 5

1. E. J. Kahn, Jr., *The China Hands: America's Foreign Service Officers and What Befell Them* (New York: Viking Press, 1975), 212–14.

2. John K. Emmerson, *The Japanese Thread: A Life in the U.S. Foreign Service* (New York: Holt, Rinehart and Winston, 1978), 311.

3. Levenson, "Caroline Service," 113–14.

4. Ibid., 112–17.

5. Ibid., 100–101.

6. Ibid., 134.

7. Robert Griffith, *The Politics of Fear: Joseph R. McCarthy and the Senate* (Lexington: University Press of Kentucky, 1970), 315.

8. Levenson, "Caroline Service," 139.

9. Ibid., 140–41.

10. Ibid., 143–44.

11. Mildred Teusler Ringwalt, "Memoirs of a Foreign Service Wife: 1938–58" (unpublished, Chapel Hill, N.C.).

Chapter 6

1. Mary Vance Trent, private communication to George A. Morgan, 19 July 1962.

2. Marvin Breckinridge Patterson, private communication to Fanchon J. Silberstein, Foreign Service Institute, 3 February 1983.

3. Trent to Morgan, 1962.

4. U.S. Department of State, "Training Wives and Other Members of Family," *Foreign Affairs Manual Circular No. 304* (Washington, D.C.: Department of State, 28 April 1965).

5. Peggy Durdin, "The Ambassador's Wife Is an Ambassador, Too," *New York Times Magazine*, 4 October 1964, 21.

Chapter 7

1. Mary Stuart [Eleanore Lee], "Belling the Cat," *Foreign Service Journal* (February 1964): 32.

2. Elsie Lyon, letter to her father, Joseph C. Grew, undated (probably June 1961), reprinted in Jewell Fenzi, interviews with Elizabeth (Elsie) Grew Lyon, 7 April and 20 August 1987, Foreign Service Spouse Oral History Program.

3. Joleen Schweitzer, ed., "Interview with Alice McIlvaine, an Ambassador's Wife," *State* (formerly *Department of State Newsletter*) (February 1990): 16–18.

4. Alice McIlvaine, "Big Mob Here—Rocks Being Thrown—Everything Smashed," *Washington Post*, 16 March 1990.

5. Jane Wilson Pool, "Foreign Service Women's Association," *Foreign Service Journal* (August 1960): 37.

6. "Ladies' Luncheon," *[American] Foreign Service Journal* (January 1929): 21.

7. "State Department Wives Give Luncheon," *Washington Times Herald*, 19 November 1953.

8. Dorothy McCardle, "Foreign Service Blues: Sofa Can Prove a Hot Seat," *Washington Post*, 19 November 1953.

9. Edward Kennedy [Duke] Ellington, *Music Is My Mistress* (New York: Doubleday & Co., 1973), 327–30.

10. Ibid.

11. Evan M. Wilson, *Jerusalem: Key to Peace* (Washington, D.C.: Middle East Institute, 1970), 99.

12. Paul Hendrickson, *Looking for the Light: The Hidden Life and Art of Marion Post Wolcott* (New York: Alfred A. Knopf, 1992), 227–31.

Chapter 8

1. U.S. Department of State, "Diplomacy for the '70s: A Program of Management Reform for the Department of State," Publication No. 8551, Department and Foreign Service Series 143 (Washington, D.C.: Government Printing Office, 1970).

2. Martha Caldwell, report to AAFSW board of directors on ad hoc women's committee open meeting, 5 November 1970.

3. Mary Lou Schertz, "Department of State Policy toward Spouse Employment:

Radical Change and Continued Need" (master's thesis, University of Oklahoma, Norman Okla., May 1981), 18.

4. Macomber, *The Angel's Game*, 128.

5. Hope Meyers, conversation with Jewell Fenzi, 1990.

6. U.S. Department of State, "Policy on Wives of Employees of State, USIS, and AID," airgram A-728, 22 January 1972.

7. Jean Joyce, interview with Richard L. Williamson, 12 and 17 April 1974 (unpublished, Schlesinger Library, Radcliffe College, Cambridge, Mass.).

8. Carol Pardon, "The Foreign Service Wife and 'Diplomacy for the '70s,'" *Foreign Service Journal* (September 1971) 34–35, 45.

9. William B. Milam, letter to Jewell Fenzi, 7 March 1992.

10. "Orientation," *Foreign Affairs Manual*, 3 FAM 820. 824.2, "Policy": "It is the policy of the Department, AID and USIA to help members of families (18 years and over) of officers and employees to *acquire a basic understanding of their responsibilities as members of the Foreign Service team with the necessary orientation and language skills for filling their roles abroad successfully*" (author's italics).

824.3, "Training at the Foreign Service Institute": "Special senior briefings on meeting the press, using an interpreter, and administrative tips are scheduled concurrently with the seminar or individually as needed for spouses of ambassadors, deputy chiefs of mission, AID directors, country public affairs officers and other *spouses with senior responsibilities* (author's italics).

11. Association of American Foreign Service Women, "The Concerns of Foreign Service Spouses and Families," Forum Committee report (Washington, D.C.: AAFSW, March 1977), 6.

12. Cynthia Chard, "Proposal to State, AID, USIS for the Development of a Foreign Service Skills Bank," submitted to the board of directors of the Women's Action Organization, Washington D.C., 6 February 1976.

13. Ricker was a prominent nineteenth-century feminist and lawyer, fluent in several languages, who also was the first woman to apply for a major U.S. diplomatic post, in 1897, but who was turned down because she was a woman; the position went to a West Virginia newspaperman.

14. Bailey Morris, "State Department Wives? Bored?" *Washington Star*, 1 October 1976.

15. Bailey Morris, "A Quiet Revolution Is Shaking the State Department to Its Core," *Washington Star*, 14 August 1977.

Chapter 9

1. Marlene Eagleburger, "'Mrs. Foreign Service' Deserves to Be Paid Too," *Washington Post*, 7 March 1984.

2. Association of American Foreign Service Women, "The Role of the Spouse in

the Foreign Service," edited by Penne Laingen, Role of the Spouse Committee report (February 1985).

3. Miryam Hirsch, "The Story of the Struggle: Benefits for Foreign Service Wives Not Covered by the 1980 Act," *AAFSW News* (February 1989).

4. Schertz, "Department of State Policy toward Spouse Employment," 2.

5. Leila Finlay Dane, "The Iran Hostage Wives: Long-term Crisis Coping" (Ph.D. dissertation, School of Psychology, Florida Institute of Technology, 1984; Ann Arbor, Mich.: University Microfilms International, 1985).

6. Moorehead Kennedy, *The Ayatollah in the Cathedral: Reflections of a Hostage* (New York: Hill and Wang, 1986), 143.

7. Barbara Parker, "Coping with IRage," *Washington Post*, 10 December 1979.

8. Gerald E. Parsons, "How the Yellow Ribbon Became a National Folk Symbol," *Folklife Center News* (Library of Congress) 13, no. 3 (Summer 1991): 9.

Chapter 10

1. Joan Plaisted, "Senior Foreign Service Women: Who Are They? Where Are They?" *State* (October 1993): 25.

2. AAFSW, "Report on the Role of the Spouse in the Foreign Service."

3. William B. Milam, letter to Jewell Fenzi, 10 October 1992.

4. Christine Shurtleff, "The Professional Foreign Service Spouse" (unpublished, Washington, D.C., 1992).

5. Sen. Joseph Biden, Jr., hearings before the Committee on Foreign Relations of the U.S. Senate, 4 May 1993.

6. *Association of American Physicians and Surgeons vs. Hillary Rodham Clinton*, 997 F. 2d 898 (D.C. Cir. 1993).

7. Lewis L. Gould, "U.S. Women Taking Centre Stage," *Daily Telegraph* (London), 30 June 1993.

Bibliography

Primary Sources

The 170 interviews conducted by the Foreign Service Spouse Oral History Program provided most of the material for the book. See the Appendix for listings.

Secondary Sources

Books

Adams, John G. *Without Precedent: The Story of the Death of McCarthyism*. New York: W. W. Norton & Co., 1983.

Bohlen, Charles. *Witness to History*. New York: W. W. Norton & Co., 1973.

Boyce, Richard Fyfe. *The Diplomat's Wife*. New York: Harper and Brothers, 1956.

Brown, Lynn Mikel, and Carol Gilligan. *Meeting at the Crossroads: Women's Psychology and Girls' Development*. Cambridge, Mass.: Harvard University Press, 1992.

Butterfield, L. H., Marc Friedlaender, and Mary-Jo Kline. *The Book of Abigail and John: Selected Letters of the Adams Family 1762–1784*. Cambridge, Mass.: Harvard University Press, 1975.

Child, Maude Parker. *The Social Side of Diplomatic Life*. Indianapolis: Bobbs-Merrill Co., 1925.

Davis, Julia McDonald. *Legacy of Love: A Memoir of Two American Families*. New York: Harcourt Brace and World, 1961.

Dodd, Martha. *Through Embassy Eyes*. New York: Harcourt, Brace and Co., 1939.

Ellington, Edward Kennedy [Duke]. *Music Is My Mistress*. New York: Doubleday & Co., 1973.

Emmerson, John K. *The Japanese Thread: A Life in the U.S. Foreign Service*. New York: Holt, Rinehart and Winston, 1978.

Evans, Sara M. *Born for Liberty: A History of Women in America*. New York: Free Press, 1989.

Faludi, Susan. *Backlash: The Undeclared War against American Women*. New York: Crown, 1991.

Francis, Russell. *The Shadow of Blooming Grove: Warren G. Harding in His Times*. New York: McGraw-Hill Book Co., 1968.

Friedan, Betty. *The Feminine Mystique*. New York: W. W. Norton and Co., 1963.

Friedman, Thomas L. *From Beirut to Jerusalem*. New York: Farrar Straus Giroux, 1989.

Gelles, Edith B. *Portia: The World of Abigail Adams*. Bloomington: Indiana University Press, 1992.

Green, Lispenard Crocker, ed. *A Foreign Service Marriage*. Washington, D.C.: private printing, 1985.

Grew, Joseph C. *Turbulent Era: A Diplomatic Record of Forty Years, 1904–1945*. Edited by Walter Johnson. Boston: Houghton Mifflin, 1952.

Griffith, Robert. *The Politics of Fear: Joseph R. McCarthy and the Senate*. Lexington: University Press of Kentucky, 1970.

Harper, Alan D. *The Politics of Loyalty: The White House and the Communist Issue 1946–1952*. Westport, Conn.: Greenwood, 1969.

Harvey, Brett. *A Women's Oral History*. New York: HarperCollins, 1993.

Heilbrun, Carolyn G. *Writing a Woman's Life*. New York: Ballantine Books, 1988.

Hendrickson, Paul. *Looking for the Light: The Hidden Life and Art of Marion Post Wolcott*. New York: Alfred A. Knopf, 1992.

Herz, Martin F. *Diplomacy: The Role of the Wife: A Symposium*. Washington, D.C.: Institute for the Study of Diplomacy, Georgetown University, 1981.

Hooker, Nancy H., ed. *The Moffat Papers: Selections from the Diplomatic Journals of Jay Pierrepont Moffat*. Cambridge, Mass.: Harvard University Press, 1956.

Kahn, E. J., Jr. *The China Hands: America's Foreign Service Officers and What Befell Them*. New York: Viking Press, 1975.

Kennan, George F. *American Diplomacy: 1900–1950*. Chicago: University of Chicago Press, 1951.

Kennedy, Moorehead. *The Ayatollah in the Cathedral: Reflections of a Hostage*. New York: Hill and Wang, 1986.

Leech, Margaret. *In the Days of McKinley*. New York: Harper and Brothers, 1959.

Leffler, Melvyn P. *A Preponderance of Power: National Security, the Truman Administration, and the Cold War*. Stanford, Calif.: Stanford University Press, 1992.

Lisagor, Peter, and Marguerite Higgins. *Overtime in Heaven*. New York: Doubleday & Co., 1964.

Luppi, Ann, ed. *American Diplomacy and the Foreign Service*. Washington, D.C.: American Foreign Service Association, 1989.

Lyon, Cecil. *The Lyon's Share*. New York: Vantage Press, 1973.

Macomber, William B., Jr. *The Angel's Game*. New York: Stein and Day, 1975.

Miller, Hope Ridings. *Embassy Row: The Life and Times of Diplomatic Washington*. New York: Holt, Rinehart and Winston, 1969.

Morin, Ann. *U.S. Women Ambassadors: 1933–1983*. New York: Twayne, 1994.

Nagel, Paul C. *The Adams Women: Abigail and Louisa Adams, Their Sisters and Daughters*. New York: Oxford University Press, 1987.

O'Shaughnessy, Edith. *A Diplomat's Wife in Mexico*. New York: Harper and Brothers, 1916.

Plowman, Janice. *A Body in a Slot: Reminiscences of the Foreign Service*. St. Louis, Mo.: Jamric Press, 1991.

Reeves, Isabella Key. *A Diplomatic Tea*. Casper, Wyo.: Oil City Press, 1938.

Sheehy, Gail. *Passages: Predictable Crises of Adult Life*. New York: Dutton, 1976.

Shirer, William L. *Berlin Diary: The Journal of a Foreign Correspondent 1934–1941*. New York: Alfred A. Knopf, 1941.

Sidey, Hugh. *John F. Kennedy, President*. New York: Atheneum, 1964.

Sperber, A. M. *Murrow: His Life and Times*. New York: Freuindlich Books, 1986.

Steinem, Gloria. *Revolution from Within: A Book of Self Esteem*. Boston: Little, Brown and Co., 1992.

Teague, Michael. *Mrs. L: Conversations with Alice Roosevelt Longworth*. Garden City, N.Y.: Doubleday & Co., 1981.

Thayer, Charles. *Diplomat*. New York: Harper and Brothers, 1959.

Waldvogel, Merikay. *Soft Covers for Hard Times: Quilt Making and the Great Depression*. Nashville: Rutledge Hill Press, 1990.

Weil, Martin. *A Pretty Good Club: The Founding Fathers of the U.S. Foreign Service*. New York: W. W. Norton & Co., 1978.

Werking, Richard Hume. *The Master Architects: Building the U.S. Foreign Service, 1890–1913*. Lexington: University Press of Kentucky, 1977.

Wilson, Evan M. *Jerusalem: Key to Peace*. Washington, D.C.: Middle East Institute, 1970.

Articles

[Anonymous]. "A Consul's Wife: An Efficiency Report by One Who Knows." *American Consular Bulletin* (January 1923): 8.

Association of American Foreign Service Women. "The Concerns of Foreign Service Spouses and Families," Forum Committee report. Washington, D.C.: AAFSW, March 1977.

———. "'The Kabul Experience'—A Model for the Future?" *AAFSW News* (December 1978): 1.

Biggar, Joanna. "Married to Uncle Sam." *Washington Post Magazine*, 14 April 1985, 28.

Brown, John L. "Abigail Adams' First Post." *Foreign Service Journal* (January 1962): 26.

Bumiller, Elisabeth. "The Indian Cloister." *Washington Post*, 27 November 1986, 1, 23–25.

Cooper, Marguerite. "Twenty Years after the 'Women's Revolution': A Personal View." *Foreign Service Journal* (January 1991): 12.

Delear, Frank J. "5,000 Miles in a Flying Gas Tank." *Yankee* (July 1981), 54.

Durdin, Peggy. "The Ambassador's Wife Is an Ambassador, Too." *New York Times Magazine*, 4 October 1964, 21.

Eagleburger, Marlene. "'Mrs. Foreign Service' Deserves to Be Paid Too." *Washington Post*, 7 March 1984.

Fales, Rose H. "The Making of Diplomacy." *Foreign Service Journal* (October 1974): 42.

Fenzi, Jewell. "The Great Divorce: Why the 'Hands-off' Policy Did More Harm than Good for Spouses." *Foreign Service Journal* (June 1992): 17.

Fenzi, Jewell, and Carl L. Nelson. "The Duke in Baghdad." *Foreign Service Journal* (August 1991): 24–26.

————. "Bon Appétit: Julia Child: From Foreign Service Wife to French Chef." *Foreign Service Journal* (November 1992): 40–43.

Finnegan, William. "A Reporter at Large (Mozambique—Part 1)," *New Yorker*, 22 March 1989, 43.

Hall, Carla. "Women of the Hidden War: The Underground Victories of 'The Ladies of the OSS.' " *Washington Post*.

"Foreign Service Jobs Are Open for 300 Women." *Minneapolis Tribune*, 26 September 1943.

Hirsch, Miryam. "The Story of the Struggle: Benefits for Foreign Service Wives Not Covered by the 1980 Act." *AAFSW News* (February 1989), 1, 10–11.

Laingen, Penne, ed. "The Role of the Spouse in the Foreign Service: A Study of Attitudes and Perceptions of Spouses toward Foreign Service Life." Washington, D.C.: AAFSW, Role of the Spouse Committee, February 1985.

Light, Nancy. "Joined in Service." *Foreign Service Journal* (July-August 1988): 34–39.

Low, Sue. "Associates of the Service." *Foreign Service Journal* (March 1985): 24.

"Marion Post Wolcott, Photographer, Dies at 80." *Santa Barbara [Calif.] News-Press*, 26 November 1990.

McCardle, Dorothy. "Foreign Service Blues: Sofa Can Prove a Hot Seat." *Washington Post*, 19 November 1953.

McGeehon, Dale. "Goodbye to a Fractured Land." *SUN [Spouses' Underground Newsletter]* (Fall 1992): 1, 13–14.

McIlvaine, Alice. "Big Mob Here—Rocks Being Thrown—Everything Smashed." *Washington Post*, 16 March 1990, C 1–4.

Morris, Bailey. "State Department Wives? Bored?" *Washington Star*, 1 October 1976.

Papachristou, Judith. "American Women and Foreign Policy, 1898–1905." *Diplomatic History: The Journal of the Society for Historians of American Foreign Relations* 14, no. 4 (Fall 1990): 493–509.

Pardon, Carol. "The Foreign Service Wife and 'Diplomacy for the 70s.'" *Foreign Service Journal* (September 1971): 34–35, 45.

Parker, Barbara. "Coping with IRage." *Washington Post*, 10 December 1979.

Parsons, Gerald E. "How the Yellow Ribbon Became a National Folk Symbol." *Folklife Center News* [Library of Congress] 13, no. 3 (Summer 1991): 9–11.

Piet-Pelon, Nancy J. "A Spouseless Service." *Foreign Service Journal* (March 1985): 22.

Raine, Alice. "Wriston Report: The Feminine View." *Foreign Service Journal* (May 1955).

Sadler, Christine. "Thursday's Child: Cornelia Bassel of Clarksburg, West Virginia." *National Historical Magazine* [Daughters of the American Revolution] (April 1938): 63–64.

Saltzman, Charles E. "The Reorganization of the American Foreign Service." Speech before the Board of Directors of National Sales Executives, Inc., 10 September 1954. Reprinted in *Department of State Bulletin* (27 September 1954): 444–46.

Schweitzer, Joleen, ed. "Interview with Alice McIlvaine, an Ambassador's Wife." *State* (February 1990): 16–18.

Shurtleff, Christine. "The Foreign Service Spouse: An Endangered Species." *AAFSW News* (January 1992): 5.

Stansbury, Dorothy. "Representational Responsibilities: Guidelines for Foreign Service Wives at Posts Abroad." *State* (June 1971): 20–22.

Stuart, Mary [Eleanore Lee]. "Belling the Cat." *Foreign Service Journal* (February 1964): 32.

———. "Guidelines for the Ambassador?" *Foreign Service Journal* (September 1971): 36.

Sullivan, Margaret. "Lots of Hours." *AAFSW News* (May-June 1978): 1.

———. "What Role for Spouses?" *AAFSW News* (May-June 1978): 1.

———. "To Be or Not to Be: Observations and Proposals on the Dilemmas of the Foreign Service Woman." *AAFSW News* (April 1975): 1.

———. "Toward Unsnarling the Foreign Service 'Wife Problem.'" *Foreign Service Journal* (April 1977): 10–15, 52–54; (May 1977): 10–16, 57–58.

Superfluous Spouses, The. "Excess Baggage." *Foreign Service Journal* (April 1975): 21.

Weisz, Morris. "Labor's Role in World Affairs: A Memoir from a Socialist in the State Department." *Horizons* (Summer 1990): 8–11.

Unpublished Sources

AID collective memoir, 1947–53 (Priscilla DeAngelis, Florence Keppel Dennis, Margaret (Marge) Luikart, Rickel Marvin, Anita Paige, Peggy Pope, Ruth Redstrom, Evelyn Strachan, Lois Hermanson [Young*])

AAFSW and WAO executive boards, draft of memorandum to M/DG—Ambassador Carol C. Laise. Washington, D.C., n.d. (Other documents substantiate that the memorandum was written before autumn of 1975.)

Anderson, Suzanne. Correspondence, c. 1930–60. Suzanne Anderson collection.

Association of American Foreign Service Women, Family Life Committee. Evacuation report (draft). Washington, D.C., 1977.

Behlen, Ann Denton. "Mary Marvin Breckinridge Patterson: From Career Broadcaster to Career Diplomatic Wife." Bachelor's thesis, Harvard University, Cambridge, Mass., 1982.

Bell, Catharine Johnson. Interview with Catharine Johnson Cluett [her mother], 1982, including 1919 correspondence. Troy, N.Y.

Boyatt, Thomas D. Letter to Barbara J. Good, 2 October 1978.

Boyd, Clemence Jandrey. Foreign Service correspondence, 1938–1959, 7 vols. AAFSW Oral History Collection, Washington, D.C.

Challinor, Joan Ridder. "Louisa Catherine Johnson Adams: The Price of Ambition." Ph.D. thesis, American University, Washington, D.C., 1982.

Chard, Cynthia. "Proposal to State, AID, USIS for the Development of a Foreign Service Skills Bank." Submitted to the board of directors of the Women's Action Organization, Washington, D.C., 6 February 1976.

(Cluett), Catharine Johnson. Letters written to her parents, Mr. and Mrs. Charles H. Requa, 6 July to 8 August 1919.

Dane, Leila Finlay. "The Iran Hostage Wives: Long-term Crisis Coping." Ph.D. dissertation, School of Psychology, Florida Institute of Technology, 1984; Ann Arbor, Mich.: University Microfilms International, 1985.

Eagleburger, Marlene. "Proposed Amendment to the Foreign Service Act of 1980 for a Spouse Compensation Allowance." Family Liaison Office, U.S. Department of State, Washington, D.C., 2 October 1981.

Eagleburger, Lawrence. "Address to the Thirtieth Anniversary Meeting of AAFSW." U.S. Department of State, Washington, D.C., 9 October 1990.

Joyce, Jean. Interview with William B. Macomber, Jr., 30 May 1974. Arthur and Elizabeth Schlesinger Library on the History of Women in America, Radcliffe College, Cambridge, Mass.

———. Interview with Richard L. Williamson, 12 and 17 April 1974. Arthur and Elizabeth Schlesinger Library on the History of Women in America, Radcliffe College, Cambridge, Mass.

Kemp, Anna Durkee Smith, and Bernette Chase Kemp. Correspondence, 1915–1925. AAFSW Oral History Collection, Washington, D.C.

Kinney, Stephanie S. "Reconsidering the 1972 Directive on Wives," memorandum under director-general's letterhead. Washington, D.C.: Department of State, 31 May 1978.

Koenig, Myron L. (acting dean, School of Foreign Affairs, Foreign Service Institute). Private communication to Regina O. Blake, 7 July 1960. AAFSW Oral History Collection, Washington, D.C.

Levenson, Rosemary. "Caroline Service: State Department Duty in China, the McCarthy Era, and After, 1933–1977," vol. 2. Regional Oral History Office, Bancroft Library, University of California at Berkeley, 1978.

Lomask, Milton. "Lively Memories: The Life of Mary Marvin Breckinridge Patterson." Washington, D.C., 1992.

Lyon, [Elizabeth] Elsie Grew. Private communication to her father, Joseph C. Grew, undated (probably June 1961). In Jewell Fenzi, interviews with Elizabeth (Elsie) Grew Lyon, 7 April and 20 August 1987. AAFSW Oral History Collection, Washington, D.C.

Macomber, William B., Jr. "Change in Foggy Bottom: An Anniversary Report." Address delivered at the Department of State, 26 January 1972.

Meyers, Hope, Carmen Williams, and Annette Buckland. Memorandum from the Women's Action Organization Study Group on Spouses to Sue Whitman, Office of the Director-General, 23 August 1975.

Milam, William B. Letters to Jewell Fenzi, 7 March and 18 October 1992.

Nelson, Judith Grummon. "Personal Prologues to Pearl Harbor: Diaries and Letters of a U.S. Diplomatic Family in China and Japan." Washington, D.C.

Patterson, Marvin Breckinridge. Private communication to Fanchon J. Silberstein, Foreign Service Institute, 3 February 1983.

———. Talk delivered to the Society of Women Geographers, Washington, D.C., 6 December 1986.

Porter, Paul R., ed. "Greece at the Turning Point." Group IV Papers. Harry S. Truman Library, Independence, MO., 1981–82.

Ringwalt, Mildred. "Memoirs of a Foreign Service Wife: 1938–1958." Chapel Hill, N.C.

Rogers, William P. Memorandum for the Department of State Open Forum Panel chairman, William R. Salisbury, 7 August 1972.

Rozek [Cordery], Stacy A. "Alice Roosevelt Longworth: Life in a Public Crucible." Ph.D. dissertation, University of Texas at Austin, May 1992.

Schertz, Mary Lou. "Department of State Policy toward Spouse Employment: Radical Change and Continued Need." Master's dissertation, University of Oklahoma, Norman, Okla., May 1981.

Smallwood, Arwin D. "A History of the Overseas Briefing Center and the Individuals Responsible for Its Development and Growth." Overseas Briefing Center, Foreign Service Institute, U.S. Department of State, Washington, D.C., 1990.

(Spencer), June Byrne. AAFSW First Annual Report. Washington, D.C., May 1961.

———. "Reflections on the Development of AAFSW." Prepared for interview with Mary Louise Weiss, 2 March 1989. AAFSW Oral History Collection, Washington, D.C.

Steven, Robert S., Penne Laingen, and Kathleen Boswell. Minutes of a discussion of the 1972 "Policy on Wives," 9 February 1983.

Summary description of the Women's Action Organization (State). Washington, D.C., n.d.

Thomas, Charles H., III. "Reform of the Policy on Foreign Service Wives." Department of State Action Memorandum to Mr. [William B.] Macomber, [Jr.], 20 October 1971.

Trent, Mary Vance. Private communication to George A. Morgan, 19 July 1962.

Department of State Publications

Register of the Department of State. Washington, D.C.: Government Printing Office, 1907.

Register of the Department of State. Washington, D.C.: Government Printing Office, 1911.

Register of the Department of State. Washington, D.C.: Government Printing Office, 1922.

Register of the Department of State. Washington, D.C.: Government Printing Office, 1925.

"Toward a Stronger Foreign Service: Report of the Secretary of State's Public Committee on Personnel." Publication No. 5458. Washington, D.C.: Department of State, June 1954.

Department of State Bulletin. 27 September 1954.

"Social Usage in the Foreign Service." Washington, D.C.: Foreign Service Institute, 1957. Revised and reprinted as "Social Usage Abroad: A Guide for American Officials and Their Families" (Washington, D.C.: Government Printing Office, 1963), and "Diplomatic Social Usage: A Guide for United States Representatives and Their Families Abroad" (Washington, D.C.: Government Printing Office, 1984).

"Training Wives and Other Members of Family." Foreign Affairs Manual Circular No. 304. Washington, D.C.: Department of State, AID, and USIA, 28 April 1965.

The China White Paper, August 1949. Stanford, Calif.: Stanford University Press, 1967. Reissued with the original letter of transmittal to President Harry Truman from Secretary of State Dean Acheson and with a new introduction by Lyman P. Van Slyke. Originally published as "United States Relations with China, with Special Reference to the Period 1944–1949." Department of State Publication No. 3573, Far Eastern Series 30.

"Diplomacy for the '70s: A Program of Management Reform for the Department of State." Publication No. 8551, Department and Foreign Service Series 143. Washington, D.C.: Government Printing Office, 1970.

"Representational Responsibilities: Guidelines for Foreign Service Employees Abroad." Management Reform Bulletin No. 20.

"Policy on Wives of Foreign Service Employees of the Department of State, Agency for International Development, and United States Information Agency" (the "1972 directive"). Airgram A-728, 22 January 1972.

Calkin, Homer L. *Women in American Foreign Affairs*. Washington, D.C.: U.S. Department of State, 1977.

"Foreign Service Associates Proposal." Airgram A-1036, 7 December 1984.

DiBacco, Thomas. "An Outsider's Historical Perspective." In *Foreign Service Associates: Concept and Controversy, A Forum*. Washington, D.C.: Center for the Study of Foreign Affairs, Foreign Service Institute, U.S. Department of State, 1986, 37–39.

Dean, Michael Ann. "Employment Options for Foreign Service Family Members." Family Liaison Office., Bureal of Management, U. S. Department of State, Washington D.C.: Government Printing Office, 1993.

Index

CLO (Community Liaison Office), xxiii,
323
CODEL (congressional delegation), 225
Cohn, Roy, 119
compensation, spouse, 143–44, 202–8,
261–62
Cooper, Magda, 251–53
croquet, 35–37
cultural surveys, 135

Dane, Leila, 215
DeAngelis, Priscilla, 80–81
Deep River Boys, 117
de Gaulle, Charles, 147–48
"deserving Democrat," 12
Diplomacy for the '70s, 177
Diplomatic and Consular Officers Retired
(DACOR), 31–32
Diplomatic Tea, A, xix
Displaced Foreign Service Partners, 209,
212–14
divorce, 209–14
domestics, xxi–xxii, 89, 105–6
Dorman, Lesley, 191–94
Dorsey, Carolyn, 105–6
dragon ladies, 100–101
Dreyfus, Grace, 96–99
Dubs, Adolph (Spike), 186, 209–11
Dubs, Jane, 209–11
Dubs, Mary Ann, 210–11

Eagleburger, Marlene Heinemann, 202–8
education, childrens', 85–87, 187–88
efficiency report, 18
Ellington, Edward Kennedy (Duke),
169–70
Emmerson, Dorothy, 151–52
employment, spouse, 178–79, 184
endangered spouses, 259–62
English, Anita Grew, 28–30
evacuation, xxiii, 3–5, 51, 121–23, 174–76,
222–24, 228

FLAG ([Iran hostage] Family Liaison Action
Group), 216
FLO (Family Liaison Office), xxiii, 259–60;
founding of, 178, 191–94, 223
Farm Security Administration, 174
Foley, Heather Strachan (Mrs. Thomas),
81–82
Foreign Affairs Manual ("the FAMs"), 274

foreign born spouse, 12–14, 251–53
Foreign Service Act of 1946, 131
Foreign Service Act of 1980, 201–4, 212
Foreign Service Associates proposal, xxiii,
202
Foreign Service Auxiliary, 58–61
Foreign Service Institute. *See* National
Foreign Affairs Training Center
Foreign Service Officers' Training School,
31
Foreign Service Spouse Oral History
Program, xviii, 265–68
Foreign Service Wives' Group, xxiii, 159

Global Training Associates (Washington,
D.C.), 249
Government Girl, 53–54
Green, Lispenard (Lisa) Crocker, 110–11,
168
Grew, Joseph C., xxiv, 20, 28, 270

Hamilton, June, xxiv, 169–70
Harriman, Pamela C. (Mrs. W. Averell), 271
Hessman, Dorothy M., 53–54
Hirsch, Miryam, 209, 214
Hitler, Adolf, 48–49, 62
Holmes, Marilyn, xxi–xxii
Hornbeck, Stanley, 35–37
Hoover, Herbert, and Mrs. Herbert, 46–47
Hoskins, Harold B., 127–29
hostages, 215–21
housing, 82–83, 85, 88–90, 153–55, 257.
See also AAFSW, Housing Office
Hull, Cordell, 35–37
Hurley, Patrick J., 77

illness, 60–61, 166
Iran Evacuee Support Network Program,
222
Iran hostage hot line, 221

Jandrey Boyd, Clemence, 96–99
Jeffrey, Robert Emmett, 12–13
Johnson Cluett, Catharine, 6–7
Johnson, Lady Bird, 132
Jones, Loretta, 85–87
Jordan, Yvonne, 13–14

Kassim, Abdul Karem, 169
Kemp, Anna Smith, 9–12
Kemp, Bernette Chase, 9–10

The Authors

As a Foreign Service spouse for 30 years, Jewell Fenzi lived in Rotterdam, Netherlands; Freetown, Sierra Leone; Rabat, Morocco; Curaçao, Netherlands Antilles; Recife, Brazil; Port of Spain, Trinidad and Tobago; and Washington, D.C. She nurtured two children (in three languages and thirteen schools, on three continents), founded an American school, studied Dutch, French, and Portuguese, wrote cookbooks, served as embassy community liaison officer, hosted thousands of official guests, and moved her household a dozen times. Her husband retired from the Department of State in 1985.

She established Foreign Service Spouse Oral History, Inc., shortly after settling in Washington, D.C., and conducted many of the interviews excerpted in the book. She speaks periodically on spouse history at the National Foreign Affairs Training Center and oversees the Association of American Foreign Service Women Oral History Collection.

Carl L. Nelson is the author of *Protecting the Past from Natural Disasters* (1991). In 1986 he won a Gold Circle Award from the American Society of Association Executives for the multi-image slide-tape presentation "A Living Part." Formerly a speechwriter at the National Trust for Historic Preservation, he also managed, researched, wrote and edited the organization's annual reports, as well as special publications and audiovisual materials. His work has appeared in the *Washington Post*, *Air and Space*, *Humanities*, *Landscape Architecture*, *Historic Preservation*, and *Historic Preservation News*. He is a contributing editor of *Stone World* and *Tile World* magazines. A native Washingtonian and CIA "brat," Nelson is a graduate of the College of William and Mary.